The American County

WITHDRAWN

The American County
Frontiers of Knowledge

Edited by
Donald C. Menzel

With a Foreword by
John P. Thomas

The University of Alabama Press

Tuscaloosa and London

JS
261
.A64
1996

The American county

BGP 8902-1/3

Copyright © 1996
The University of Alabama Press
Tuscaloosa, Alabama 35487-0380
All rights reserved
Manufactured in the United States of America

∞

The paper on which this book is printed meets the minimum
requirements of American National Standard for Information
Science–Permanence of Paper for Printed Library Materials,
ANSI Z39.48-1984.

Library of Congress Cataloging-in-Publication Data

The American county : frontiers of knowledge / edited by Donald C.
    Menzel ; with a foreword by John P. Thomas.
    p.   cm.
    Includes bibliographical references and index.
    ISBN 0-8173-0803-2 (pbk. : alk. paper)
    1. County government—United States.   I. Menzel,
Donald C.
    JS261.A64   1996
    352.073—dc20
    95-41592

British Library Cataloguing-in-Publication Data available

RECEIVED

MAY 1 5 1997

Kennedy School Library

For Kay . . . love and thanks!

Contents

Tables and Figures

TABLES

FIGURES

Foreword

John P. Thomas

PERHAPS IT SHOULD come as no surprise that so little is written or generally understood about county government. Governments are generally recognized by their services, politics, and finances. Many county services deal with unpleasant topics: corrections, courts, mental illness, indigent health care, welfare, communicable disease, and property-value assessments. At the same time, other county government activities appear so mundane that they are of little interest: garbage disposal, pollution control, arterial and collector roads, vital statistics/records, and regulatory standards.

In addition to their unglamorous activities, county governments are overlooked for other reasons. Politically, power is dispersed among a variety of officials. While some decisions are made by county board members, many other entities make decisions for the county as well: legislatures, Congress, courts, municipalities, special districts/authorities, and county constitutional officers. This dispersal contrasts sharply with the focused political role of a mayor or governor.

From a financial standpoint, counties often spend far more money indirectly through third-party providers than through direct services. Functional areas, like health, welfare, and roads, constitute a majority of county expenditures. To a great extent these services are delivered by contract or third-party providers rather than by county employees. Consumers are often unaware that these are county services. Only when services are provided directly by county employees is it clear to recipients that county funds are used.

While many governmental entities can be readily understood, counties are not easily definable. Generic similarity, but no clear consistency, exists among the forty-eight versions (Connecticut and Rhode Island do not have counties), but each state has multiple variations. Patterns of county governments are hard to find, harder still to document, and almost impossible to aggregate on a national scale. The only thing truly fixed and easily understood about counties seems to be geographic boundaries, and even they are invisible except on a map. For those willing to persevere, there is a fascinating world to explore.

Collectively counties are a huge government that has existed for a long time. The first American county, James City, Virginia (1634), predates all states and the U.S. government. Today, counties in the aggregate spend more than $100 billion. While the history and magnitude of county government are well documented, their operation can be quite complex.

Counties can serve three distinct governmental roles. Historically, they have served as administrative arms for state governments in the administrative categories of health, welfare, courts, corrections, roads, tax administration, vital statistics, and elections. In recent years this role has expanded as the federal government has increased state responsibilities, many of which have been passed on to counties.

Second, the fastest-growing role for urban and suburban counties has been as provider of municipal services. Traditional city services, such as police, fire, streets, garbage collection, and utilities, are often provided in unincorporated areas by counties. In some states, the majority of the population now lives in such unincorporated areas. In these locales, citizens look to the county as their "city" government.

A third substantially expanded role for counties is as provider/coordinator/regulator/negotiator of city services that cross municipal boundaries. Pollution control, emergency medical services, public communications, drug enforcement, and mass transit lead a growing list of interjurisdictional activities.

In response to recent decades of increased responsibilities, modern counties operate in dramatically new ways. Both administrative and financial mechanisms have become consistent with advanced management practices of the public and private sectors. One indication of these changes is found in urban and suburban counties of more than 250,000 citizens, which represent 52 percent of the American population. All of these counties have adopted new management structures with professional administrators and/or elected executives. At the same time, state statutes have been revised to allow use of the latest tools and techniques of financial management. In addition to the traditional property tax and intergovernmental transfers, counties now employ a variety of fees and user charges as well as sales and income taxes. Sophisticated debt financing mechanisms are also used by most counties.

The public is generally unaware of this dramatic transformation of county government. Traditional researchers, writers, and teachers focus their study of government on federal, state, and city jurisdictions. Most of what we learn about county government comes from those counties that choose to tell their own stories, organizations that represent counties, media coverage, census data and other reports, and the few scholars who choose to examine a specific aspect of county government. Seldom is the information comprehensive.

Don Menzel and his colleagues have created a treasured resource in *The*

American County: Frontiers of Knowledge. The book is broad in scope, independently analytical, and easily understood. The authors explore the breadth of county government and guide readers to sources of data and research that expand their knowledge of county government.

These authors have also achieved a second goal. This work is a serious publication that serves as a springboard for other governmental researchers to shift their focus to counties. This text raises many scholarly challenges that will generate lively and spirited dialogue. On behalf of all who have spent their careers toiling in the field of county government, I express sincere appreciation and gratitude to Dr. Menzel and his colleagues.

Preface

THIS BOOK HAS three objectives: (1) to provide a state-of-the-art review of the major issues and questions facing American counties; (2) to expand the knowledge base of the American county; and (3) to identify gaps in our understanding of American counties, especially in relation to the governance and management of these often-maligned units of local government. As the subtitle suggests, this volume seeks to identify and advance the knowledge frontier of the American county.

This book has its origins in panels convened by the editor at two national conferences, one held in 1990 at the American Political Science Association meeting in San Francisco and the other held in 1991 in Washington, D.C., at the annual conference of the American Society for Public Administration. The scholars who participated in these panels were in full agreement about the need to investigate a host of issues and problems confronting American counties. They also agreed that American counties in many states are rapidly becoming important service providers and participants in local and state governance. Given these conditions, the panelists believed strongly that efforts should be made to stimulate scholarly interest in American counties.

Consequently, two steps were taken. First, the members of the panels— J. Edwin Benton of the University of South Florida, Beverly A. Cigler of Penn State–Harrisburg, Vincent L. Marando of the University of Maryland, Donald C. Menzel of the University of South Florida, Roger B. Parks of Indiana University, Mavis Mann Reeves of the University of Maryland, Tanis J. Salant of the University of Arizona, Mark Schneider of SUNY at Stony Brook, Gregory Streib of Georgia State University, James H. Svara of North Carolina State University, Robert D. Thomas of the University of Houston, and William L. Waugh, Jr., of Georgia State University—drafted a research agenda for the study of the American county. This agenda was published in the *Public Administration Review* in the spring 1992. That agenda is revisited in both chapters 1 and 12. Second, it was believed important to develop the agenda set forth in the *Public Administration Review* article. Thus, this volume reflects that effort. Because it seemed unlikely that any single author or a collaborator could undertake a state-of-the-art examination of important policy and governance issues facing counties, experts on county government were invited to contribute to this volume.

This book is an avowedly scholarly examination of issues and problems facing many American counties in the 1990s. This does not mean, however, that the following chapters are irrelevant to ongoing issues of county governance and management. Indeed, thoughtful practitioners of county government, including elected and appointed executives and legislators, should find valuable insights and suggestions in these chapters.

Some comment is in order about what the reader will not find in this volume. Among other things, only a brief history of county government is recounted in this volume. Those who feel a need to ground themselves more fully in the historical evolution of the American county should consult Lawrence L. Martin's "American County Government: An Historical Perspective" published in David R. Berman, ed., *County Governments in an Era of Change* (1993), or Kirk H. Porter's *County and Township Government in the United States* (1922). There is also little contained in this volume about the legal status of the American county. Excellent treatments of this subject can be found in Blake R. Jeffery, Tanis J. Salant, and Alan L. Boroshok, *County Government Structure: A State-by-State Report* (1989), and although dated somewhat, Herbert S. Duncombe's *Modern County Government* (1977).

Finally, it should be noted that neither rural nor urban counties are singled out for special treatment, although some authors draw primarily on the experiences of large counties to amplify their topics.

To provide a framework for the authors to address their subjects, each contributor was asked to focus on three broad questions: (1) What do we know about the topic (e.g., county conflict and cooperation) under consideration? (2) How should we go about finding out more about the topic? And (3) how does our existing knowledge of the topic aid or hinder county governance? The contributors were not asked to devote equal attention to each question and, as is evident in the chapters that follow, the contributors address these questions in their own stylistic ways. The contributors were also asked to speculate about their topics, often resulting in either the specification of hypotheses or the collection and reporting of data to test hypotheses.

ACKNOWLEDGMENTS

The original pieces published in this volume, along with what is perhaps the most extensive bibliography ever assembled on the American county, result from the work of dedicated scholars who are committed to advancing the knowledge frontier of the American county. And they have done just that. As editor, I learned much from each author, and for that I am grateful and appreciative.

A volume like this is, of course, the product of many helpful hands. The initial drafts of each chapter were subjected to two sets of blind reviews. First, each author was asked to review another author's chapter. Second, the editor solicited reviews from a number of experts throughout the United States. Those who graciously gave of their time and constructive criticism included David R. Beam (Illinois Institute of Technology), David M. Hedge (University of Florida), Jeff Luke (University of Oregon), Lawrence L. Martin (Florida Atlantic University), Roger B. Parks (Indiana University), John P. Pelissero (Loyola University of Chicago), Laura A. Reese (Wayne State University), Alvin D. Sokolow (University of California–Davis), and William L. Waugh, Jr. (Georgia State University). These reviewers made an invaluable and appreciated contribution to this volume.

Others who made important contributions to this volume include two graduate research assistants, David Whitmer, who has moved on to a Presidential Management Internship, and Susan Schubert, who labored hard to develop the bibliography. Finally, the editor would like to give a special acknowledgment to a colleague and friend, J. Edwin Benton, who freely provided his advice and expertise.

Of course, the final responsibility for the overall merit or lack thereof of this volume rests solely with the editor.

Donald C. Menzel
Tampa, Florida

PART I

Change and Continuity

1

Introduction

Donald C. Menzel

THE AMERICAN county is an important yet often neglected and maligned unit of local government. Indeed, in certain respects it has taken on mythical qualities, having been described as the "dark continent of American politics" (Gilbertson 1917), ramshackle, and the "plague spot of American politics" (Childs 1925). Although the words are less harsh in recent years, phrases such as the "still-forgotten governments" are invoked to describe the county's role in the American federal system (Schneider and Park 1989). But are American counties the forgotten governments of the 1990s?

Interest in the American county is growing rapidly as a result of several developments. First, as federal and state governments shift functional duties and responsibilities to local governments, scholars and public officials alike are attempting to ascertain the importance of counties as service providers and actors in the American federal system.

Second, there is a growing recognition that the pace of change (sometimes characterized as modernization) of the American county has increased significantly over the past several decades. Many American counties have been transformed in both form and function. Some have changed from boss- and patronage-ridden governments to governments that emphasize merit and ethics in the day-to-day business of making county government work. Other counties have changed from keepers of vital statistics to governments that compete, cooperate with, and at times resemble full-service American cities. At the same time, the arrival of regional problems such as water usage and rapid urbanization has propelled counties into the public's consciousness.

Finally, interest has been stirred by a growing realization that counties, although historically little more than arms of the state, may become the local governments of the future. Neither fish (city) nor fowl (state) nor Council of Government (COG), some counties reach across city limits and beyond county lines. Megacounties, like Baltimore County (Maryland), Dade County (Florida), and Los Angeles County (California), are realities in many parts of the nation. Other large and rapidly growing although less densely populated counties, such as Fairfax County (Virginia) and Hillsborough County (Florida), may soon achieve

3

megacounty status. These large, growing counties may become the urban weather vanes of the future.

It is somewhat misleading to speak of the American county as if it were a monolithic social, economic, political, and governmental entity. Diversity characterizes American counties more aptly than homogeneity. Such diversity poses a substantial challenge to those who study these often enigmatic governments. Nonetheless, the time has arrived to move counties out of the backwaters of local government study and begin the serious task of understanding them.

This volume takes a modest step in this direction. What we know and do not know about the American county occupy the pages that follow. It is also necessary to discuss what is needed to learn more about the American county. The first step toward identifying what we know begins with a review and assessment of Progressive-era authors.

COUNTIES AND THE PROGRESSIVE ERA

Early writing on the American county was rooted in the Progressive movement that swept the nation at the turn of the twentieth century. As noted earlier, Gilbertson (1917) called the county the "dark continent of American politics," contending it was a largely unknown and mysterious institution. Childs (1925), the father of the council-manager plan of municipal government, labeled county government as ramshackle. He asserted that counties lacked professional administration, were not responsive to the public, lacked accountability, and had archaic and fragmented organizational structures. (Historical milestones in the evolution of the American county preceding the Progressive movement are highlighted in figure 1.1.)

Kirk H. Porter, an Iowa academician who wrote about the American county in *County and Township Government in the United States* (1922), described the legal status and the offices and functions of county government. He advocated reform measures that he believed would "modernize" county government in America. County reform, he argued, required substantial changes in function and structure. Counties should assume new functions such as maintaining parks and libraries and take over from townships some existing functions such as poor relief. Moreover, counties should have more centralized decision making, with authority vested in an appointed county manager. Porter also maintained that counties should have home-rule powers like those held by municipal governments, and, in some instances, he called for counties to be consolidated with cities.

A handful of authors (Fairlie and Kneier 1930; John P. Duncan 1950; Wager 1950), writing in the legalistic-structural-functional tradition of the era, continued to call for the reform of county government. Paul W. Wager in particular

800–900 A.D.	Kingdom of England is divided into governmental districts called shires
	Shires consist of a shire court with both judicial and legislative powers and three shire officials—the earl, the sheriff, and the bishop, who shared executive power. The primary governmental functions were the administration of police and military functions, the operation of the court system, public works, poor relief, and taxation. The earl, who was appointed by the king, presided over the shire and was in charge of military personnel. The shire court was comprised of twelve landholders who enacted ordinances and passed judgment on criminal and civil complaints brought by citizens. The legal status of the shire was that of an administrative district, or arm, of the crown.
1066	Norman Conquest of England
	The shire was reconstituted as a county, and the powers of the earl and bishop were greatly reduced. The bishop was removed entirely from county affairs and the sheriff emerged as the preeminent county official.
1300–1400	King Edward III
	The Justice of the Peace was established, assuming many duties and responsibilities previously belonging to the sheriff. Later, other county officers, such as the coroner and the constable, were added, thus pluralizing executive power.
1634	First American county governments established in the Commonwealth of Virginia
	Eight counties became the basic administrative districts of the state and functioned much as they did in England. This "strong" form of county government eventually spread to other southern states.
1643	County Governments established in the Massachusetts Bay Colony
	Because cities and towns were regarded as more important units of local government, counties were regarded as weak. This "weak" form of county government spread to eastern states such as New York and Pennsylvania where other permutations occurred. Midwestern states created counties modeled on eastern states. The Pennsylvania form of county government, with its county commissioners elected at large, eventually diffused throughout most of the western United States.
1868	Dillion's Rule Established—Judge John F. Dillon of the Iowa Supreme Court rules that municipalities, and by extension counties, are exclusively administrative arms of the states. Thus, counties were required to have enabling state legislation to act.
1911	California is the first state to amend its constitution to permit home rule for counties

Fig. 1.1 Historical Evolution of the American County. From Lawrence L. Martin, "American County Government: An Historical Perspective," in *County Governments in an Era of Change,* ed. David R. Berman (Westport, Conn.: Greenwood Press, 1993), and the National Association of Counties.

noted several important shifts in county functions. On the one hand, states were steadily assuming some county functions, such as the maintenance of primary roads and crime control, through the establishment of state police systems. On the other hand, some states were steadily conferring on counties powers and responsibilities typically held by municipalities including "planning and zoning, housing, health, public works, and regulatory activities" (1950, 20).

These changes were the topic of an important essay written in 1952 by Clyde F. Snider. His essay identified ten issues confronting the American county at midcentury:

1. Consolidation—greater economy and efficiency in local affairs could be achieved by merging rural counties and city and county governments in some urban communities.

2. Home Rule—counties, like municipalities, should be granted home-rule powers to govern themselves more effectively.

3. County Executive—greater centralization of authority and decision making would make counties, particularly urban ones, more responsive and effective policy-making bodies.

4. Ballot Reform—shorter ballots would enhance popular control and interest in county government.

5. Merit System—civil-service systems based on merit would contribute to general county reform.

6. Size of County Board—smaller boards would promote administrative effectiveness.

7. Transfer of Functions—some sorting out of state-county and county–special purpose district functions should be undertaken.

8. Revenue Diversification/Constraints—growth in state grants-in-aid and shared taxes along with limitations imposed by the state on property levies has complicated county service delivery.

9. Financial Reform—improvements needed in budgeting, purchasing practices, and expenditure auditing.

10. Functional Consolidation—increased use of interjurisdictional agreements to provide health protection, welfare services, recreation, libraries, fire protection, jails, and other services has occurred.

Snider concluded that "county reform, though under way, is still in its infancy," and what is most needed is "a further application of principles and techniques already tried and proved successful" (29). He was referring to enacting the agenda described above and, among other things, elimination of townships and transferral of their functions to county government.

BEYOND THE PROGRESSIVE ERA

The Progressive era agenda, with its strongly stated prescriptions, occupied the attention of most local government scholars well into the 1960s. Moreover, in combination with the growing prominence of President Lyndon B. Johnson's Great Society agenda, few investigators focused their energy or attention on county government. The few that did, however, were more data-oriented, analytical, and comparative. Herbert S. Duncombe (1966), for example, with the support of the National Association of Counties, published *County Government in America,* which described the structure, functions, service responsibilities, and administration of five counties. He also relied on national survey data to profile service-delivery activities of 221 counties. Moreover, he claimed that counties were at a historical crossroads and that "continued progress requires further change in the organization, services, finances, and intergovernmental relations of county government" (251).

Thomas D. Wilson (1966) noted the growing presence of elected county executives. He was interested in determining whether this form of executive reorganization resulted in improvements in how "urban counties confronted the problem of providing increased services" (568). Drawing on a small number of cases, he concluded that "some improvement in management can be secured through executive reorganization" (568).

A still more ambitious study of elected and appointed county executives was published by William H. Cape in 1967. He was interested in determining if and how more centralized executive control in counties affected the operations of county government. Like Wilson, his database was meager: Cape could identify only forty counties with International City Management Association (ICMA)–recognized council-manager governments and twelve counties with elected chief executives whose positions were based on charter provisions and who were elected separately from the county governing body by the people in the entire county (114).

These studies, although limited in scope, pointed to a wider set of issues associated with advancing knowledge of the American county. Those issues included the need to be more behavioral, systematic, analytical, and theoretical. Although written more than twenty years ago, John C. Bollens's (1969) criticism of county research echoes loudly in the 1990s:

1. County research customarily employs a structural, legalistic, and descriptive approach and does not attempt to undertake systematic analysis within a theoretical framework (15).
2. Although behavioral methods have become widely used and important re-

search tools in the discipline of political science generally, only a very small, though significant, group of behavioral studies have been made of county government, politics, and elections (16–17).

3. The absence of an adequate structure for analysis in the literature of county government may largely account for the dearth of empirical analysis and theorizing in county government research (17).

4. Basically, most research into county government has suffered from a lack of concern about relationships (31).

These shortcomings prompted Bollens (18–31) to offer his own research agenda, which emphasized: (1) the patterns of relationships between county governing bodies and other officials such as row officers; (2) the extent to which counties experienced integrating influences caused by reform efforts and disintegrating influences caused by the proliferation of special districts and independent boards and authorities; (3) the impact of increased professionalization on the operations of county government; (4) how "new" services are administered in contrast to how "old" services (such as those under the jurisdiction of the clerk, treasurer, and so forth) are administered; (5) the relationships between the governmental leadership of counties and the political leadership, including that of the state; (6) the extent to which counties have viable interlocal relationships, including contracting for services and overlapping memberships between county governing boards, independent authorities, and special districts; (7) how services are delivered among counties and what might explain differences that exist; and (8) the role of the county as a metropolitan government, including the question of whether counties can effectively assume this role.

Scholarly interest in counties grew at a more rapid pace in the 1970s, although it could still be regarded as modest. City-county consolidations between 1967 and 1976 in places like Jacksonville–Duval County, Florida and Lexington–Fayette County, Kentucky, sparked some interest. W. E. Lyons (1977), for example, studied the Lexington–Fayette County experiences to understand the dynamics of merger politics. Lyons stopped short of assessing the results of consolidated government. Studies along these lines would necessarily come later (see Benton and Gamble 1984; Owen and Willbern 1985).

The ICMA and the National Association of Counties (NACo) also played important roles in kindling interest in county government through the joint publication of an annual county yearbook. This collaborative effort resulted in four yearbooks published between 1975 and 1978 that included compilations of statistics and articles that explored important issues facing counties. The *1975 Year Book,* for example, devoted chapters to regionalism and counties, financial trends, forms of county government, characteristics of county administrators, environmental management programs, law enforcement, and county solid-waste management. Among other things, the *1978 Year Book* contained data and articles dealing with county home rule, labor relations, budgeting, contracting for services, and coastal zone management.

Another NACo-sponsored effort during this period was the publication of Duncombe's second book, *Modern County Government* (1977). This book provided comprehensive information about American counties. Timeless subjects such as organizational structure and functions were addressed, as were topics such as counties as urban service providers and their role in the intergovernmental system. Like Bollens, Duncombe concluded by sketching out a research agenda, which emphasized a search for the factors that "contribute to county modernization such as the use of intergovernmental contracts and agreements, the use of the most current techniques in staff services such as budgeting, and achievements in program innovation" (256). Duncombe defined county modernization as the trend toward modern, optional functions, such as consumer protection and growth management, and away from state-mandated functions; some version of council-executive government; and "extensive cooperation with other units of local government" (254).

Duncombe's work, although a welcome addition to the literature, was not the only voice in the wilderness of county government research. Other voices could be heard. Vincent L. Marando and Robert D. Thomas in *The Forgotten Governments* lamented that "too much of what we know about counties is based on 'logic' and on the reform ethic, not research" (1977, 140). Heeding their own advice, they studied county commissioners in Georgia and Florida to understand how these officials performed their policymaking roles. Their study represented a pioneering effort to apply "modern social science to the comparative study of county government within a systematic framework" (Bollens 1969, 32). Marando and Thomas used a political-systems framework, modern survey research techniques, and sophisticated statistical analyses to uncover how and why county commissioners perceive their policy-making roles as they do.

One other study, published in 1977 by Keith Baker, examined county expenditures in California. His research attempted to assess the extent to which "balkanization" (operationalized as the number of incorporated jurisdictions in a county) influenced expenditure policies. He also assessed socioeconomic influences on county expenditures, finding that such factors explained a large percentage of the expenditure variance and that balkanization change factors explained very little. However, when state and federal aid were dropped from the expenditure data, socioeconomic influences such as urbanization explained merely 14 percent of the variance. These "disappointing" findings (his words) prompted him to call for studies that would combine county-by-county data with case studies to more directly reveal the relationships he believed existed.

THE REAGAN YEARS

President Reagan's bold proposal to restructure federal-state roles and responsibilities never materialized along the lines outlined in his 1981 inaugural address. Still, in combination with growing fiscal pressures and constraints in the 1980s, it significantly influenced state and local governments. Indeed, by the end of the decade, many cities and counties were providing more services to more people than ever before in their history—and straining harder and harder to do so.

The forgotten governments were becoming the remembered governments. Studies were launched across a broad front. Many studies focused on single states and addressed a number of issues. Giles, Gabris, and Krane (1980) surveyed elected county supervisors and chancery clerks in eighty-two Mississippi counties to obtain their views on public policy issues such as the need to provide more services and their attitudes toward county administration. They found no evidence that administrative development precedes policy development, which contradicts a theme frequently found in the municipal literature.

Svara's research on North Carolina counties (1985b, 1990a) center on county leadership roles and specifically how they resembled or differed from city leadership roles. He examined five cities and the counties in which they reside and concluded that although there are similarities, there are also important differences in city-county leadership roles. Two variances are especially noteworthy: county commissions are more heavily involved in the operational dimensions of government than are city councils; and "the mayor has more ceremonial responsibilities and is more commonly perceived to be a political leader than the chairman" (1985b, 22). To examine these findings more thoroughly, Svara (1990a) surveyed city and county managers in North Carolina. The survey data showed that, contrary to what was expected, mayors are as active in administrative matters as are chairpersons and "are more commonly perceived to be excessively involved" (1990a, 19). More generally, Svara found that mayors, and chairpersons, roles are more similar than dissimilar. This finding led him to conclude that the "council-manager form can function in much the same way in cities and counties" (1990a, 20).

Other students of county government examined home rule in Arizona (Berman, Martin, and Kajfez 1985; Salant 1989), discretionary authority and state-county relations (Martin 1990; Sokolow 1993b), the roles and attitudes of county clerks/administrators in Alabama (Smith, Sauser, and Salinger 1984), county revenue capacity and effort in Arkansas (Hy et al. 1993), and the effects of local government complexity on county property tax and debt policies (Thomas and Boonyapratuang 1993). Still others focused primarily on county services. Benton and Rigos (1985), for instance, were the first to compare the service role of cities with that of urban counties. Cigler (1990) studied contracting practices and behaviors in North Carolina counties to determine how many counties contract for services, what types of services are contracted, and how those who receive contracts are held accountable. Accountability problems, according to her survey, were a great concern to county administrators.

Like Cigler, Menzel and Benton (1990, 1991b) employed statewide survey data to document the number and types of county services delivered in Florida. Their study detailed the expanding service menu of county government. It also examined the extent to which counties provided services through contracts, franchises, and intergovernmental agreements (see also Benton and Menzel 1992a).

Some county government studies have focused on single counties. The best-known studies are those supported by the U.S. Advisory Commission on Intergovernmental Relations (1988b; 1990a). In their studies of St. Louis and Pittsburgh (Parks 1990; Parks and Oakerson 1989, 1993; Oakerson and Parks 1988, 1989) Roger B. Parks and Ronald J. Oakerson have attempted to assess the extent to which cities and counties can govern themselves in an effective manner in the face of significant jurisdictional fragmentation. Parks and Oakerson argued that cities and counties engage in creative methods to govern in the absence of metropolitan government. More directly, they contended that "a set of relatively small local governments, when embedded in a structure of overlapping jurisdictions and coordinated service delivery arrangements, is a viable alternative for organizing large metropolitan communities" (Parks and Oakerson 1989, 11).

Small multicounty studies are not numerous but are growing in number. Susan A. MacManus (1991b), for example, studied government contracting by focusing on the attitudes held by more than three thousand business leaders toward county purchasing and bidding practices in Hillsborough County, Florida, and Harris County, Texas. Her research identified a number of variables that discourage businesses from seeking contracts from counties. These impediments, she concludes, are likely to diminish competition and therefore limit cost savings that governments should accrue from subcontracting efforts (343).

Studies of single counties and of multiple counties within and across states should advance the knowledge base of county government (see Brasher 1994; Hawkins and Hendrick 1994). At the same time, research on counties nationally has been conducted and more is underway (Waugh 1988; Waugh and Streib 1990; Streib and Waugh 1990; Waugh and Hy 1988; Lewis 1986; Lewis and Taylor 1990; and Schneider and Park 1989). William L. Waugh, Jr., and Gregory Streib have relied primarily on surveys of county officials throughout the United States conducted in 1984 and 1989 to investigate questions of state-county trust, responsibility, and organizational capacity. Their efforts have also centered on policy issues facing county leaders in an attempt to profile the rapidly changing roles of counties (Streib and Waugh 1990). Their findings point to a need to rethink state-county relationships and assess whether counties are accorded too little discretion.

Edward B. Lewis and George Taylor (1990) also take a national perspective toward the study of counties. However, their research centers primarily on the attitudes and roles of county administrators. Their overall objective is "to understand what the county manager does, why, and what difference it makes" (11). While similar research on the role of the city manager at the municipal level is abundant, it is a rare commodity at the county level.

Mark Schneider and Kee Ok Park (1989) take a different approach to the study of counties nationally. Their research examines metropolitan counties as service-delivery agents. More specifically, they attempt to assess the effects of several influences (region, metropolitan age, and government structure) on county expenditures. Their findings show that government structure has a significant, independent influence on the role of county government as a service provider. As they put it, "the data show that county governments with reformed structures (especially elected county executives) spend more and provide more services than counties with the traditional commission form of government" (350). This is the first documented relationship at the county level between government structure and policy outputs.

Schneider and Park conclude that counties are the "still forgotten governments." Perhaps. But as this review suggests, this situation may not last much longer. Indeed, at nearly the same moment that Schneider and Park uttered these words, the National Association of Counties released a useful document *County Government Structure: A State-by-State Report,* by Blake R. Jeffery, Tanis J. Salant, and Alan L. Boroshok (1989). This document contains detailed information about county governments and is a valuable reference tool. Also in 1989, Victor DeSantis provided an overview of a century of change in county government. His review covered county home rule, city-county consolidation, form of government, elected head of county government, the county legislature, and county finances.

EMERGING THEMES AND DIRECTIONS

The literature reviewed above points to several themes that have dominated county research over the years. Perhaps the strongest theme is change—frequently called county modernization. This theme has an important history in challenging past practices—indeed, abuses—in the exercise of governmental power and authority. Still, its utility as a guide for conducting more rigorous research could be quite limited. Modernization too often connotes that counties are or should become more like cities: highly centralized, professional, accountable—reformed. As appealing as this perspective seems, the tradeoff may be a blind spot in the conduct of theoretical and rigorous empirical research.

Vincent L. Marando and Mavis Mann Reeves (1991a), for example, caution that it may not be wise to study counties in the same way and with the same theories that have guided research on cities. As they put it, "Some of the variables frequently applied to cities may be appropriate for county research. Others are not. The transfer of municipal research approaches to the study of counties should be pursued in recognition of city-county differences" (52).

The American county remains an enigma whose future is difficult to predict. Fiscal strain as well as the altered global landscape following such events as the breakup of Soviet bloc nations, the Persian Gulf War of 1991, the disintegration of the former Yugoslavia, the passing of apartheid in South Africa, and shifts in world trade patterns are likely to make the ordinary business of running county government more than ordinary.

Indeed, if the fiscal plight of California counties in 1993–94 is any indication, counties cannot simply be reactive, second-class partners in accomplishing things for the American public. And they are not. When the 1993 California legislature, with the support of Governor Pete Wilson, set about transferring $2.6 billion in property taxes raised by counties and cities to fill a state budget shortfall of $9 billion, county officials were furious. "Elected officials in the state's 58 counties," a New York Times reporter wrote, "are howling in protest, with law-enforcement officials, who rely almost entirely on county financing, leading the charge with dire warnings that criminals will go unprosecuted" (June 17, 1993, A8).

The chapters in this volume do not predict what the future may hold for American counties. However, separately and collectively, they provide a rich trove of ideas, suggestions, and guidance that will serve as a basis for thinking about the future of the American county.

ORGANIZATION OF THE BOOK

This volume is organized into five parts or subthemes, excluding chapter 1, which provides an overview of the issues, topics, and questions that delineate the broad contours of our existing knowledge of the American county.

Part I: Change and Continuity

Part I contains two chapters that illustrate how American counties are and have been subject to change and continuity, both as an agent and as an object. Indeed, one paradox of counties viewed in the aggregate is the fact that some have changed very little over the past two hundred years while others have changed dramatically.

David R. Berman and Tanis J. Salant begin this discussion in chapter 2 by focusing on the changing role of the American county in the intergovernmental system, noting that change is occurring in both the vertical and horizontal dimensions of the federal system. Counties, they contend, are no longer passive pawns on the federal-state-local chessboard. Rather, many counties are asserting themselves in an effort to obtain a fair hearing, if not a fair share of rights, responsibilities, and resources. Their discussion of issues and trends in the vertical intergovernmental relations system is followed by an in-depth analysis of the forces that encourage or discourage counties to seek greater autonomy in the form of home rule. Finally, Berman and Salant discuss the increasingly important role played by counties in interlocal (horizontal) patterns of governance. Among other things, the authors contend that many counties are assuming the responsibilities of regional governments, particularly in the area of economic development. Although the county presence is growing in the federal system, much remains to be learned about county-city, county-county, county-state, and county-national relationships, not to mention an astonishing variety of county–private sector relations.

In chapter 3, Kee Ok Park examines counties as the objects of change, including how and why they grow as governments. He notes that county governments, particularly urban and urbanizing counties, are (except for special districts) the fastest growing of all local governments. In 1987, for example, U.S. counties in the aggregate spent $98.2 billion, a jump of 430 percent in just fifteen years. Why? What is happening in county government that accounts for this astronomical rate of growth? Park's review of the literature on the growth of government led him to identify a number of factors that could be responsible for the growth of county government, including the multiplier effect of demands made by state or national governments through intergovernmental aid and mandates, the form of government (commission or elected executive/administrator), population pressures and growth rates, availability of local resources to provide services, and regional location.

To examine these influences on the growth of county government, Park develops a regression model and tests it with data assembled from 244 counties in fifty-six of the largest metropolitan statistical areas. Moreover, the expenditures-growth-determinants model is tested in the aggregate across four policy domains—developmental, redistributive, allocational, and public safety. The author concludes that counties with more service functions and reformed governmental structures and whose population is growing fast in states with a propensity to impose mandates grow faster than counties that lack these characteristics. Most importantly, Park concludes by detailing what needs to be done to investigate the expected growth of county governments in the decade ahead. The study results presented in this chapter, as Park acknowledges, constitute only a starting point for much needed research into why counties are growing and what the consequences of that growth mean to residents and public policy-makers.

Part II: Structure and Governance

Part II of this volume examines the board structure, governance processes, and policy expenditures of American counties. Susan A. MacManus leads off in chapter 4 with a comprehensive description and assessment of governing boards—form, name, size, partisanship, term of office. Using survey data from ninety-one large counties, she then details their composition with reference to gender, race/language, and age. Finally, she explores campaign and election trends, including questions of ballot access, competitiveness, campaign expenditures, and political life after serving on the county board. MacManus's findings and observations are too numerous to recount here, but suffice it to say that her chapter adds much to the previously sparse knowledge and points clearly and forcefully to the terrain that needs further exploration.

In chapter 5, Victor S. DeSantis and Tari Renner heed one of MacManus's pleas when they investigate an important and complex question: Do county structures make a difference in policy expenditure levels? Are more centralized structures such as the county administrator form, likely to spend more on public programs than are noncentralized, traditional structures such as the commission form of county government? Moreover, how do other variables, such as state fiscal aid, political culture, region, suburbanization, wealth, and so forth, attenuate or amplify policy-expenditure levels? In reviewing previous research in this area, DeSantis and Renner note that these questions have received considerable attention from students of municipal governments but have been all but ignored by students of county governments. DeSantis and Renner attempt to remedy this situation by reporting and analyzing survey data collected from 1,295 American counties.

In chapter 6, Kenneth Klase, Jin W. Mok, and Gerald M. Pops address governance issues from the point of view of conflict and cooperation. Indeed, they develop a conceptual model of county conflict, arguing that counties, unlike many other local governments, are highly vulnerable to conditions that promote conflict. At the same time, conditions such as fragmentation of authority, lack of centralized decision making, and politically powerful constituencies that coalesce around certain functions and offices such as law enforcement and sheriffs can promote continuity or stability.

These authors further argue that counties can and do engage in cooperative patterns of interaction. They agree with James Svara's thesis (1990b), which evolved from research on municipal structures of government, that the presence of conflict does not necessarily imply the absence of cooperation, and, conversely, the absence of conflict does not necessarily imply cooperation. Klase, Pops, and Mok provide a conceptual road map that discerning readers can use to understand more fully many points and arguments developed by other contributors.

Part III: Management Issues and Challenges

Part III explores management issues and challenges facing elected and appointed county officials, including the civil servants who staff thousands of county departments. Counties, as Svara correctly points out in chapter 7, have been largely on the sidelines as the Progressive reform initiatives that swept across municipal America nearly one hundred years ago brought new forms of leadership and professionalism to those governments. Unlike most municipal governments, American counties remain largely partisan and structurally fragmented. These factors along with the unique nature of counties as hybrid governments (local/state) have made it difficult for effective leadership to be exercised and have confounded efforts to professionalize county management. The irony of this conclusion, Svara argues, is that county leaders, particularly managers, have found it necessary to become able negotiators, able bargaining agents, and effective conflict managers—skills increasingly held out as those needed to manage more successfully in the increasingly complex world of local government (see also Kettl 1993).

Svara's chapter provides insightful comparisons between county and municipal elected and appointed leadership styles, drawing on data collected in North Carolina, and addresses key issues such as chairperson leadership styles, governing board roles, and commission–county manager relationships. He concludes by providing a study agenda that, once pursued, should greatly advance the knowledge frontier of the American county. Svara presents a picture of county leadership and professionalism that has both challenge and opportunity woven throughout for those who work in America's courthouses.

Svara's broad outline of professionalism in county government is extended and complemented in chapter 8 by Gregory Streib's thoughtful assessment of what needs to be done to strengthen county management. Streib sets forth a three-pronged agenda that, if put into place, would raise the level of managerial leadership and competence in every American county. Counties, Streib contends, must build government support networks involving universities, professional associations, other governments, and consultants. In addition, county leadership capacity must be improved by securing greater home-rule powers and shaping governance structures to fit particular needs and by the acquisition of practical knowledge of important management tools such as management by objectives, planning-programming-budgeting, strategic decision making, and Total Quality Management (TQM), the management rage of the mid-1990s.

Furthermore, Streib advocates a rethinking of the role of the county manager, suggesting that effective managerial leadership will hinge greatly on the ability of managers to embrace a wide range of values, including a commitment to openness, participation, intergenerational impacts of county decision making, and a genuine interest in what people think and do. The pursuit of efficiency, the hallmark of the effective public manager of the Progressive era, is no longer a singularly sufficient value. Strengthening county management will require elected and appointed leaders to have a well-developed set of values that will serve as a road map for navigating through the frequently stormy environments that typify county rule by many masters—commissioners, row officers, state and federal authorities, and others.

Part IV: Fiscal Issues and Policies

Part IV directs attention to what may be the most pressing set of issues confronting counties in the 1990s—fiscal issues such as intergovernmental aid, costly mandates, revenue growth and diversification, and economic development. In chapter 9, J. Edwin Benton surveys the literature on intergovernmental aid and the impact of mandates and challenges scholars to be inventive in examining how these two vitally important fiscal matters (separately and jointly) constrain—perhaps even undermine—the ability of county officials to deliver public services. Benton's wide-ranging review makes it abundantly clear that fiscal entrepreneuralism is required of counties in an era of declining intergovernmental aid and multiplying policy mandates imposed by state and federal authorities. His review also highlights how thin the knowledge base is with regard to counties as recipients of intergovernmental aid and as targets of burdensome mandates.

The twin forces of dwindling intergovernmental aid and mandate mania have motivated county officials throughout the land to intensify their search for alternative sources of revenue, thereby leading to a diversification of the revenue base. And, as Beverly A. Cigler details in chapter 10, the movement along these lines has been brisk and imaginative. After reviewing the fiscal and policy complexities associated with the incessant demand for county services, she discusses five broad options that states can choose to enable counties to achieve greater revenue flexibility: (1) change the level of state-local intergovernmental assistance; (2) alter county tax options, perhaps allowing counties in many states to mix and match sales taxes, local income taxes, and others; (3) revise property taxes by allowing counties to exercise options, such as tax-increment financing, that municipalities enjoy; (4) broaden the base for user charges or fees; and

(5) restructure local governments through greater use of multicounty special districts, tax-base sharing, and intergovernmental agreements that foster new forms of metropolitan government.

Cigler concludes that county revenue systems are undergoing fundamental change. Such change, she argues, is likely to be complicated by the unending struggle to be a municipal-type government, a political subdivision of the state, and a regional if not metropolitan government.

The penultimate chapter in this volume focuses on a topic of growing importance for American counties—the design of economic development strategies aimed at stimulating local public economies. In chapter 11, William J. Pammer, Jr., reviews the short history of counties as agents of economic development and carefully delineates supply-side and demand-side strategies that many counties are adopting. More specifically, Pammer explores and assesses the strategies employed by more than one hundred large counties to attract, retain, and expand businesses in their jurisdictions. The data drawn from a 1989 International City/County Management Association (ICMA) national survey of county managers and economic development directors, indicate that demand-side strategies that employ marketing approaches and emphasize public-private partnerships are more successful in achieving the goal of attracting new businesses than are supply-side strategies such as providing tax abatement incentives and investing in infrastructure development.

Pammer is careful to point out that his findings are far from definitive in light of the sparseness of available data. Consequently, he urges students of the American county to turn their attention to this important but little-explored area. He provides important guidance for would-be investigators by closing the chapter with a set of questions and suggested hypotheses that constitute a research agenda in their own right.

Part V: The Future

Chapter 12 draws together many of the findings offered in the preceding chapters. The rediscovery of the American county is continuing from both scholarly and political perspectives. Still, much remains to be accomplished, and chapter 12 provides some guidance in this regard. Finally, it is argued that the future of the American county is bright, promising, and challenging—although difficult to predict.

The authors in this volume have taken an important step toward advancing the knowledge frontier of the American county. Ignorance about American counties is rapidly vanishing in light of the many insights, findings, critiques, and suggestions offered by these scholars. Still, the task of illuminating the role and place of the American county in the nation's governance has only begun.

2

The Changing Role of Counties in the Intergovernmental System

David R. Berman and Tanis J. Salant

RELATIONS AMONG governments in the United States are highly complex and dynamic. Rather than a federal system in which the functions of the national, state, and local governments are clearly defined and neatly separated in a layer-cake fashion, national, state, and local government activities in the U.S. federal system run together much like a marble cake (Grodzins 1966). At the local level alone, governmental authority is shared and divided among nearly 87,000 units—schools, cities, counties, special districts, public authorities, and so forth.

Some reformers have been anxious to sort out local governing functions in a more rational manner, shifting responsibilities to larger units or, if necessary, creating new units to handle problems that spill over the boundaries of existing local governments. Yet where some observers see an ineffective fragmentation of local governing authority, others see a highly integrated and effective network of local government units (USACIR 1987; Hamilton and Wells 1990; Schneider 1989; Kenyon 1990). Given the complexity of the intergovernmental system, governments regularly collide. As political scientist Thomas Anton notes, "With each bump an opportunity is provided to challenge or affirm existing understandings regarding who should do what, on whose budget" (1989, 2).

Of all the units of government in the United States, few have experienced as much change as county governments. Generally, one finds a considerable strengthening of their authority, responsibilities, structure, and operation. Much of the impetus for change has come in response to pressures generated by increased urbanization and suburbanization and by the growth of regional problems. Other developments propelling a shift toward greater county authority and responsibility are the demise of federal revenue sharing to local governments in the 1980s and the fiscal plight of states in the 1990s.

To some extent, change has been simply a matter of counties drawing on existing authority to restructure their governments, create new agencies, hire more technically trained personnel, or devise service arrangements in cooperation with other local governments. Adjusting to changed conditions in most states, however, has also produced statutory or constitutional changes at the state level that give county governments more authority. Some of the legal change has resulted from bottom-up pressure—that is, from county officials and other groups making demands on the state. Other changes affecting counties have been made in a top-down fashion by state officials, sometimes over the opposition of county officials. In the broad perspective, counties have experienced both gains and losses in regard to self-rule.

Counties historically have been both administrative arms of the state government and units of local government responding to local needs. They appear destined to continue to play both roles. As a unit of local government, they are likely to be of increasing importance in providing services on a regional basis. They are also likely to continue as administrative arms of the state and the federal governments in a top-down system in which they will have to struggle to exert influence over the framing of policies and the implementation of programs.

This chapter examines how and where county governments fit into the intergovernmental system. It begins with an overview of problems and trends in the vertical relations among county governments, state governments, and the national government. Next, the discretionary authority of county governments and the varied and changing roles of counties in the pattern of local government are examined. The conclusion suggests topics requiring further inquiry.

ISSUES AND TRENDS IN THE VERTICAL SYSTEM

The vertical intergovernmental system in which counties function has become both more permissive and, in many respects, more coercive. Counties have received more discretionary authority but have had less assistance from other levels of government and have been forced to undertake expensive functions typically paid for out of local taxes.

Although the new federalism of the Reagan-Bush years was ballyhooed as decentralizing authority, the system actually became even more coercive, with preemptions of state and local authority and the imposition of costly federal mandates on states and localities in many policy areas, including air and water quality, solid waste, transportation standards, courts and corrections, and health services (Zimmerman 1992).

Some observers contend that state and local governments have been abandoned by Congress, which has an obligation to protect them from the intrusion of national authority (Hero 1989; Derthick 1986). Others, including state and local officials and their organizations, have condemned the federal courts for allowing an erosion of state and local authority (Berman and Greene 1993; Kearney and Sheehan 1992). Making life even more difficult for counties is the increasing concern with the federal debt, which has brought about a philosophy of fend-for-yourself federalism that has led to reductions in federal aid (John P. Thomas 1991).

THE MANDATE ISSUE

The problems of costly mandates and declining aid have also generally characterized state-local relations. In many cases, states have passed on mandates laid down by the federal government. One law of intergovernmental relations is that in periods of economic stress, local officials can expect less intergovernmental aid and more intergovernmental mandates (Berman 1992). Mandates allow federal and state officials to satisfy policy demands and take political credit for so doing while shifting the financial burden to local taxpayers. As a U.S. Advisory Commission on Intergovernmental Relations (USACIR) study notes, "In the absence of sufficient funds—whether by legislative choice or economic constraint—there is a strong temptation to satisfy policy demands by mandating that functions be performed by other governments (USACIR 1990a, 2). Moreover, recent events also lead to the prediction that in times of economic stress, relief to localities from the states is particularly likely to take the form of authorizing increased local taxing authority or reducing or eliminating state revenue sharing, so that local government officials must take the political heat for raising taxes.

County officials have fewer complaints over the goals of mandated programs than with the fact that they are not adequately involved in shaping the programs and are often stuck with the bills. Some of the new mandated roles for counties, for example in regional land-use planning or solid-waste management, have been imposed by states over the objections of counties, particularly small ones with limited funds and professional capabilities, that worry about the costs and their ability to perform the function (Fix and Kenyon eds., 1989).

State mandates to counties without funding are a major problem for counties, if not the key intergovernmental issue. In a survey of forty-four county associations in 1991, twenty-three respondents included unfunded state mandates as one of the three biggest issues facing counties. The California legislature, for example, passed down 1,240 mandates to counties and provided funding for only eleven. Out of the six thousand bills introduced in the 1991 session, 92 percent affected counties (Salant 1991b). State county associations were asked again in 1992 what the most critical issues facing their counties were. Out of the forty-three states that responded, twenty-six listed unfunded state mandates as the most critical and several others named intergovernmental funding issues such as sorting out proper financing responsibilities and program and fiscal realignment as major issues (Salant 1992).

Although mandates and financial problems have no doubt grown more onerous because of recession pressures and reduced federal funding to the states, they are hardly new problems. Catherine Lovell's work more than a decade ago documented the types and fiscal impacts of unfunded mandates (Lovell 1981 a and b; Lovell and Tobin 1981). What has changed in the 1990s is the propensity of county officials to fight such mandates. In 1990, New York county commissioners, for example, instituted a successful lawsuit against an administrative mandate involving county nursing homes that would have cost $27 million. County officials claim that the successful litigation sent a message to state agencies that "counties are taking a selectively aggressive attitude toward state mandates" (Salant 1991). In 1991, South Carolina counties successfully pushed an amendment to strengthen the state's fiscal-note statute, and Colorado counties helped to pass a mandate reimbursement law in 1990. In addition, in 1992 Nevada county officials campaigned for defeat of an advisory question that asked voters if the Nevada legislature should be able to tell local governments to provide new services without providing money to pay for them. More than 80 percent of voters in each county opposed the question (Hadfield 1992).

PROBLEMS OF INFLUENCE

County officials have a long-standing image of passivity with respect to exercising their authority—the good soldiers—unwilling to seek out new responsibilities and powers, challenge state authority, or even use the powers they have without clear expressions of state approval (Salant 1993). Many county officials apparently have preferred to let the state assume responsibility for complicated or expensive programs. Moreover, for various reasons, county officials at times have been the leading opponents of home rule. Recent research, however, suggests a new aggressiveness on the part of county officials in seeking out greater authority and, as noted, fighting off unwanted state actions (Waugh 1988; Waugh and Streib 1993; Salant 1993).

County officials, as a whole, have both sought and resisted greater discretionary powers and have welcomed and attempted to avoid new responsibilities imposed by mandates. A more common and consistent goal has been minimizing financial burdens, which has led to an insistence that states not only fund state mandates but also assume greater financial responsibility for state programs supported out of county revenues, such as trial courts. Counties, too, have sought greater federal assistance and fewer federal regulations.

Some research suggests that county and other local officials, working individually or through associations, may have considerable influence on the development of state and federal policies affecting them, the distribution of state and federal funds, and the extent to which state and federal policies are implemented (Rich 1989; Nathan 1983, Hamilton and Wells 1990). The bottom line may be that when it comes to state-local and federal-local relations, local units "are not passive objects allowing themselves to be willy-nilly shoved anywhere. The shoved can and do sometimes become the shovers" (Hamilton and Wells 1990, 153). Six county sheriffs, for example, have challenged the constitutionality of the federal Brady Law, which requires potential handgun buyers to wait five days while authorities run a background check. A federal judge in Montana threw out the requirement that local police run a background check, citing the Tenth Amendment (Rotstein 1994).

Current knowledge of the specifics of how counties seek to exert influence on the federal and state activities and the extent to which they are able to do so is very limited. In exploring the status and influence of counties within the intergovernmental system, more research must be directed at the activities and influence of groups that represent counties in their dealings with federal and state governments.

The influence of the National Association of Counties (NACo) and other local-government lobbying groups in Washington apparently has varied with the condition of the national economy, the partisan complexion of Congress and the national administration, and, though difficult to judge, the quality of the lobbying effort (Berman and Greene 1993; Farkas 1971; Glendening and Reeves 1977; Haider 1974; Hale and Palley 1981; Hays 1991).

Over the years the broad coalition of groups speaking for state and local governments in Washington has had varying degrees of access to public officials. The 1980s were a particularly bleak period. The demands of state and local officials for an increased federal role were frustrated by growing concerns over federal spending levels and the mounting national debt. In the Reagan White House, moreover, cutbacks in domestic programs were often seen as a matter of defunding the Left and reducing subsidies for selfish special interests (Reed 1993; Levine and Thurber 1986). The 1990s, however, appear to be characterized by greater activism. NACo initiated a nationwide effort to educate the public about the federal proactive of imposing, without funding fully, costly mandates to states and local governments. "National Unfunded Mandates Day" (NUMday) was staged on October 27, 1993, and followed by a "Stop the Mandate Madness" protest rally on Capitol Hill in March 1994. Congress responded by introducing legislation (the "no money, no mandate" bill) to relieve state and local governments from all obligations to carry out future federal mandates unless federal funds were provided (S.993/H.R.140). The 103rd Congress took no action on either bill. The 104th Congress, however, did take action, and on March 22, 1995, President Clinton signed into law the Unfunded Mandates Reform Act of 1995. (Jones 1994).

County success at the state level also appears to depend on the condition of the economy, the ideological dispositions of governors and legislators toward the programs pursued by counties, and the energy and talents of the county lobby (Cigler 1991; Salant 1993; Wright, 1988).

Survey information suggests that county association directors are generally positive about county relations with legislators in their states. They are quick to point out, however, that such good relations do not necessarily lead to legislative decisions favoring counties. Thus, although county officials may be trusted, even respected, by legislators, other factors make it difficult for them to secure policy objectives. As one county association official remarked, "Our relationship is cooperative and the legislature is accessible, but ultimately we are not a high priority." Another observed that, "Legislators are fine in the coffee shop back home, but when they get to the capitol, they clearly work for the state" (Salant 1993, 110).

Some county lobbyists also report that legislators continue to treat them in a paternalistic and disrespectful way and to regard them as a special interest no different than a tavern association or tobacco lobby (Salant 1993). To some extent, county officials may be engaging in the habit of poor-mouthing. As one southern legislator has defined it, "When you contend that you don't have anything, can't get anything, and have no hope for the future, you're poor mouthing" (Bragg 1988).

In recent years, as economic times have become tougher, county officials have often been on the defensive at both the federal and state levels, trying to prevent further cuts and fend off costly mandates. They have also had to fight off the image of being special pleaders with large appetites. Many county officials tend to view themselves, perhaps increasingly so, as partners or cogovernors in the intergovernmental system and have not given up the quest for strengthening cooperative relations with state and national governments (Stewart 1991).

CONFLICT AND PROGRESS IN THE STATES

To a considerable extent, the status and activities of county governments as well as those of other local governments are the product of decisions made at the state level. Many of the most important choices were made long ago, when state constitutions were written. State courts have historically regarded counties as administrative arms of the state rather than as entities with self-governing powers. As a result, state legislatures have exercised virtually unlimited authority in prescribing the limits of county discretion and intervening in county affairs by stipulating various rules and requirements that mandate the performance of certain functions. For those concerned with understanding trends and variations in county responsibilities and discretionary authority, the proper unit of analysis would be the state rather than the county.

Political conflict at the state level involving counties has generally resulted from three different types of demands: (1) those of citizen groups, community leaders and, sometimes, county officials that counties be given more general authority (the home-rule movement); (2) those of state officials that counties assume more responsibilities and, at the same time, pay for them out of local taxes; and (3) those of county officials and the groups representing them that states take various courses of action designed to reduce the financial problems of counties.

States have generally responded to demands of others for home rule and to some of their own problems, particularly in raising revenues, by increasing the discretionary authority of county governments. At the same time, however, overall county authority has diminished because of the growth of state mandates. Because of mandates counties are doing more but have less control over their overall agenda and operations. In an effort to provide fiscal relief for counties, moreover, there has been a movement in the states to shift financial responsibility for traditional county services such as jails, courts, transportation, and health and human services. Increased state financial involvement, in some cases at least, has reduced county control over activities (Todd 1991). States have attempted to fill in for the decline of federal aid, but the record has been spotty and the aid has been unreliable (Berman 1992, 1993a). Moreover, elected county officials have little confidence in the state's willingness to provide adequate funding for the programs they must administer (Waugh 1988). A more common state response to county distress has been to encourage and authorize counties to raise their own revenues.

On the bright side, state courts seem more willing to protect county home-rule powers and fend off costly state mandates. According to executive directors of state-level county associations around the country, the spread and success of county home rule along with the emerging willingness of county officials to challenge state actions in court have contributed to judicial rulings in favor of counties (Salant 1993). On mandates, for example, a Texas court ordered the state to reimburse counties for the costs of housing state felons, and in 1987 the Pennsylvania high court ruled in favor of counties by declaring that the state's refusal to fund the lower-court system is unconstitutional. Pennsylvania counties also won a significant case that obligated the state to fund health and children's programs. As noted above, in New York the State Supreme Court upheld an appellate decision that the state department of health had "overstepped its bounds of authority" when it sent to counties an administrative mandate involving county nursing homes that would have cost counties millions of dollars (Salant 1991b).

Information gathered in a 1992 survey of county association officials suggests that state court decisions regarding county authority are just as likely to be resolved in favor of counties as they are against them (Salant 1992). The .500 batting average is significant when considering the fact that courts have nearly always ruled in favor of states because counties were viewed as mere administrative appendages. Such legal domination by the state over counties has been called "state predominance under the rubric of state concern" (Salant 1988).

COUNTY HOME RULE AND DISCRETIONARY AUTHORITY

Over the past several decades there has been a gradual increase in the number of states giving counties general home-rule powers. Thirty-eight states grant counties various forms of general home rule; only eighteen did so in 1965. Arizona became the most recent state to permit counties to adopt home-rule charters when a constitutional amendment was approved in November 1992.

What factors facilitate or inhibit efforts to secure more authority for county governments? What are the consequences of the reforms? How much discretion do counties have? How do the discretionary powers vary? What state characteristics or policies are associated with this variation? Although much remains unknown about these matters, some preliminary observations can be offered.

Reform Efforts

Reform efforts aimed at giving county officials greater general discretion or home rule have, by all accounts, faced considerable opposition in most states. Change, apparently, has been difficult because state officials have clung to the notion that counties are little more than subservient units of the state and cannot be trusted with more discretionary authority. Legislators, regardless of ideology, party, or type of constituency served, have been unwilling to relinquish control and have tended to view more county discretion as producing undesirable results (Berman, Martin, and Kajfez 1985). In some places at least, fear of county home rule has been coupled with the fear that it would lead to new local taxes (Salant 1989).

Even where state officials may have been willing to respond to demands for more county authority, the opposition of others in the political process apparently has prevented action. Demands for a readjustment of local governmental responsibilities, for example, have often encountered the strong resistance of municipalities and their lobbyists. In addition, business groups have been concerned about their ability to defend and promote their interests if responsibilities are shifted from friendly state legislatures to county governing boards (Berman 1992).

It should also be noted that even certain groups of county officials have opposed home rule. Such proposals usually engender the strong opposition of constitutionally elected officers such as sheriffs, attorneys, and assessors. They perceive home rule as inviting structural reform that threatens their autonomy and jobs (Salant and Martin 1993). County legislators at times have also been reluctant to seek greater authority. For example, in speaking of the home-rule effort in Arizona in the late 1980s, one state legislator asserted, "The big problem has been that supervisors have never pushed for it because they trade off home rule for pay raises and financial bailouts" (Salant 1989, 9). County officials who are hit hardest by increased population growth are more likely to be in the forefront of the effort for home rule and an expanded role of counties than are county officials in slow-growing or declining rural areas.

Faced with so many difficulties, it seems remarkable that the bottom-up approach for more authority has produced any change at all. It is difficult to tell from existing research if, how, and why the attitudes of state officials regarding the status and competence of counties have changed or how and why the barriers erected by municipal, county constitutional, business, and other groups to reform have diminished—if, indeed, they have diminished. Research suggests some softening in the attitudes of state legislators in regard to county officials. Such softening, however, may result from the previously mentioned state court decisions placing limits on state control over county authority.

The movement toward allowing greater discretion at the county level has been particularly significant in encouraging structural changes. Several counties, for example, have taken advantage of the discretion given them to opt for the replacement of the traditional commission form with the more centralized county administrator or county mayor form (Jeffery, Salant, and Boroshok 1989). Counties also regularly move to centralize their governments by eliminating or consolidating the elective positions of constitutional officers under the governing board. Many states even permit this type of structural change regardless of home rule or charters. In a 1992 survey of state county associations, counties in nineteen out of forty-one states responding indicated some type of change in the status of elected constitutional officers. The most common change was to consolidate the offices of recorder, assessor, and/or auditor with the treasurer or to move the treasurer's functions into the department of finance under the governing board (Salant 1992).

Less change has been forthcoming in state law allowing counties greater discretion over what functions they may perform or what revenue they may raise, though some progress has been made, particularly on revenues (John P. Thomas 1991). Research suggests that rapid population growth encourages legislatures to give counties more authority in regard to structure. Changes as to what functions a county can perform, however, are more difficult to bring about because of deeply rooted state practices concerning the distribution of authority (Berman and Martin 1988). Financial pressures resulting in a decline of intergovernmental aid account for the new authority given in regard to revenues in recent years. Grants of this authority have often bypassed the formal home-rule route by applying home rule to all counties.

Although much of the increased activity on the county level results from grants of general home rule or greater discretion to undertake certain specific activities, there is a considerable gap between the potential authority and actual authority of county governments. Relatively few counties, for example, have taken advantage of the opportunity to adopt home-rule charters. By the late 1980s, only 117 of the 1,307 counties eligible to take this action actually had done so (Salant 1988). And, between 1990 and 1992, only ten of twenty-eight county charter adoption attempts were successful at the polls, bringing the number of charter counties to about 130 (Salant 1992).

Several disincentives discourage counties from pursuing charter status. For example, many states are simply giving all counties greater authority regardless of home-rule status, which tends to blur the distinction between charter powers and general law (Salant 1988). Further, charters do not mitigate against restrictive court rulings or onerous state mandates, as the role of counties as administrative units of states is generally unaffected by adopting a charter. Many county officials simply do not see the point in spending valuable time and resources on adopting changes that will not address their major problems.

County home rule has had somewhat less appeal in rural than in urban areas. Voters in heavily populated counties are more likely than voters in lightly populated counties to adopt charters (Salant 1992). While reformers often complain about elected county constitutional officers and call for greater centralization in county government, many rural residents apparently feel that what might be gained in efficiency through such a move would be matched by losses in accountability and governmental responsiveness (Weaver 1992).

In evaluating trends, it should also be noted that in some cases the idea of giving counties more discretion and more responsibility has had as much if not greater support at the state level than at the county level. Grants of greater discretion to counties in regard to raising revenues, for example, may have had less to do with the demands of county officials than with the fact that it suits state purposes by shifting the political blame for increased taxation or the failure to reach program objectives to the county level.

Variations in Discretionary Authority

How much discretion do counties have? How does it vary from state to state? One particularly useful index of state policies affecting county governments in this respect—although it needs updating—was developed by Joseph Zimmerman for the USACIR in 1980 (USACIR 1981; Zimmerman 1983). Zimmerman found that counties have considerably less general discretion than cities and less discretion in regard to raising revenues than, say, in regard to restructuring their governments.

What factors seem to explain the amount of discretion provided by states to counties? One factor is the period effect, which is a belief or practice that is unusually important in a particular historical era. Regarding local government discretion, a useful place to look for period effects is in state constitutions. State constitutions adopted in different historical periods reflect different attitudes toward the status of local government. The more recent the state constitution, the more discretion given counties. Moreover, there is evidence indicating that county and city discretionary authority are linked. As one of these local governments receives more authority, so does the other (Berman and Martin 1988).

Finally, research conducted for this chapter suggests that the amount of discretion accorded a county is also related to other measures reflecting the status of county government. More specifically, the number of county governments compared to the number of other local governments, the revenues of county governments compared to those of other local governments, and the extent to which state governments contribute to the revenue sources of county governments are related in a positive fashion to the amount of discretionary authority. Making counties more salient in the pattern of local government in terms of their numbers and revenues apparently has gone hand in hand with giving them greater discretion. Giving counties greater discretion is also linked to giving them increased amounts of state aid as a percentage of all county revenues. Apparently, those states most willing to trust in the discretion of county governments are also those most willing to lend financial support to these governments (and vice versa).

COUNTIES AND INTERLOCAL PATTERNS OF GOVERNMENT

Counties, to some extent, muddle the picture of local government. As they have become more involved in providing urban and regional services, they have also helped to make the urban delivery system more complex, adding to public confusion over the assignment of responsibilities and to the competition among governing units. Still, in many places, counties are central actors in the local government network. They are major collaborators with other units through contracts and agreements, important participants in regional organizations such as councils of government, and direct providers of areawide services such as solid waste, transit, and health. Indeed, one observer has noted after looking back at the 1980s, "If counties had not existed at the beginning of the decade, something like them would probably have been invented by the end of it to deliver sub-regional and regional services" (Dodge 1990, 358).

Counties sometimes provide services to everyone within their jurisdictions. At other times, they provide services such as law enforcement only to those who reside in unincorporated areas. An important new role played by counties is as service provider for suburbanites in unincorporated areas (Schneider and Park 1989). These services include parks and recreation, libraries, land use, and garbage collection.

In some places, such as Allegheny County, Pennsylvania, jurisdictional fragmentation is overcome by county governments playing leadership roles in coordinating activity (USACIR 1992a; Oakerson and Parks 1991). Allegheny County government is concerned mainly with delivering state-mandated services, but as a local government it has five basic roles: (1) providing countywide services such as an arterial highway network and a park system; (2) providing service components that benefit from economies of scale or broad-based coordination, such as police and fire training, the investigation of serious crimes, and forensic analyses; (3) planning, information gathering, and facilitating coordination, including an important problem-solving component for issues that spill over municipal boundaries; (4) funding innovative municipal programs that take on an interlocal character; and (5) providing backup services to municipalities or councils of government (USACIR 1992a, 83).

As an example of innovative activity in regional problem solving, Montgomery County, Ohio, has forged an arrangement with Dayton and twenty-two other municipalities whereby the county sets aside revenues out of its sales tax to fund selected economic-development projects proposed by participating cities and townships. William J. Pammer, Jr., and Jack L. Dustin (1993) contend that this type of tax-sharing program is unique because it is integrated into regional economic development and involves the voluntary participation of local governments.

The most intricate local networks are found in metropolitan areas. Increasingly, however, rural counties are becoming involved in cooperative ventures with municipalities and other local units (Cigler 1993c). Counties and municipalities in rural as well as urban areas have discovered that interlocal cooperation through contracts and agreements can cut costs, improve administrative and professional capacities, and enhance the provision of services.

From a practical perspective, cooperative activities have been encouraged because of the difficulties of securing voter approval for restructuring local governments through consolidation. Although consolidations have been difficult and even more unpopular with local officials than with voters, numerous functions have been transferred from municipalities to counties on a voluntary basis.

The larger jurisdiction of counties often enables them to get a better grip on regional problems than can municipalities. Compared to special districts and authorities, alternative means of meeting regional service demands, counties offer the advantages of being well-known general-purpose governments that are directly accountable to the voters. In some places, however, one might question if counties are actually large enough geographically to handle regional problems. In these places, publicly accountable multi-purpose councils of government, covering two or more counties, are the more logical organizing unit (Berman 1993a).

Counties as well as other local governments are constantly entering into intergovernmental agreements (IGAs), which cover such matters as solid waste management, landfills, libraries, and parks and recreation. IGAs include a variety of partners—neighboring cities, school districts, and even Indian tribes. Agreements range from the handshake variety to the highly formal, such as that involving the joint use of a facility. The number of IGAs between counties and federally recognized Indian tribes, for example, is increasing, particularly for law enforcement and road services. Cross-deputization between sheriff's deputies and tribal police is one manifestation (Whittaker 1993). Most cooperation is also voluntary and conducted without interference by higher levels of government, such as one county's attempt to define its role with the Navajo Nation (Salant 1994). On the other hand, as suggested earlier, an increasing amount of the local cooperation found in the states is the product of state mandates. One common type of top-down regionalism has been legislation such as the Florida Growth Management Act of 1985, which requires counties and other local governments to prepare multipurpose plans regarding growth management, environmental protection, and the provision of an adequate infrastructure. Such mandates have often placed great strains on the administrative abilities of local governments.

National legislation may also disrupt the pattern of local cooperation. An example is the Intermodal Surface Transportation Act passed in 1991, the implementation of which should be of considerable interest to county researchers. This act theoretically not only brings local governments into the transportation-planning process but also increases the role of councils of government (of which counties are a part) in coordinating approaches to transportation, air quality, and growth-management problems.

Counties are likely to play an increasingly important role as participants in regional problem solving in the years ahead. Their specific roles, however, are likely to vary from region to region and within regions over time as specific functions are shifted and alliances are made and, at times, broken. Researchers have much to learn about the varying roles that county governments play in local government networks and how particular networks evolve.

COUNTIES AT THE INTERGOVERNMENTAL FRONTIER

Over the past several decades county governments have assumed greater importance in both the horizontal and vertical dimensions of the intergovernmental system. Many counties have become full-service governments, especially in metropolitan areas where counties provide a number of urban services, often on an areawide basis, and in midsized counties experiencing growth. Rural counties also find themselves grappling with complex issues—solid waste management, economic development, environmental mandates—that necessitate more interaction with local, state, and federal governments. They, too, are more active—and sometimes dominant—in regional and intergovernmental settings. Further, officials of counties situated along the border with Mexico often find themselves responsible for dealing with international issues once exclusively the domain of the federal government (Rivas 1994).

Assumption of new service responsibilities by county governments in rural as well as urban areas has come, in part, as the result of state legislation allowing them more discretion and, in part, as the result of state mandates. In the broad scheme, county officials have both sought out responsibilities and have had responsibilities thrust upon them. They have gained importance both as units of local government, deeply involved in local governing networks, and as units through which the state and federal governments implement programs. Through self-help and aid from the state and national governments, many counties have responded well to the new demands placed on them.

As part of the modernization movement, many counties have restructured themselves and have recruited professionally trained personnel. Thus far there is little evidence of the actual significance of adopting more centralized forms of county government (DeSantis and Renner 1993). Perhaps the most immediate significance of these changes is that they reshape the image of and confidence in these units. The growing professional parity between county and municipal administrators, for example, has encouraged greater communication, interaction, understanding, and cooperative activities (Marando and Reeves 1991b). The growing professionalism of local officials on the municipal as well as the county level has also helped facilitate the implementation of federal-local programs (Peterson, Rabe, and Wong 1986).

Much of the strength of the intergovernmental system rests on the ties or networks among administrators or policy professionals. Elected officials, however, are also well integrated into the system. County legislators are regularly involved in intergovernmental activities. They sit as members of multicounty agencies or multicity/county agencies such as regional planning councils, maintain contact with a variety of state departments, and regularly attend meetings with other county officials (Sokolow 1993a). Organizations like NACo and county associations on the state level not only further the policy objectives of county legislators but also provide forums through which county legislators (and managers) from different states or regions network, exchange ideas and information, and devise solutions to common problems.

With the assumption of more duties, structural changes, growing professionalism, and increased networking among elected and appointed officials, many counties have become more fully integrated into both the horizontal and vertical IGR systems. There is, however, still much to learn about intricacies of these relationships and the overall influence of counties within the intergovernmental system. What factors explain the variation in state policies regarding counties? What are the various roles played by counties in local networks? What determines these roles? Looking at the dynamics of change, one might also ask what factors have propelled the bottom-up drive for county reform in various states. What tactics have been the most or least successful in securing changes at the state level?

County scholars also need to focus on two historic attitudinal or behavioral problems affecting state-county relations: (1) the unwillingness of state officials, especially state legislators, to view counties as little more than administrative subunits that cannot be trusted with increased authority; and (2) the timidity or unwillingness of some county officials to seek authority or to use the authority they have. Existing research suggests a shifting of these attitudes, yet we have little definitive knowledge about their historical antecedents, why they have changed, and what the actual effects are.

Finally, taking a broader perspective, there must be a more pronounced effort to identify the conditions, strategies, and techniques affecting the ability of county officials to exert influence in the vertical IGR system—a system that has become less friendly and more coercive.

3

Determinants of County Government Growth

Kee Ok Park

County governments in the United States provide a variety of services to their residents. They perform many local functions, such as provision of streets and highways, water and sewer services, zoning and community development, parks and recreational facilities, and economic development. Counties also implement a growing number of federally or state mandated functions including health, welfare, and other social services; court and law enforcement; and even education. The number and level of services has expanded substantially.

This chapter will examine the factors that influence the growth of county government, describing county government growth, reviewing the relevant literature, providing data to test several growth-determinants hypotheses, and—based on the findings—discussing how knowledge of the growth of county government can be improved.

BACKGROUND

County governments are growing faster than all local governments except for special districts. Although the total amount of expenditures and number of service functions of counties are lower than those of municipalities, county growth rates are steeper (Schneider and Park 1989; USACIR 1992b). For example, in 1972, county governments nationwide spent $22.3 billion. By 1987, this number had more than quadrupled, reaching $98.2 billion. Moreover, it is increasing steadily in the 1990s (U.S. Bureau of the Census 1990a).[1]

Also, the service-dominance index developed by the U.S. Advisory Commission on Intergovernmental Relations (USACIR), which counts the number of functions for which counties are dominant service providers, rose from forty-one in 1962 to sixty in 1987. As a consequence, county governments in the 1990s are serving more residents, providing more service functions, and employing more persons than ever before in their history.

Metropolitan county governments are growing the fastest among all counties. Indeed, they take a special place in delivering services to metropolitan residents. As urban dwellers moved out of central cities to suburbs in past decades, metropolitan county governments expanded their service delivery by providing state and local services to residents living in unincorporated areas and, in some instances, to those living in incorporated areas. Because the expansion of metropolitan areas into suburbs and exurbs is continuing and fewer areas are incorporating (becoming municipalities), county governments are expected to serve more residents and play even more important service roles in the 1990s. In fact, they are increasingly touted as the local government that can effectively deal with many metropolitan if not regional issues such as zoning, pollution control, and transportation planning.

The magnitude of the growth of metropolitan county governments is illustrated in table 3.1, which shows the per capita expenditures and number of functions of 244 county governments in fifty-six of the largest metropolitan statistical areas (MSAs). The table shows that metropolitan county governments grew in both spending and service functions in the 1972–87 time period. The average per capita expenditures by metropolitan county governments jumped from $262.27 in 1972 to $434.36 in 1987 (in constant 1982 dollars), or by 65.6 percent. The average number of county functions rose from 14.12 to 15.04, or by 6.5 percent.

Table 3.1 also shows expenditures and functions by developmental, redistributive, allocational, and public safety policy areas. According to Paul E. Peterson's 1981 policy-classification scheme, developmental policies—highways, utilities, water transportation, parking, sewage, and sanitation—improve the economic position of a locality by facilitating economic growth. Redistributive policies benefit low-income residents but at the same time hurt localities by impairing economic growth. Redistributive policies include public welfare, housing and community development, health, and hospitals. Allocational policies include employee security, general public buildings, parks and recreation, general government, and financial administration and are neutral in their impact on the economic position of the community. Public safety includes police, fire protection, and corrections.

As Table 3.1 shows, all expenditures and functions except for redistributive functions increased between 1972 and 1987. The largest increase in expenditures occurred in the allocational area, with the smallest increase in the redistributive area. The largest increase in the number of functions occurred in the developmental area, with the only decrease in the redistributive area. These figures suggest that housekeeping expenditures increased the fastest as the size of overall government grew and many counties began to expand their economic development plans to compete with other localities. Although the number of redistribu-

Table 3.1 County Expenditures and Functions

	1972	1977	1982	1987	1972–87	
Expenditures						
					Change	%change
Total	262.27	380.77	345.08	434.36	172.09	65.61
Developmental	53.92	59.28	54.11	64.73	10.81	20.04
Redistributive	97.39	101.12	96.59	104.49	7.10	.07
Allocational	32.52	79.49	71.05	100.32	67.80	208.48
Public Safety	20.48	30.27	32.48	48.55	28.07	137.06
Number of functions						
Total	14.12	14.32	14.59	15.04	.92	6.52
Developmental	2.16	2.49	2.52	2.64	.48	22.2
Redistributive	2.85	2.49	2.70	2.73	-.12	-4.2
Allocational	5.56	5.70	5.70	5.73	.17	3.1
Public Safety	2.38	2.48	2.53	2.55	.17	7.1

Note: Totals also include education and payments to general debt. All expenditures are in dollars per capita.

Sources: Bureau of the Census, *Census of Governments: County Finances, 1972, 1977, 1982, 1987.*

tive functions declined somewhat between 1972 and 1987, the general trend is clear—county governments grew during that time period, and their growth is continuing.

WHY IT IS IMPORTANT TO STUDY COUNTY GROWTH

Scholars study the growth of county government to test general theories about why government grows. They want to see if general growth theories can be applied to the growth of county government. If these theories are supported by empirical data from counties as well as from other types of governments (e.g., cities, states, nations), the external validity of their theories is strengthened.

There are also practical reasons to study the growth of county government, especially in metropolitan areas. First, if the factors that influence growth can be identified, then policy makers may be able to control or manage excessive government growth. Controlling government growth is important at all times, but it is even more vital during economically hard times. Because many counties are experiencing fiscal stress in the 1990s because of a slow-growth economy and declining federal and state aid, many county leaders are searching for ways to control the growth of government. Knowledge of the determinants of county growth could contribute to sound fiscal policy.

Second, knowing the patterns and determinants of county government growth could help policy makers shape the future of their county. Understanding government growth will enhance the ability of county leaders to plan and predict future government growth and respond more effectively to demands for services. Among other things, policy makers may forecast future expenditures and services when they set long-term budgets or devise comprehensive plans.

Third, the growth of county government is likely to be related to the growth of counties in many areas—including residents, households, vehicles, and business establishments. In the 1980s, many suburban megacounties experienced unprecedented growth that created a host of policy problems such as traffic congestion, strain on health care and welfare systems, and environmental pollution. County policy makers can attack these problems more effectively if they know the factors affecting government growth.

What do we know about county government growth? How can knowledge of county government growth be improved? To answer these questions, the remainder of the chapter reviews the literature on county government growth, reports and analyzes data that test hypotheses regarding county government growth, and discusses the results with discussion directed at describing alternative measures and models that can expand our knowledge of county government growth.

DETERMINANTS OF GOVERNMENT GROWTH

A myriad of explanations of government growth and empirical tests of those explanations are available at the aggregated international, national, state, and local levels. These studies provide an overall picture of the factors that explain the growth of government in general. For example, at the international level, David Cameron (1978) investigated eighteen Western nations and found a significant positive relationship between government growth and the length of time a country has been ruled by leftist parties. At the national level, Michael Lewis-Beck and Tom Rice (1985) examined the size of the U.S. government between 1932 and 1980 and found that, among other things, national defense commitment, foreign trade, economic hardship, and demographic change influenced the size of government.

Among American states, James C. Garland (1988) found that the power of bureaucrats and intergovernmental grants explain government growth. At the local level of government, Thomas R. Dye and Susan A. MacManus (1990) showed that the growth determinants of the state public sector and those of the local public sector are different. More specifically, they report that the size of the public bureaucracy, intergovernmental aid, size of the youth population, and less visible methods of revenue collection (reliance on hidden taxes) are the primary determinants of the size of the state public sector, whereas the size of the youth population is primarily responsible for the large size of the local public sector.

These studies, however, do not directly address the growth of county government because they focus on international, national, state, or local government growth at the aggregate level. As a consequence, applying the determinants of national or state government growth to counties may be inaccurate, because these indicators may not reflect the contributions made by individual governments at the local level. Furthermore, several studies use federal-level indicators to determine the size of overall government in the United States. For example, federal-level political indicators such as percentage of Democrats in Congress or presidential party identification are often used to measure preferences of elites (Lowery and Berry 1983; Lewis-Beck and Rice 1985). However, political indicators at the national level may not directly affect the size of state and local government because national political actors have only limited control over the policies of state and local governments. Thus, federal-level variables such as national politics, foreign trade, and defense commitment are not likely to be helpful in explaining the growth of county government.

More specific studies of local expenditure determinants suggest various factors that may influence the growth of local government. After Lawrence Herson (1957) bemoaned the lack of research on municipal governments, many scholars identified various factors that affect the size of municipal government. For example, Edward Banfield and James Q. Wilson (1963) and Susan Welch and Timothy Bledsoe (1988b) used demographic characteristics and government structure to explain the size of city governments. Roland Liebert (1974, 1976) and Thomas R. Dye and John A. Garcia (1978) explained municipal spending with the total number of functions for which cities are responsible. Following Charles Tiebout's (1956) theory of local expenditures and Peterson's (1981) strategic budgeting, Schneider (1989) tested the influence of competition among jurisdictions on suburban city expenditures. Emphasizing the role of states in local budgeting practices, Vincent L. Marando and Mavis Mann Reeves (1991a) used state debt and expenditure limits as determinants of local expenditures.

Although these studies provide many variables that can be used to explain the size of local government in general, the same variables have rarely been operationalized and tested with county government data. Only studies by James Henderson (1968), Keith G. Baker (1977), Gordon Myer (1979), and Herbert Duncombe, William Duncombe, and Richard Kinney (1992) examine some of these variables with county-level expenditures, but even these studies are not comprehensive. They do not control for other important variables, and they do not include many counties in their data base. Although both counties and municipalities often perform similar local functions, counties typically perform state functions as well as local ones. Therefore, the municipal-growth-determinants variables should be tested controlling for the strong linkages that counties have with their state (see Marando and Reeves 1991a).

Although the study described later in this chapter adopts many municipal growth determinants to explain county-government growth, it differs from previous studies in several important respects. First, it stresses the uniqueness of counties by examining the influence of state-imposed mandates on county expenditures. If counties are substantially different and have different working relationships with their state, as Marando and Reeves (1991a) argue, then it is necessary to examine these relationships. Second, this study pools several years of data to test the significance of the variables held out to be determinants of county-government growth. More specifically, the change in the size of government is used as the dependent variable instead of the size of government at a given point in time. This relationship captures the dynamic nature of the influence of determinants on growth. Third, this study examines the growth of county government in four different policy areas as well as in the overall policy area. That is, the determinants of government growth are disaggregated by type of policy area—developmental, redistributive, allocational, and public safety.

INDICATORS OF GOVERNMENT GROWTH

Many scholars equate government growth with the size of government expenditures, and scholars use different indicators to represent the size of government expenditures (Lowery and Berry 1983; Dye and MacManus 1990).[2] One indicator is the ratio of government expenditures to total economic output, which measures government growth relative to the private sector. Another indicator is the ratio of government expenditures to personal income, which measures government growth relative to residents' ability to sustain the policies and programs of government. Another indicator is per capita expenditures, which measures government growth relative to the size of population.

These three measures are relative measures and are useful for different research purposes. For example, if the question concerns why government expenditures grow relative to the overall economy, the first measure is most appropriate. The third measure is most appropriate if the subject is why some county government expenditures are larger than those of other county governments relative to the size of their population.

The study presented later in this chapter employs per capita expenditures, a measure that has been used widely by researchers and is less susceptible to the influence of the size of population than is the actual amount of expenditures. Per capita expenditures measure the size of government, taking into account jurisdictional size rather than economic resources or service needs (Stipak 1991). In estimating growth determinants, the growth of county government is measured by the change in per capita expenditures (in constant 1982 dollars).

DETERMINANTS OF COUNTY GOVERNMENT GROWTH

The change in the size of county expenditures may be influenced by residents' ability to support county services. Counties with more resources can spend more on developmental expenditures than counties with fewer resources. Generally, affluent counties face higher demand for local services because of the homogeneity of their population, which increases with community income (Schneider 1989). In addition, affluent counties may desire more growth-oriented services such as police protection and education, while poorer counties need more stable social services. In addition, counties with greater resources may be able to attract more matching grants from higher level governments.

The growth of county expenditures may also be influenced by federal and state fiscal aid. Intergovernmental aid increases the resources available to counties and stimulates counties' own expenditures, often through matching requirements. Although the influence of intergovernmental fiscal aid on local expenditures is always positive in absolute terms, it is not necessarily positive in relative terms. Thus, the influence of intergovernmental aid on local expenditures is not automatic or trivial. Given that counties rely heavily on states for revenues, the influence of state aid may be even greater than that of federal aid.

According to Liebert (1974), Dye and Garcia (1978), and Robert M. Stein (1982), local expenditure levels depend on the range of functions that local government performs: those that provide a greater number of service functions consequently spend more than others. Functional responsibilities represent not only the current scope of services but also the tendency to expand existing services and adopt new ones. Thus, counties with more service functions are likely to grow faster than counties with fewer service functions.

Counties have different forms of government, and the growth of county expenditures may depend on the form of government they adopt. Under the traditional commission form of government, county administration is frequently divided among competing branches, factions, or personalities and is therefore not centrally controlled. Under the commission-manager form or elected-executive form, county administration is more centralized under the authority of a chief executive or professional administrator. With centralized control and greater expertise in specific policy areas, these counties can embrace more policies and put large-scale projects into place quickly. In addition, elected executives may target service and spending levels at residents or constituents who can help advance their political ambitions.

Counties are legal entities of the state and are susceptible to state control in many administrative and policy areas. Counties have to fulfill state mandates such as enforcing state water-quality standards, meeting jail safety and security standards, and establishing special-education programs. In many states, counties also are bound by state tax, debt, and expenditure limitations. Marando and Reeves (1991a) note that it is difficult to explain county expenditures without considering the presence of state influences on local expenditure decisions. Thus, the growth of county expenditures may be heavily conditioned by state-imposed restrictions.

The growth of county government is also affected by demographic characteristics such as jurisdictional age, region, population size, population growth rate, and poverty rate. County governments in older, established areas tend to provide more comprehensive services to residents because they demand more services (Liebert 1974). Southern counties perform more functions than counties in other regions as a result of historical circumstances and the diminished presence of municipalities within their boundaries. Population size and population growth rate impel counties to expand services, and concentrations of poor residents may require additional services such as health and welfare.

In sum, the growth of county expenditures can be attributed to residents' wealth, intergovernmental fiscal aid, functional responsibility, government structure, state mandates, and demographic characteristics of counties. Initially, the influence of these variables on county government growth as a whole is examined in this research with total county expenditures. However, these variables may have more influence on specific policy expenditures but less influence on other policy expenditures. Therefore, the influence of these variables is also examined with developmental, redistributive, allocational, and public safety expenditures. This disaggregation of county expenditures is congruent with the disaggregation of the concept of government growth advocated by David Lowery and William Berry (1983), allowing the identification of different determinants of government growth within and across policy expenditure categories.

Peterson (1981) claims that each policy area has distinctive politics associated with it. That is, developmental politics are largely consensual, and redistributive politics are virtually nonexistent at the local level. Allocational politics is conflictual and pluralistic. Likewise, the influence of the growth determinants may not be identical across policy areas. For example, local wealth may have more influence on the growth of developmental and public safety expenditures because counties with more resources can allocate more money for economic development and public safety. Federal and state fiscal aid and state mandates may have a greater effect on redistributive expenditures because the latter are largely subsidized by the federal and state governments.

Reformed governments may pursue economic development more vigorously than other types of government by utilizing their expertise and professional ability to control county agencies, thereby resulting in higher developmental expenditures (Sharp 1990). Population growth may produce higher public safety expenditures than other demographic variables, because the movement of population or the influx of new residents can result in social unrest and conflict. Finally, region is likely to influence the area of developmental expenditures because population and job growth has been most acute in southern and western metropolitan counties.

STUDY DATA

Data have been assembled on the expenditures of 244 counties in 56 of the largest MSAs. Consolidated city-county governments are excluded because the Bureau of the Census counts them as municipalities. Also, counties in Rhode Island and Connecticut are excluded because they exist in name only, and those in Virginia are omitted because they are completely independent from their municipalities.[3] The data are pooled from four data points—1972, 1977, 1982, and 1987—to increase the sample size, enhance the efficiency of the estimates, and provide reliable estimates. As a result, all four annual expenditures of 244 counties are included in the analysis. To measure change in the size of county government, the following regression model is estimated:

Expenditures (Exp_t) = Expenditures$_{t-1}$ + Independent Variables$_{t-1}$ + Error.

This model uses lagged variables to predict the actual change in the size of county government. The dependent variables are county government expenditure levels at time t, and the independent variables are expenditure levels at time $t-1$ and other county characteristics.[4] This lagged analysis reduces the number of counties in the data from 976 to 732 because the dependent variables in 1972 do not have lagged independent variables. The expenditure levels at time $t-1$ are included as a control variable because the type of growth examined here is the change in expenditures rather than the size of expenditures. Therefore, the influence of the independent variables on the current expenditures is obtained after controlling for the influence of previous expenditures. Because this lagged model purports to explain the change in the size of county government with lagged variables as well as with other independent variables, it captures the dynamic nature of growth, which is often missed in cross-sectional studies.

The measurement of the independent variables is straightforward. Residents' ability to support county services is measured by per capita personal income. Intergovernmental fiscal aid is measured by per capita aid from the federal and state government in total and in four functional areas. The functional responsibility of counties is measured by the number of service functions each county government performs, regardless of budgetary outlays. The form-of-government variable is a dummy that differentiates the council-administrator or elected-executive form from the traditional commission form. State tax and debt limitations are measured by two dummy variables that denote the existence of state tax and debt limitations. Finally, region is represented by a series of dummy variables dividing the county into north, midwest, west, and south regions, and jurisdictional age is measured by counting from the year of county incorporation.

FINDINGS

Table 3.2 presents the results of regression estimates of the influence of the independent variables on county government growth as measured by total county expenditures per capita in constant 1982 dollars.[5] The income variable has the expected sign but is not statistically significant, indicating that it may not facilitate or hamper county government growth at the aggregate level. The state-aid variable is significant. In fact, except for the strong influence of previous expenditures, state fiscal aid is the most important determinant of aggregate county expenditure growth. State mandates, state tax-rate limitations, and state debt limitations imposed on counties all show the expected signs, and the influence of two state linkage variables is statistically significant, strongly suggesting that county government growth at the aggregate level is affected by state-imposed mandates.

The number of functions that each county performs, government structure, and population growth also show significant influences on expenditure growth. Counties with more functions, reformed structures, or high population growth rates grow faster than those with fewer functions, unreformed structures, or lower population growth rates. At the same time, the size of population, poverty rate, and jurisdictional age are not statistically related to expenditure growth. Another conspicuous result is the regional pattern of county government growth. County governments in the South (base category) are growing faster than those in other regions, a finding that is fully consistent with documented population migration to Sunbelt states.

Table 3.3 reports the results of regression estimations of expenditure growth determinants in four functional areas. Developmental, redistributive, and public-safety expenditures are significantly influenced by residents' income, controlling for other variables. As Peterson (1981) notes, the growth of government in the developmental, redistributive, and public-safety areas seems to be facilitated by the ability to pay rather than by need. State and federal fiscal aid variables show uneven influences across policy areas. State aid is significant only in the redis-

Table 3.2 Regression Estimates of Total Expenditure Determinants

Variable	Unstandardized Coefficient	Standard Error	Standardized Coefficient
Intercept	-151.61		
Total exp$_{t-1}$	0.51	0.06	0.38***
Income	0.00	0.00	0.00
Federal aid	0.38	0.46	0.02
State aid	0.67	0.11	0.24***
State mandate	3.26	1.82	0.08**
Tax rate limit	-43.47	21.22	-0.05**
Debt limit	-2.46	2.66	-0.02
Functions	18.22	4.63	0.12***
Administrator	67.96	26.83	0.07***
Executive	45.63	27.62	0.04*
Population	-0.00	0.00	-0.02
Pop growth (%)	185.99	74.60	0.07***
Age	0.01	0.01	0.02
Poverty rate (%)	-2.37	2.33	-0.03
West	-134.33	35.61	-0.12***
Midwest	-75.89	32.00	-0.09***
North	-100.76	43.41	-0.10**
R–square		.60	
N=732			

Note: All expenditures and intergovernmental aid are in per capita terms. Tax and debt limitations, political structure, and region are dummy variables.

* $p < .10$; ** $p < .05$; *** $p < .01$

Sources: Bureau of the Census, *Census of Governments: County Finances, 1972, 1977, 1982, 1987.*

tributive and allocational areas, and federal aid is significant only in the developmental area. Heavy infusions of federal highway funds are probably responsible for the strong influence of federal aid on county expenditure growth in the developmental area.

Most state linkage variables have the expected signs, and many are signifi-

	Developmental			Redistributive			Allocational			Public Safety		
	CO	SE	SC	CO	SE	SC	CO	SE	SC	CO	SE	SC
Intercept	11.20			-15.84			-20.93			-4.34		
Exp$_{t-1}$	0.65	0.03	0.60***	0.93	0.02	0.84***	0.48	0.18	0.13***	1.06	0.04	0.72***
Income	0.00	0.00	0.05**	0.00	0.00	0.05***	-0.000	0.00	-0.00	0.00	0.00	0.08***
Federal aid	0.00	0.00	0.11***	-0.22	0.32	-0.01	-0.26	0.39	-0.02	-0.00	0.06	-0.00
State aid	0.04	0.07	0.01	-0.33	0.05	-0.17***	0.69	0.42	0.07*	-0.07	0.07	-0.02
State mandates	1.63	0.72	0.07**	7.09	1.31	0.15***	2.41	1.29	0.12**	0.27	0.26	0.03
Tax rate limit	-2.30	3.49	-0.01	-0.64	4.20	-0.00	-9.31	14.48	-0.02	-1.84	2.29	-0.02
Debt limit	0.58	0.45	0.03*	-0.72	0.55	-0.02*	-3.15	1.89	-0.07**	-0.05	0.31	-0.00
Administrator	11.88	4.25	0.08****	10.30	5.56	0.04**	24.48	18.65	0.05*	7.03	2.77	0.07***
Executive	16.16	4.76	0.09***	3.02	5.72	0.01	23.56	19.22	0.04	1.89	3.15	0.01
Population	-0.00	0.00	-0.06**	0.00	0.00	0.03**	0.00	0.00	0.00	0.00	0.00	0.00
Pop growth(%)	2.21	12.87	0.00	-48.48	15.43	-0.06***	238.51	51.02	0.19***	29.30	8.20	0.10***
Age	0.00	0.00	0.05**	0.00	0.00	0.03**	-0.00	0.01	-0.01	-0.00	0.00	-0.00
Poverty rate(%)	-0.26	0.40	-0.02	0.88	0.50	0.04**	-0.30	1.62	-0.00	0.07	0.26	0.00
West	-14.09	6.12	-0.07**	10.49	7.59	0.03*	-39.61	25.23	-0.07*	-8.16	3.87	-0.06**
Midwest	-15.43	5.22	-0.11***	6.99	6.31	0.02	-20.29	21.15	-0.05	-4.69	3.41	-0.05*
North	-19.34	6.14	-0.11***	13.44	7.29	0.04**	-21.34	29.26	-0.04	5.70	4.21	-0.05*
R-square	.56			.78			.11			.61		

Note: All expenditures and intergovernmental aid are in per capita terms.

CO = Unstandardized Coefficient, SE=Standard Error, SC=Standardized Coefficient

N = 732

* p < .10; ** p < .05; *** p < .01

Sources: Bureau of the Census, Census of Governments: County Finances, 1972, 1977, 1982, 1987.

cant, reaffirming the influence of state mandates on the growth of county expenditures and suggesting that county governments grow not only because of residents' demand for services but also because of basic obligations imposed by state authorities. The influence of state restriction variables is slightly stronger in the redistributive area than in the developmental area. Because the impact of state-imposed obligations is stronger in the redistributive area, where counties' policy activities are most prominent, counties are probably (and expectedly) more susceptible to state influence than are municipalities.

Population growth and reformed government also positively influence the growth of county expenditures in many functional areas. In the redistributive area, however, the influence of population growth is negative, suggesting that not all functional expenditures increase when the population grows. Finally, the growth of county expenditures in the South is most notable in the developmental and public-safety areas. The fact that the developmental and public-safety expenditures of southern counties tend to grow faster but their redistributive expenditures grow slower than those of other counties suggest that these counties focus on economic development.

The results in table 3.3 also show that the determinants of growth in different policy areas vary somewhat. In the developmental policy area, growth is mostly determined by local wealth, federal aid, form of government, and region. In the redistributive policy area, it is determined primarily by state mandates and demographic variables. Although federal and state aid may increase the absolute amount of redistributive expenditures, it does not seem to increase the amount in per capita terms. In the allocational policy area, the per capita amount is determined primarily by state mandates and population growth. Population size, which may indicate the population diversity, is not significant. In the public-safety area, per capita spending is determined by local wealth, government form, and population growth, indicating that the ability to pay, professionalization, and diversity of population all result in more public-safety activities.

IMPLICATIONS

This chapter examined the determinants of county government growth with an emphasis on metropolitan counties. County governments have grown significantly over the past twenty years. This growth results from intergovernmental fiscal aid, government structure, and state mandates. Moreover, the influence of these factors appears to vary in different policy areas. The influence of state mandates on county government growth is particularly notable because the functions of counties are somewhat different from those of other local governments. For example, counties generally cannot shift state-imposed functions such as welfare, health, and corrections to other local governments. Given that the number of state mandates in these areas increases constantly, the size of county government is likely to grow even more.

What can county policy makers do to control, slow, or perhaps even reverse this growth? The study results suggest that there are no easy or quick answers to this question. In the first place, it is not clear whether county-government growth in all policy areas should be controlled. For example, growth in the developmental policy area may contribute positively to the local economy. If this is the case, then counties should control the growth of government in the allocation and redistribution areas rather than in the area of development. However, county government growth in the areas of allocation and redistribution is facilitated, if not stimulated, by population growth, implying that county governments may have to discourage population growth to reduce government growth. Given that developmental policy activities may attract new residents, counties may end up reducing developmental policy activities such as economic development and infrastructure improvement in an effort to slow population growth.

The absolute growth of county government, of course, may be inevitable because of population growth and suburbanization. Even in terms of controlling the relative growth of county government, some determinants such as population growth and region are not easily amenable to manipulation by public officials. However, other determinants, such as state fiscal aid, mandates, and number of functions, may be controlled to slow the rate of government growth. For example, states may reduce fiscal aid and mandates to counties simultaneously, thereby preventing counties from becoming dependent on the state for their revenues and easing the burdens imposed on them. Also, county officials may negotiate with the state and other local governments to shift functional responsibilities so that resources and efforts can be concentrated in policy areas deemed essential. This effort, however, may entail long, arduous bargaining with federal, state, and local authorities who have their own incentives to retain popular, low-cost programs and jettison high-cost programs with marginal political returns.

FUTURE RESEARCH DIRECTIONS

This study employed census data collected every five years. Because year-to-year changes may show more detailed patterns of growth, it would be desirable to examine these relationships with annual data. Also, an examination of county government growth in more detailed policy areas may reveal additional knowledge of growth trends. For example, in the redistributive policy area, the proportion of welfare policy expenditures decreased, while the portion of health and corrections increased between 1972 and 1987. Furthermore, just as the determinants of county government growth in the four broad policy areas are somewhat different, those in more specific policy areas may vary as well.

There may also be other growth determinant factors not examined in this study that should be explored. One such factor is political ideology. Research on the influence of ideology on the size of county government may reveal that the desires and opinions of residents are reflected in the size of county government. For example, the political ideology of progrowth or antigrowth county residents and the level of service demands by residents may determine the level of county government growth. Because most county officials are elected and want to retain or seek higher public office, they may have little choice but to respond to the service demands of residents. Similarly, it may well be that county growth is stimulated by interparty electoral competition. This hypothesis certainly has some validity at the state-government level and is plausible at the local level, especially given the fact that most county governments, unlike their municipal counterparts, have retained partisan elections.

Another pertinent question may be whether the growth of county government better reflects the political ideology of residents or the behaviors of budget-maximizing bureaucrats, another variable often mentioned as an important growth determinant (Buchanan 1977). A combination of survey research and census-data analysis could contrast these two possible growth determinants to assess their comparative influence on growth rates.

One often-neglected but potentially significant variable is the policy-driven interaction between county officials and other local-government officials. In metropolitan areas, what counties do is often determined by the functions performed by municipalities or special districts. For example, if municipalities compete with one another to attract businesses and affluent residents, the county may have to follow suit by spending more on economic development and related growth stimulus policies. Otherwise, the county may not survive as a fiscally sound entity because its tax base may shrink and new firms may choose not to locate in the county's unincorporated areas (see Tiebout 1956; Peterson 1981; Schneider 1989). Thus, economic competition among local governments in metropolitan areas may spur growth in the size of county government. Because the actions of local governments have reciprocal effects on one another, this type of relationship should be examined with simultaneous models.

Related to policy interaction and economic competition among local governments, the growth rate of the population in incorporated areas and that in unincorporated areas may have different effects on the growth of county government. That is, the growth of population in unincorporated areas of the county is more likely to increase the size of county government than the growth of population in incorporated areas. People residing in unincorporated areas receive most services from the county government, while those residing in incorporated areas receive services mainly from their municipal governments.

Probably the most underresearched aspect of county government growth, as well as government growth in general, is the consequences of growth. The impact of government growth on residents' taxes, income, employment, and other factors is not well known. What are the consequences of the overall growth of county government? Do developmental, allocational, and redistributive expenditures have differential impacts on residents' taxes and income? Peterson (1981) claims that growth in the developmental area should increase residents' income, while growth in the redistributive area should decrease it. The evidence, however, is sketchy. Mark Schneider (1989, 145) reports that the fiscal and budgetary policies most directly under the control of local governments have only marginal impact on changes in the distribution of wealth. He notes that developmental expenditures have only slight positive influences on the change in median income and the affluent. Similar research is needed to measure the impact of county government growth in general and to test Peterson's strategic-budgeting proposition in particular.

Another aspect of the impact of county government growth is the change in the quality of life when county government grows. As county government enlarges, service-delivery personnel may become more impersonal, nonresponsive, and consumed by paperwork—more bureaucratic. Do residents who experience growth in county government feel less satisfied with services than residents who do not experience growth? Similarly, are residents who live in larger counties less satisfied with county services than those in small counties? William E. Lyons and David Lowery's (1989) survey of residents in Louisville/Jefferson County and Lexington/Fayette County, Kentucky, suggests that residents of small jurisdictions operating in highly fragmented systems are not significantly better informed, more efficacious, more participatory, or more satisfied than their counterparts living in large, consolidated settings. This type of survey research should be directed to residents in different growth settings to answer the fundamental question of how the quality of life may differ in growth stimulated environments.

County growth, as this chapter documents, is real and significant; it has also received little systematic inquiry. This chapter takes a step toward remedying this oversight and suggests several fruitful lines of inquiry that could yield valuable information and new knowledge about the American county.

NOTES

1. The change from 1967 to 1990 is even more dramatic. Expenditures grew from $11.8 billion to $121.2 billion, or by 927 percent (178 percent in constant 1982 dollars).

2. In strict terms, the size of government does not measure the dynamic nature of government growth because size measures the consequence of growth rather than growth itself. If the

question is why some governments are larger than others, the size of government is the appropriate measure. If the question is what factors make governments grow, the change in government growth is a better measure.

3. The primary data sources are from U.S. Bureau of the Census 1989. The changes in per capita county expenditures, intergovernmental aid, functional responsibility, population, and population change are taken from the primary sources. Percentage of residents under poverty come from U.S. Bureau of the Census 1988; state tax and debt limitations are from USACIR 1992b; and government structure and jurisdictional age are from the *Census of Governments: Government Organization* (computer file).

4. Two alternative dependent variables are the current-year expenditures and actual change in per capita expenditures. The former does not capture the dynamic nature of expenditure growth because it simply explains the size of government, not the change in the size of government. Change in per capita expenditures and the current dependent variable produce virtually the same results.

5. All regression models are statistically significant at the .0001 level. Because they include lagged variables, the Durbin Watson *h* test is done for each model. Results show that there is no first-order serial correlation in these models. If changes in independent variables such as intergovernmental aid are included, the explained variation slightly increases in each regression model. However, such changes are not included because their correlation to their own base or lagged variables is high. For example, federal aid and change in federal aid are highly correlated.

PART II

Structure and Governance

4

County Boards, Partisanship, and Elections

Susan A. MacManus

THE GOVERNING boards of U.S. counties approve the taxing, spending, and borrowing of billions of dollars annually. These legislative bodies play major roles in providing a wide array of government programs and activities. The irony is that very little is known about the political landscape in which these decisions are made. In contrast, studies on the electoral systems of city councils abound (MacManus and Bullock 1993). This chapter takes a modest step toward filling a huge gap in our knowledge of the governing boards of U.S. counties. The chapter begins by identifying the various names used to refer to county governing bodies and then focuses on the different types of election formats used to select county legislators, the form of government most commonly associated with each format, and the size of the governing board. This chapter also examines other elected boards and commissions, such as those concerning soil conservation, drainage, school, road, and fire departments. This discussion is followed by a look at other electoral system features—ballot format, majority vote requirement, length of term, term limits, term structure, and timing. The legalities of running for office, such as filing fees, ballot access by petition, and campaign contribution limits are described as well.

Structural features are but one dimension of county election systems. Other dimensions include representativeness and openness, both of which are examined in this chapter. Board representativeness is probed by focusing on partisanship, gender, race and ethnicity, and age composition. Board openness is analyzed by looking at the frequency of vacant seats, the incumbency return rate, new types of candidates (women, minorities, young), and trends in electoral competition. The chapter concludes with an examination of the frequency with which large counties change electoral systems. The factors prompting these changes (court rulings, state mandates, threats of litigation, citizen initiatives, and referenda) are highlighted. The hypothesis that litigation prompts this change is tested.

The data for this assessment are derived from three sources: a 1985 survey by the National Association of Counties (NACo), a 1988 survey by the International City/County Management Association (ICMA), and the author's December 1992–January 1993 survey of governing-board clerks in large counties (hereafter referred to as the 1993 survey). This survey solicited information from county board clerks in the nation's 110 largest counties. These counties had 1990 populations over 423,380 and together contain 45 percent of the nation's total population. Usable responses were received from 91 counties—an 83 percent return rate, which far exceeds the normal response rate for national mail surveys.

The focus on large counties is valuable in two respects. First, big counties are typically the most likely to modernize their governmental structures. Second, they have more diverse populations than smaller counties, thereby permitting hypotheses related to representation to be tested.

GOVERNING STRUCTURES

In recent years, large counties have abandoned structural features associated with the reform movement, such as at-large elections, and adopted structures resembling those used by large cities. However, the pace of abandonment has not been as fast among counties as municipalities, often because the rate at which states have granted home-rule authority to counties has lagged behind that of cities.

Form of Government

The 1988 ICMA county survey identified three prevalent forms of government (Urban Data Service 1988). The first, popularly known as the commission form, is one in which "each elected commissioner or board member [may] serve as [the] director of one or more functional departments in addition to their policy-making roles. The presiding officer may be chosen from the board or elected directly."[1] Under the council-administrator (manager) form, "an elected board sets policy, adopts legislation, and the budget. The council appoints an administrator to conduct the day-to-day county business, to prepare the budget, to oversee department heads, and to recommend policy to the board." The form paralleling the strong mayor–council structure is referred to as the council–elected executive form.[2] Under it "the commissioners or supervisors are the legislative body responsible for making policy. The executive, elected at-large, implements county board policies, prepares the budget, and acts as county spokesperson. The executive often has veto power, which can be overridden. There is a full separation of the legislative and executive powers" (Urban Data Service, 1988).

The 1988 ICMA survey found that 40 percent of all counties operated under the commission form, 38 percent under the commission-manager form, and 22 percent under the commission-elected executive form. The ICMA survey included counties of all sizes. Smaller counties are more likely to have maintained the traditional commission form because they are not as likely to have been granted home-rule status by their states (DeSantis 1989).

The 1993 survey of large counties shows that a mere 7 percent operate under the traditional commission form. More than half (54 percent) are governed by a commission-administrator form and 39 percent have a commission–elected chief executive format (see table 4.1). The latter tend to be the very largest counties, again mirroring the pattern observed among cities and reflecting the influence of the urban county movement.

City-County Consolidation

Paralleling the home-rule movement, which peaked in the early seventies, was state legislation permitting city and county governments to become city-county consolidation governments. Supporters argue that consolidated structures improve efficiency and accountability. However, in recent years, this rationale has come under attack by public-choice theorists, who maintain that efficiencies are best achieved through the competition inherent in fragmentation, especially in large metropolitan areas (USACIR 1991d).

As of 1991, there were twenty-two consolidated city-county governments—a small proportion of all 3,042 American counties (Salant 1991a, 6). Of the ninety-one large counties in the 1993 study, twelve (15 percent) were actually consolidated governments. These types of counties tend to be governed by commission–elected executive forms (64 percent). They also have larger governing boards, usually elected using a single-member district (58 percent) or mixed method (33 percent). Mixed or combination election formats select some board members from at-large seats and others from single-member district seats.

Name of Governing Board

County governing boards take on a variety of names (seventeen different ones according to Blake, Salant, and Boroshok 1988). The unusual names arise from the unique functional responsibilities assigned to them in the early stages of their development (Salant 1991a). The 1993 survey found that county governing boards are most commonly referred to as county commissions (31 percent), boards of supervisors (19 percent), or county councils (18 percent).

Method of Electing Governing Board

There are numerous methods used to elect county board members. In the few analyses that have examined county election systems, the tendency has been

Table 4.1 Governing Structures of Large U.S. Counties

Structure	n	% of n
Form of Government	83	100.0
Commission	6	7.2
Commission-Administrator (Manager)	45	54.2
Commission–Elected Chief Executive	32	38.6
City-County Consolidation	81	100.0
Yes	12	14.8
Name of Governing Board*	91	100.0
Commission	28	30.8
Board	9	9.9
Board of Commissioners	5	5.5
Board of Freeholders/Chosen Freeholders	5	5.5
Board of Supervisors	17	18.7
Council	16	17.6
City-County Council	1	1.1
Legislature	4	4.4
Fiscal Court	1	1.1
County Court	5	5.5
Method of Electing Board Members	91	100.0
Pure at-Large	15	16.5
At-Large by Post	3	3.3
At-Large from Residency Districts	9	9.9
SMD	47	51.6
Mixed (Combination at-Large, SMD)	17	18.7
Size of Governing Board*	91	100.0
3 Members	16	17.6
4 Members	1	1.1
5 Members	26	28.6
7 Members	20	22.0

(continued on next page)

Structure	n	% of n
9 Members	9	9.9
10–15 Members	4	4.4
17–20 Members	5	5.5
21–25 Members	6	6.6
More Than 25 Members	4	4.4
Other Elected Boards (Multiple Responses)*	66	100.0
Soil Conservation	19	28.8
Drainage	5	7.6
Fire	16	24.2
Road	1	1.5
Public Utility	5	7.6
School Board	57	86.4
Hospital Board	1	19.7
Agriculture	2	3.0
Environmental	1	1.5
Board of Estimate	1	1.5
Citizen/Neighborhood Advisory Board	4	6.1
Mosquito Control	1	1.5
Water	6	9.1
Tax	2	3.0
Parks and Recreation	2	3.0
Community College	1	1.5
Library	1	1.5
Deed	1	1.5
Community Service	1	1.5
Emergency Service	1	1.5

Note: Data are as of January 1, 1993.

*Figures in the % columns may not add to precisely 100 due to rounding or to the multiple-response format of a question.

Source: Mail survey of county governing board clerks in largest U.S. counties, December 1992–January 1993, by author. Tampa: Department of Government and International Affairs, University of South Florida.

to lump election formats into three groups—at-large, single-member district (SMD), and mixed (DeSantis 1989; DeSantis and Renner 1992; for exceptions, see Bullock 1990, 1993). In general, at-large systems are seen by their advocates as promoting broader, countywide perspectives rather than narrow district-specific ones. Proponents of SMDs stress their superiority in creating diversity in representation and in fostering a more direct link between citizens and their representatives. Those promoting mixed systems argue that having representatives with both broad and narrow perspectives on the same governing body is better than having just one or the other.

It is important to note that there are substantial differences in the various types of at-large and mixed formats. For example, in a pure at-large system, candidates are voted on countywide and the winners are those who receive the highest vote count. If there are five seats, the five highest vote getters are elected. In an at-large-by-post system, candidates run for a designated position (e.g., seat a, position 1) but are voted on countywide. In the at-large-from-residency-district system, candidates run from geographically defined districts but are voted on countywide. With regard to mixed, or combination systems, there is substantial variation in the ratio of the at-large seats to the SMD seats. Generally, the number of SMD seats exceeds the number of at-large seats. Among the counties in the study sample with mixed systems, at-large seats on average comprise 25 percent of all seats, and SMD seats comprise 75 percent.

The overwhelming majority of large counties elect their legislators from SMD (52 percent) or mixed (19 percent) election formats. Of those still using at-large methods, the most prevalent is the pure at-large (16 percent) type, followed by the at-large-from-residency districts (10 percent) and the at-large-by-post (3 percent).

Size of Governing Board

Almost half of the governing boards of large counties have between three and five members. Nearly 70 percent have seven or fewer seats. The 1993 survey found that larger boards are more common in counties with city-council consolidated governments, commission–elected executive forms, and SMD and mixed electoral formats, although the size difference between those with consolidated governments and those without is not statistically significant.

Governments have tended to abandon at-large elections in favor of SMD or mixed formats to enlarge their governing bodies, most often to enable the creation of a majority-minority district. In a few Voting Rights Act cases, the federal courts ordered jurisdictions to increase the size of their governing bodies for this purpose, although other judicial rulings held that such decisions should be made by the voters or their representatives, not by the courts (Renner 1988b).

Other Elected Boards

Historically, counties have been characterized as fragmented electoral landscapes. In addition to the elected board members, there are often a number of other officials elected countywide, such as the sheriff, attorney, recorder, tax assessor, tax collector, treasurer, or election supervisor. Often forgotten are other elected boards, which typically govern special districts or authorities. A 1985 survey by NACo found that 15 percent of the 1,323 counties responding reported having at least one such elective body. School, road, fire, and hospital boards were the most common special districts.

The 1993 survey reveals that large counties have a much higher incidence of other county elected boards; with 72 percent of them reporting at least one of these entities in their jurisdiction. This pattern may result from the larger number of counties from the West and South among the respondents. Special districts are the most prevalent in these regions. Among the large counties, school (86 percent), soil conservation (29 percent), fire (24 percent), and hospital boards (20 percent) are the most common other elected bodies.

The average number of other elected boards is two, but eight counties have five or more. Of these, seven are located in the West—six in California alone. This fact is not surprising in light of California's long history of creating special districts to address specific functional activities and the state's propensity for direct democracy.

ELECTIONS

The preference for nonpartisan elections has never taken hold in counties like it has in cities. ICMA's 1988 survey of counties found that 82 percent used partisan ballots (DeSantis 1989, 64). In contrast, a 1986 ICMA city survey revealed that 73 percent used nonpartisan ballots (Adrian 1988, 8).

The 1993 large county survey shows that a strong preference for partisan ballots still prevails—82 percent of the counties elect their board members in such a manner (see table 4.2). Although partisan ballots are the predominant format regardless of the type of government, the highest incidence of nonpartisan ballots (24 percent) occurs among commission-administrator (manager) counties—consistent with the reform movement.

Majority-Vote (Runoff) Requirement

In jurisdictions with a majority-vote requirement, a runoff election is held if no candidate receives a majority of the votes cast in the first election. The basic premise behind such a requirement is that to govern effectively, officeholders

Table 4.2 Election System Characteristics: Large U.S. Counties

Characteristic	n	% of n
Ballot Format	91	100.0
Partisan	75	82.4
Nonpartisan	16	17.6
Majority Vote (Runoff) Requirement	88	100.0
Yes	34	38.6
Length of Term	91	100.0
2 Years	9	9.9
3 Years	7	7.7
4 Years	73	80.2
Other (Combination)	2	2.2
Term Limits	91	100.0
Yes	12	13.2
Maximum Number of Terms (Where Limited)	11	100.0
2 Terms	8	72.7
3 Terms	3	27.3
Term Structure	91	100.0
Staggered (Overlapping)	59	64.8
Simultaneous	32	35.2
Timing of Board Election	91	100.0
Odd Years	17	18.7
Even Years	61	67.0
Both (Staggered)	13	14.3
Election Timing Relative to Other Elections*	83	100.0
Same Year as Presidential Election	8	9.6
Same Year as Gubernatorial Election	10	12.0
Same Year as Both President and Governor	38	45.8
Time Unique to Local Government	26	31.3
Other	1	1.2

Note: Data are as of January 1, 1993.

*Figures in the % column do not add to precisely 100 due to rounding.

Source: Mail survey of county governing board clerks in largest U.S. counties, December 1992–January 1993, by author. Tampa: Department of Government and International Affairs, University of South Florida.

should be elected by a majority of the voters (not a plurality). Such requirements are found in local governments with partisan or nonpartisan ballot formats. Runoff requirements are most prevalent in the South and emerged when it was a one-party (Democratic) region and the possibility "that a majority of votes were not cast for the candidate finishing first seemed wrong because it was in fact a final result" (Adrian 1988, 4).

Nearly 40 percent of the large counties have a majority-vote requirement, which is not surprising in light of the fact that 32 percent of them are located in the South. A majority (52 percent) of the commission-administrator (manager) counties have majority-vote requirements, as do only 17 percent of the commissioner–elected executive counties.

Interest in the presence or absence of a majority-vote (runoff) requirement intensified following the 1982 amendments to the federal Voting Rights Act. These amendments established the "totality of the circumstances" test for determining the extent to which structural features dilute minority votes. Under this test, federal courts must now determine whether "unusually large election districts, majority vote requirements, anti single-shot provisions [and] other voting practices or procedures" dilute minority participation in the electoral process. The "other voting practices and procedures" that have occasionally been attacked are staggered terms, small legislative bodies, and long terms of office (Bullock and MacManus 1993).

Opponents of the majority-vote requirement argue that minority candidates winning a plurality of the vote in the first primary (because of splitting of the white vote among several white candidates), will lose in the runoff primary when forced to run against a single white. They argue that in the runoff whites will unite to defeat the minority candidate. However, others maintain that the majority-vote requirement may actually benefit minority candidates, who may be able to form winning coalitions with white liberals, especially in jurisdictions where a minority group comprises only a small proportion of the total population.

Among the few studies involving counties as units of analysis, Bullock and Smith (1990) found that in the 1970s, runoff requirements somewhat disadvantaged black candidates in Georgia counties who led in the initial primary but faced a white in the runoff. However, since 1977, "black primary front-runners do about as well as whites" (1205). The negligible negative impact of the majority-vote requirement found in this study is consistent with the conclusions of similar studies focusing on city council elections (MacManus and Bullock 1993).

Length of Term

Debates over term length often elicit differences of opinion based on estimates of how long it takes a newly elected official to learn the job well enough to get legislation passed and how much time and money are spent campaigning. Most elected officials prefer longer terms—four years for most local offices. But challengers, most recently women and minority candidates, often express support for shorter terms, which they believe promote turnover, thereby increasing the number of open seats and loosening the grip of incumbents. A contrary view is that "longer terms are better at promoting female and minority candidates with more resources to run, i.e., better educated, more affluent individuals who are willing to risk running for office if they do not have to be running for reelection every other year" (MacManus and Bullock 1993, 81).

The 1993 survey shows that four-year terms are the norm among large counties—more than 80 percent have terms of this length. Although there is no statistically significant relationship between length of term and form of government, there is a correlation between length of term and method of election. Only counties with SMD or mixed elections have two-year terms for their county board members, although the proportions with two-year terms are still relatively small in each (17 and 6 percent, respectively).

Term Limits

Term limits for governing-board members are in place in just a few large counties (13 percent). A two-term limit is the most common (73 percent). Those supporting the notion of term limits say they are the only sure way to break the incumbency lock on elective posts because officeholders typically have higher name recognition and more campaign money than their challengers. Opponents of term limits contend that they violate the democratic right of voters to elect the candidate of their choice, regardless of how often that person has held office. These opponents insist that the ballot box affords voters the best opportunity to get rid of incumbents who lose favor with their constituencies. Generally, the term-limit issue has been far less visible at the local than at the congressional and state legislative levels.

Staggered versus Simultaneous Terms

Term structure (staggered or simultaneous) has been a more visible issue, mostly as a consequence of staggered terms being cited in the totality-of-the-circumstances test as a factor to be considered in minority-vote-dilution cases. Proponents of simultaneous terms (all seats up for election at the same time) claim that such a scenario makes slating and group coalition building easier and reduces campaign costs if group advertising is utilized. They also maintain that it is easier to wipe a slate clean if an entire board falls out of favor with the voters. Proponents of staggered (overlapping) terms insist that they make it easier for challengers to gain name recognition and beat incumbents. A more philosophical argument holds that staggered terms ensure some continuity on the board so that there are always some experienced board members in office.

Staggered terms are the most common type of term structure in large counties, with nearly two-thirds possessing them. They are most frequently found in combination with commission (67 percent) and commission-administrator (80 percent) forms of government. In contrast, simultaneous terms are more often found in combination with the commissioner-elected executive form of government. More than half (56 percent) elect their county commissioners simultaneously.

There have been no empirical tests of the actual effects of term structures on candidacies, campaign strategies and costs, incumbent victory rates, or policy making.

Election Timing

Holding elections separate from national and state elections, along with the nonpartisan ballot and at-large elections, were seen by Progressive-era reformers as ways to minimize the influence of state and national political parties in local affairs. But just as the 1993 survey found that the partisan ballot has been retained by most large counties, it shows that only 31 percent hold county board elections at a time unique to local government. Instead, most hold board elections in even years, usually in the same year as elections are held for the president and/or governor. The relatively low incidence of holding county board elections at unique times supports the claim that "the political reform movement that occurred so profoundly at the city level has never been felt as great at the county level" (DeSantis 1989, 62).

Legal Requirements for Running for the County Board

Critics of county-board representation often complain about the incumbent lock and the paucity of female and minority candidates. To entice more candidates to challenge incumbents, reformers advocate lowering filing fees, lowering the number of signatures needed to get on the ballot via petition, and limiting campaign contributions. The major premise is that many potential candidates either do not have as much money or do not believe they can raise as much money as white male incumbents. Proponents of change argue that challengers are particularly disadvantaged when it comes to raising large sums of money from the business community and political action committees, although studies are now finding that successful female and minority candidates are raising amounts comparable to their white male counterparts (MacManus and Bullock 1993).

Those in favor of higher filing fees and higher petition signature requirements contend that they effectively reduce the number of frivolous candidacies. They argue that more candidates make it more difficult to raise money, gain voter recognition, and win, especially when running against an incumbent.

Those opposing campaign-contribution limits contend that there is little comparative empirical evidence supporting the proposition that women and minority candidates are not able to raise money as effectively as white males. They further argue that in large jurisdictions, challengers (increasingly women and minorities) must have the opportunity to raise sufficient funds to use the electronic media, most notably television, or it is difficult to unseat an incumbent.

The 1993 survey shows that in large counties, filing fees actually are quite low. Twenty-nine percent have no filing fee; one-third have fees between one and one hundred dollars. Filing fees exceed $1,000 in only 11 percent of the counties (see table 4.3). In most of these jurisdictions (82 percent), candidates can get on the ballot via the petition route. There is no relationship betwen these filing fees or petition options and forms of government or board election methods.

Campaign contribution limits are in place in one-fifth of the large counties. They are more prominent among counties with commission–elected executive forms (30 percent) and SMD election systems (29 percent). In these counties, the limit is below $500 in 38 percent and below $1,000 in 62 percent. There are no patterns to the contribution-limit amounts among these counties insofar as form of government or board election method are concerned.

COMPOSITION OF COUNTY GOVERNING BOARDS

Large, metropolitan counties have become important providers of a wide range of services, and as a result, much greater prestige is now associated with holding a seat on a county board. Partisan, gender, and racial/ethnic groups closely monitor their representation on the board and work hard to increase it.

Partisan Composition

Neither the 1985 NACo nor the 1988 ICMA county survey elicited information regarding the partisan affiliation of those elected to county governing boards. The 1993 survey asked the partisan affiliation of each board member in counties with partisan elections. Of the 683 commissioners (the total number of board seats in all respondent counties with partisan elections), 58 percent were Democrats and 42 percent Republicans. There is no statistically significant difference in the proportional party composition of boards by form of government

Table 4.3 Legal Requirements for Running for the County Governing Board

Legal Requirement	n	% of n
Filing Fee*†	77	100.0
None	22	28.6
$1–$25	4	5.2
$50	13	16.9
$100	9	11.7
$200–$500	9	11.7
$501–$1000	12	15.6
$1001–$2000	2	2.6
$300–$5000	3	3.9
More Than $5000	3	3.9
Petition Alternative to Filing Fee	83	100.0
Yes	68	81.9
Campaign Contribution Limit	83	100.0
Yes	17	20.5
Actual Campaign Contribution Limit†	13	100.0
$100	1	7.7
$200–$399	3	23.1
$400–$499	1	7.7
$500–$999	3	23.1
$1000–$1999	2	15.4
$2000 and Over	3	23.1

Note: Data are as of January 1, 1993.

* Values not covered by categories did not appear in the responses.

†Figures in the % column add to greater than 100 due to rounding.

Source: Mail survey of county governing board clerks in largest U.S. counties, December 1992–January 1993, by author. Tampa: Department of Government and International Affairs, University of South Florida.

or board election method. No doubt the best predictor of the partisan makeup of governing board members is the party affiliation breakdown of the county's registered voters, although data to test this hypothesis were not available.

To determine the extent to which there is partisan diversity on large county boards, the boards where each party holds at least 40 percent of the total seats were identified. One-quarter (nineteen counties) meet this threshold. Of these party-diverse boards, nine are located in Texas, New York, and New Jersey, which are generally regarded as party competitive states.[3] Of the highly party-balanced boards, 68 percent elect their commissioners from SMDs, and 21 percent do so from mixed systems. This pattern suggests possible socioeconomic (and thus partisan) differences in the composition of the districts. One likely pattern is the presence of Democrat-dominated urban districts and Republican-dominated suburban districts.

Gender Composition

Studies show that the proportion of women serving on county governing boards is smaller than for any type of elective body other than the U.S. Congress (Center for the American Woman and Politics, 1992, 2; Bullock 1990). There are several reasons for this pattern. First, county offices have not been highly visible until recently. Second, there is still a fairly widespread idea among women that counties deal mainly with roads, bridges, and jails and are dominated by good-old-boy and contractor networks. Thus, politically ambitious females have often preferred to run for the state legislature, school board, or city council, although changes have recently been occurring.

While women still do not hold county board seats to the degree that might be expected based on the proportional makeup of the population, there is a trend toward greater female representation. The 1988 ICMA county survey found that women held 9 percent of all county board seats. More telling was the fact that 61 percent of the counties had no women board members. By the 1993 survey, however, women held 27 percent of the board seats in large counties, and only 18 of these counties had no women on the board (see table 4.4). While the 1988 and 1993 figures are not fully comparable because the 1993 sample is restricted to large counties, there does appear to be greater representation of women on county governing boards today than in the past.

One would expect female representation to be higher in larger counties, where the board position is more visible and women's networks are more extensive. According to Robert Darcy, Susan Welch, and Janet Clark, "larger communities tend to be more cosmopolitan and less traditional [and] there are more groups such as the League of Women Voters, the National Women's Political

Table 4.4 Female Composition of the Governing Boards of Large U.S. Counties

% Females on County Board	# of Boards	% of Boards
0	16	17.6
1–9	1	1.1
10–19	13	14.3
20–29	14	15.4
30–39	13	14.3
40–49	25	27.5
50–59	5	5.5
60–69	3	3.3
70–79	0	0
80–89	1	1.1
90–99	0	0
100	0	0
Total	91	100.0

Note: The % column actually adds to greater than 100 due to rounding.

Source: Mail survey of county governing boards in largest U.S. counties, December 1992–January 1993, by author. Tampa: Department of Government and International Affairs, University of South Florida.

Caucus, and the American Association of University Women that . . . give support to women candidates" (1987, 40).

The mean percentage of females on county boards is highest in the large counties with commission-administrator governments (32 percent), followed by commission–elected executive (26 percent) and commission (12 percent) forms. Counties using the at-large-by-post board election method have higher proportions of women board members (44 percent) than those electing board members using SMD (32 percent), at-large-from-residency-district (30 percent), mixed (29 percent), or pure at-large (9 percent) methods. This pattern differs from that observed among municipalities, where election method makes little difference to the proportion of women serving on city councils, although women historically have fared slightly better under at-large systems (Bullock and MacManus 1991; MacManus and Bullock 1993).

The 1993 survey data also reveal that female representation is more extensive where there are four-year terms, majority-vote requirements, term limits, and elections held in even years in the same year as the presidential and/or gubernatorial elections. Whether a county has nonpartisan elections, a petition ballot access option, campaign-contribution limits, or staggered terms makes little difference. These findings should allay the concerns of women's advocates who oppose longer terms, runoff requirements, staggered terms, partisan elections, unlimited campaign contributions, and elections held in times not unique to local government. These structural features either do not significantly affect female board representation or they do so in a positive manner. There does, however, seem to be solid evidence showing the utility of term limits.

Racial/Language Minority Composition

The population of the United States is increasingly diverse from a racial and ethnic perspective. As of 1990, blacks comprised 12 percent of the population; Hispanics, 9 percent; Asian/Pacific Islanders, 3 percent; and American Indians, Eskimos, and Aleuts, nearly 1 percent. These groups, while underrepresented relative to their size in the population, have made significant inroads into county governing boards.

Blacks. The 1988 ICMA survey found that only 4 percent of all county board members were black. More than 83 percent of the boards had no black members, 10 percent had only one, and just 6 percent had two or more. In contrast, the 1993 survey revealed that in large counties, blacks comprise 13 percent of all board members. Twenty-nine percent have one black member, and 21 percent have two or more. Larger counties tend to have more racially diverse populations, so black representational levels in them might be expected to be higher. The data reported in table 4.5 clearly show that where the black population is sizable, blacks hold a greater proportion of the county board seats.

Black women are also making gains. A study by Victor DeSantis and Tari Renner based on the 1988 ICMA data reported that the number of black women on county boards at that time was negligible (1992, 146). The 1993 survey shows that 5 percent of all commissioners are black females, although they still trail black males (9 percent). Some have argued that black females may be doubly disadvantaged by gender and race (Karnig and Welch 1979; Darcy, Welch, and Clark 1987; Darcy and Hadley 1988).

Only a few structural variables are significantly related to the proportion of blacks serving on county boards (board election method, term structure, size of board). The proportion of blacks on county commissions is highest in counties with mixed elections (21 percent), followed by at-large-post (11 percent), at-large-from-a-residency-district and SMD (10 percent each), and pure at-large

Table 4.5 Relationship between Size of Minority Population and Proportional Makeup of County Government Board

Group/% of 1990 pop	# of Boards	% of Boards With No Minority Group Member	Total # of Minority Group Members	Average % of Minority Group Members on Board
Asians[1]	90	96.7	8	0.9
Less than 10%	85	98.8	1	0.4
10–14%	2	100.0	0	0
15–19%	2	50.0	1	10.0
20–29%	0	--	--	--
30–39%	0	--	--	--
40–49%	0	--	--	--
50% and Over	1	0	6	66.7
Blacks[2]	90	50.0	112	13.5
Less than 10%	45	77.8	23	2.9
10–14%	17	29.4	24	14.2
15–19%	12	25.0	11	0.9
20–29%	10	20.0	30	15.6
30–39%	0	--	--	--
40–49%	5	0	22	44.6
50% and Over	1	0	2	22.2
Hispanics[3]	89	83.1	28	3.4
Less than 10%	62	91.9	13	1.0
10–14%	9	88.9	1	0.6
15–19%	1	0	1	20.0
20–29%	11	72.7	4	7.3
30–39%	4	25.0	4	17.8
40–49%	1	0	2	40.0
50% and Over	1	0	3	60.0

Note: The figures are as of January 1, 1993.

[1]For the relationship between the size of the Asian population and the proportion of Asian governing board members, r^2=.68; Adj. R^2=.68; F=184.97914, significant at .001 level.

[2]For the relationship between the size of the black population and the proportion of black governing board members, r^2=.48; Adj. R^2=.48; F=81.12261, significant at .001 level.

[3]For the relationship between the size of the Hispanic population and the proportion of Hispanic governing board members, r^2=.50; Adj. R^2=.50; F=88.11013, significant at .001 level.

Source: Mail survey of county governing board clerks in largest U.S. counties, December 1992–January 1993, by author. Tampa: Department of Government and International Affairs, University of South Florida.

(nearly 1 percent). Higher proportions of black commissioners are found in counties with larger boards and simultaneous council terms. However, none of these structures is as strongly related to black county board representation as the size of the black population itself. DeSantis and Renner (1992) report a similar finding.

None of the other structural features (e.g., form of government, ballot type, term limits, campaign contribution limits, and so forth) is statistically significant to black representation on county boards, a finding consistent with research on city councils (MacManus and Bullock 1993). Structural variables are even less powerful in explaining Hispanic and Asian representation.

Hispanics. In 1988, only 1 percent of all county board members were of Hispanic origin. More than 95 percent of the boards had no Hispanic members and just 2 percent had two or more. The 1993 survey showed that the percentage of Hispanics on large county governing boards was slightly over 3 percent. The proportion of boards with no Hispanic representatives was 83 percent; 5 percent had two or more Hispanic commissioners. Counties with higher concentrations of Hispanics have more Hispanic board members, a fact reinforced by the data in table 4.5. In fact, the size of the Hispanic population accounts for 50 percent of the variation in Hispanic board representation. None of the structural variables, including form of government and board election method, are significant predictors, a finding consistent with research on Hispanics on city councils (Bullock and MacManus 1990).

Three-quarters of all Hispanic board members are male, a pattern also observed among Hispanic city councillors. Typical explanations for the low level of Hispanic female representation are culturally based. Previous studies have found that Hispanic men have traditionally assumed the dominating role in matters outside the home, including politics (Bullock and MacManus 1990).

Asians/Pacific Islanders. The 1993 survey is the first to examine the degree of Asian/Pacific Islander representation on county governing boards.[4] Asian populations are concentrated in the West, but even there the proportion is small (with the exception of Hawaii, where a majority of the population is Asian/Pacific Islander). The 1993 survey showed that Asians are represented on only three large county boards. Of the eight Asian county board members in the study, six (75 percent) serve on the same board—in a county with a majority Asian population. With such small numbers, attempts at statistically based explanations of the impacts of various structures are ill advised. However, studies of Asian representation on city councils have found that structure is a far less important predictor than the size of the Asian population and the community's resources and educational level (Alozie 1992).

A Comparative Perspective. This examination of minority representation on county governing boards yields results consistent with those conducted using city councils as the unit of analysis. In both groups, the general conclusion is that electoral structures seldom have an independent unconditional negative impact on minority voting strength. Electoral structures vary in their impacts on specific racial/ethnic groups due to differences in each group's size, political cohesiveness, participation rates, resources, and ability to build coalitions with others and the degree of a group's residential concentration (MacManus and Bullock 1993).

Age of County Board Members

The generational-politics issue that surfaced during the 1992 presidential election prompted the 1993 survey's examination of the ages of those who serve on county boards. A larger proportion of older commissioners was expected for several reasons. First, the high visibility and intensely competitive nature of the position necessitate substantial resources for a candidate to wage an effective campaign. One would anticipate that older candidates have more extensive networks and greater access to money (personal and contributor) than younger candidates, thereby making it a less-desirable starting place for young, politically ambitious candidates. The increasingly older configuration of the population at large is another reason to expect proportionately more older county board members.

Although the data to test the propositions stated above were unavailable, the basic premise of an older board is confirmed by the 1993 survey data. More than half of all county board members are fifty years of age or older. In contrast, only 2 percent are in their teens or twenties and just 15 percent are between thirty and forty years of age.

The age makeup of a county board can make a difference in how counties raise their revenue and in how they decide to spend it. Aging trends have already caught the eye of youth advocates, who have begun to express concern that exponential increases in older member–dominated boards may result in sharp decreases in the dollars allocated for youth-oriented programs and facilities. However, researchers have yet to test the relationship among age, policy preferences, and spending decisions by county board members.

CAMPAIGN AND ELECTION TRENDS

Greater county visibility has probably sparked more interest in running for county board seats among a wider range of individuals, many of whom may have chosen to get on the ballot via petition. With more candidates running, one would expect greater competition and higher campaign costs.

Candidacy Trends

In the 1993 survey, respondents were asked which of the following characterized their county's commissioner elections over the preceding eight years: More/fewer open seats; more/fewer candidates seeking office; more/fewer women running; more/fewer racial/language minorities running; more younger persons (under thirty) running; more older persons (sixty and over) running.

As table 4.6 shows, in nearly half (48 percent) of the jurisdictions, the number of candidates has increased, far in excess of the proportion of counties reporting decreases (14 percent). Most dramatic is the proportion of jurisdictions in which the number of female candidates increased (72 percent). The percent of counties reporting more racial/minority candidates running is 30 percent, far greater than the instances where the number dropped (8 percent). The larger, more racially diverse counties reported the sharpest increases in women and minority candidates.

The responses with regard to candidate age are quite surprising. Instead of more older candidates as the board composition figures and demographic trends might suggest, the most commonly observed pattern has been an increase in the number of persons under thirty running (observed in 23 percent of the counties), not of those sixty or over (seen in only 1 percent). This finding may provide comfort to youth advocates concerned with the graying of county boards. However, we do not know how the success rate of younger candidates compares to that of older candidates. There has been no research on this topic.

Another somewhat unexpected finding involves the number of open seats. As shown in table 4.6, nearly twice as many counties cited a decrease in the number of open seats (29 percent) as noted an increase (17 percent), although most counties indicated no change in the number of open seats over the past eight years. The data offer little insight into what distinguishes those counties reporting fewer open seats from those indicating more. It can only be surmised that such differences may relate to citizen satisfaction or dissatisfaction with the performance of individual county board members and/or the overall performance of the board.

Ballot Access: Use of the Petition Route

Most counties offer candidates a petition access option. The 1993 survey asked respondents to indicate whether candidates increasingly are utilizing this option. Although most counties indicated no change (69 percent), more counties said yes (20 percent) than no (11 percent) (see table 4.6).

Ballot access by petition (versus filing fee) can be a stimulant to larger, more diverse candidate pools. To test the diversification theory, 1993 survey respondents were asked, if the number of candidates using petitions has increased, who tended to use this access route most. Most respondents said there have been no differences based on age, gender, race, party, or candidate experience. However, in counties where differences existed, first-time candidates appeared to rely most heavily on the petition route (as reported by 36 percent of the counties). The next most frequent users were independents (referenced by 21 percent of the counties): a petition is often the only way independents can get on the ballot in states with partisan elections. What is surprising is the relatively low use of petitions for ballot access by women and minority candidates. It may be that the signature requirement is too onerous for them to meet with limited resources, although the data to test this hypothesis have not been collected.

Competitiveness Trends

The 1993 survey results leave little doubt that elections in large counties have become more competitive. When asked to assess the competitiveness of the county's commission elections over the previous eight years, more than half the respondents (56 percent) said that such elections had become more competitive, and only 8 percent said less competitive. Nearly three-quarters described their most recent board election as very or somewhat competitive, whereas only 9 percent classified it as not competitive at all. Competition is keenest where there are fewer incumbents running for office and where the incumbency victory rate is lowest. For example, in counties classifying their most recent elections as very competitive, the mean percent of incumbent board members running for reelection was 62 percent. In contrast, 92 percent of incumbents ran for reelection in those counties with virtually noncompetitive elections. The mean incumbency victory rate was also significantly lower in jurisdictions classified as highly competitive (48 percent) than in the noncompetitive counties (78 percent).

Campaign Expenditures

The perception that it is expensive to win a seat on a county governing board is widespread. But is it accurate? The 1993 survey asked how much successful candidates spent (on average) during the most recent election campaign. In more than one-fifth (21 percent) of the counties, the average expenditure was $10,000 or less; in another 21 percent, it was between $10,001 and $25,000; and in 22 percent, it ranged between $25,001 and $50,000. In only 20 percent did average expenditures exceed $100,000 (see table 4.6).

There is a significant relationship between the size of a county's population and the average amount spent to win a county board seat. For example, in the most recent election, where the average winning candidate spent less than $5,000,

Table 4.6 Candidacy, Ballot Access, Competitiveness, and Campaign Cost
Trends among Large U.S. Counties

Campaign/Election Trend	n	% of n
Candidacy Trends	83	100.0
# of Open Seats		
More	14	16.9
Less	24	28.9
# of Candidates		
More	40	48.2
Less	12	14.5
# of Female Candidates		
More	60	72.3
Less	5	6.0
# of Racial/Language Minority Candidates		
More	25	30.1
Less	7	8.4
Age of Candidates		
More under age 30 Running	19	22.9
More 60 or Over Running	1	1.2
Ballot Access		
Use of Petition to Get on Ballot (Past 5 Years)	91	100.0
Increased	13	20.3
Decreased	7	10.9
Stayed the Same	44	68.8
*Candidates Most Using Petition Route (Multiple Responses)**	14	100.0
Younger	1	7.1
Older	0	0
Female	1	7.1
Male	2	14.3
Racial/Language Minority	0	0
Whites	2	14.3
First Time	5	35.7
Incumbents	2	14.3
Democrats	1	7.1
Republicans	1	7.1
Independents	3	21.4
No Difference in Type of Person Using	9	64.3

(*continued on next page*)

Campaign/Election Trend	n	% of n
Competitiveness Trends		
Competitiveness Trends (Past 8 Years)	91	100.0
More Competitive	51	56.0
Less Competitive	7	7.7
No Change	33	36.3
Competitiveness (Most Recent Election)	90	100.0
Very Competitive (Close Vote All Races)	13	14.4
Somewhat Competitive (Close Vote Few Races)	54	60.0
Not Very Competitive (Very Few Close Votes)	15	16.7
Not at All Competitive (Lots of Uncontested Seats)	8	8.9
Incumbent Behavior (Most Recent Election)[†]		
% Seeking Reelection	87	76.5
% Reelected (Who Ran)	86	80.1
Campaign Costs		
Campaign Expenditures of Average Winning Candidates (Most Recent Election)*	76	100.0
Less Than $1,000	0	0
$1,000–$5,000	11	14.5
$5,001–$10,000	5	6.6
$10,001–$25,000	16	21.0
$25,001–$50,000	17	22.4
$50,001–$75,000	6	7.9
$75,001–$100,000	6	7.9
$100,001–$250,000	11	14.5
More than $250,000	4	5.3
Expenditure Typical for Winning Candidates	72	100.0
Yes	58	80.6
Expenditure Different Than Usual	14	100.0
Higher	4	28.6
Lower	10	71.4

Note: Data are as of January 1, 1993.

*Percentages in the category may not add to 100 due to rounding or to the multiple-response nature of the question.

[†]For this variable, *n* is the number of jurisdictions that reported data on incumbency and the % of *n* is actually the percent of incumbents seeking reelection and the percent of incumbents reelected, respectively.

Source: Mail survey of county governing board clerks in largest U.S. counties, December 1992–January 1993, by author. Tampa: Department of Government and International Affairs, University of South Florida.

the mean county 1990 population was 772,815. In contrast, where winning candidates spent $250,000 or more, the mean county population was 1,354,378.

Contrary to conventional wisdom, campaign spending is not significantly related to board election method. In large jurisdictions, even candidates running from district seats in SMD or mixed systems typically rely as much as those running at large on the electronic media (television), which is expensive.

Campaign spending is also considerably higher in counties where members of each political party make up at least 40 percent of the board (i.e., highly partisan diverse jurisdictions). For example, 67 percent of the counties reporting that the average expenditure of winning board candidates exceeded $250,000 are those classified earlier as partisan diverse. Campaign spending is also higher in jurisdictions with highly competitive elections.

The amount spent by winning candidates in the most recent election was judged typical by 81 percent of the large county clerks. Where rated as atypical, the county's most recent election was seen as more or less competitive than usual (usually measured in terms of whether there were more or fewer open seats). This research shows that open seats are often created when county board members leave to run for another elective post.

Life after the County Board:
Other Elective Posts Sought by Ex-Board Members

The political-career progression of board members leaving to run for another post has not been examined by previous researchers (Sokolow 1993a). To bridge this gap, the 1993 survey asked respondents what offices were sought by commissioners who left the board within the preceding eight years to seek other elective posts.

The most common path for politically ambitious board members to take leads to a countywide executive or administrative post (e.g., administrator, tax assessor, surveyor, clerk, or election supervisor). More than 37 percent of the clerks report a county board member leaving to run for such a position. Less common is a board member running for mayor (16 percent of the counties) or city council (12 percent).

Of the ex–board members seeking a state office, more seek another legislative office (state assembly or senate) than an executive position (governor, attorney general, secretary of state, state auditor, and so forth). In 27 percent of the counties, ex–board members have run for the state senate. The same figure holds true for those running for the state house of representatives. In contrast, just 8 percent report a board member campaigning to be governor, and only 14 percent had a board member running for another statewide office. About an equal proportion of counties report ex–board members running for U.S. Congress as for judicial posts (16 percent and 18 percent, respectively).

There are no discernible patterns in the types of counties whose ex–board members tend to seek other elective posts. It may well be that an individual's personality and political ambition are stronger predictors of career progression than are demographic or structural variables. But it is safe to say that serving on a county governing board is not a political dead end.

CHANGES IN ELECTION SYSTEM STRUCTURES SINCE 1988

Counties, like other local governments, occasionally change features of their county board electoral system. Alvin D. Sokolow observed that "population growth, suburbanization, state and federal mandates, and more demanding constituencies have pushed county governments" to make changes (1993, 40). This section will explore the extent to which counties have changed their structures since 1988 and the pressures producing these changes.

Extent and Nature of Change

The 1993 survey found that one-fifth of the large counties had changed their board election system since 1988, most often by altering the size of the board and/or the election method. There were few reported incidences of changes in the term structure, majority-vote, term limit, partisan-ballot, filing fee, or petition-signature requirements. More than 46 percent of the counties altering their electoral system changed the size of their board. Forty percent of the counties that changed did so by enlarging the board; only one county reduced the number of seats. Half of those enlarging their boards also adopted a mixed election system.

Overall, 60 percent of the changers adopted a different type of board election method. One-third switched to a SMD method: all but one of the counties moving in this direction abandoned some type of at-large format. Mixed systems were adopted by 27 percent, and again, all but one of these counties abandoned an at-large format in favor of a mixed plan. The trend away from at-large elections parallels that observed at the city, school board (where elected), and state legislative levels.

The growing popularity of mixed election systems at both the city and county levels results from the perception that minority representation is enhanced, whether defined in partisan or racial/ethnic terms. The presence of at-large seats permits groups with geographically dispersed memberships to coalesce and have a chance at winning the seat or being the swing vote that determines the winner. The inclusion of SMDs bolsters the chances of geographically concentrated groups to do the same. In addition, having some at-large seats and some SMD seats in the same electoral system "promotes representation of both neighborhood areas and [countywide] concerns, operating much like a bicameral legislative body encouraging coalition-building" (MacManus 1992, 638).

Factors Prompting Change

Electoral system changes can be prompted by a variety of factors. Because of the prominence of Voting Rights Act lawsuits following the 1982 amendments, it was expected that most counties would identify litigation-related factors as the major impetus for changing their board election methods. However, the 1993 survey showed that of those identifying a reason for change, only one-third cited a federal court ruling (17 percent), a state court ruling (8 percent), or the threat of litigation from a racial/language minority group (8 percent)—covered classes under the Voting Rights Act. In contrast, well over three-quarters cited a citizen initiative (58 percent) or referendum (25 percent) as the source of change.

Surprisingly, when just those counties changing their method of electing board members (the most common target of litigation under the Voting Rights Act) are isolated, the changes were still citizen driven. In only one case was the change in board election method made because of a court ruling, and it was a state court ruling.

One possible explanation for the low incidence of litigation-driven changes in structure may be that the representation of minority groups on county governing boards closely mirrors their proportion of the total population, regardless of board election method, thereby deterring lawsuits based on the Voting Rights Act. Another equally plausible explanation may be that most of the litigation-based changes occurred in the period right after the 1982 Voting Rights Act amendments rather than between 1988 and 1993. At a minimum, the change data show that civic activism plays an important role in the restructuring of county election systems.

County election systems are quite diverse, reflecting the marked differences in their historical evolution and in their demographic, socioeconomic, and political makeup. This study of a wide range of electoral system attributes (and outcomes) has reconfirmed that counties have rarely been the focus of researchers. Only a few electoral system studies could be identified in which counties were the unit of analysis.

FUTURE RESEARCH DIRECTIONS

This chapter has begun to fill the void in the knowledge of county governing boards, partisanship, and elections. It is apparent, however, that little is known about whether the changes and trends observed in this chapter have made county government more effective, efficient, responsive, or accountable. Thus, a top priority for students of the American county should be to examine the effects, if any, of structure, partisanship, political competitiveness, and board composition on both policy-making processes and outcomes. To make such determinations, it is essential that national surveys of counties be conducted in the same methodical way and with the same frequency that surveys of cities are conducted by the ICMA and the National League of Cities. Academics and practitioners alike should encourage ICMA and the NACo to move in this direction and support them when they do.

In addition, the knowledge frontier of the American county can certainly be advanced by carefully conducted, systematic case studies of similar and dissimilar counties within single states. Both quantitative and qualitative research are needed to more fully understand the dynamics of county governing boards and their often-diverse political constituencies.

NOTES

1. Under the earliest form of county-commission government, which emerged in New England during the Revolutionary War, board members were not elected to head specific departments (Wager 1950). However, counties in the middle colonies, with broader functional responsibilities, featured the election of board members with specific functional responsibilities (DeSantis 1989). Today, the commission form of government varies in the degree to which individual board members are actually elected to serve as department heads. It is more common for an individual commissioner to be assigned an oversight role for a department or set of departments.

2. It should be noted there are some elected county executives, like mayors, whose powers are weaker than those of other executives because of the separate election of various officials with executive powers (e.g., sheriff, treasurer, clerk, assessor).

3. Although Texas historically has been classified as a Democratic-dominated state, elections have increasingly become more competitive, especially in its large metropolitan areas. Republican party strength has increased significantly in the suburban counties surrounding Texas's largest cities (Houston and Dallas). In the state's metropolitan counties, there are usually both Democratic and Republican contenders for elected offices of all types.

4. The survey also asked about American Indian, Eskimo, and Aleut representation, but no board members were reported from these groups.

5

Structure and Policy Expenditures in American Counties

Victor S. DeSantis and Tari Renner

AMERICAN COUNTY governments have experienced substantial change as service providers and intergovernmental actors over the past several decades. They have acquired increasing authority over a wide range of policy functions as a result of state and federal mandates and increased service demands, particularly from suburban residents in unincorporated areas (DeSantis 1989; Schneider and Park 1989). This situation stands in stark contrast to the traditional role of counties—providing routine systems-maintenance functions such as tax collection, voter registration, and depository for vital statistics. In addition, counties have rarely been afforded much policy-making authority or administrative discretion to carry out their responsibilities.

Academic research on county governments has been sparse. Recent literature has begun to focus on counties, primarily because of their increasing importance as service providers. This chapter adds to this emerging body of research by exploring the factors that affect public policy outcomes in American counties. To what extent are policies influenced by the social and political characteristics of a county's population? How are these relationships affected by different policy-making structures? Practitioners, academics, and political activists often assume that different ground rules have different biases. Unfortunately, the evidence regarding the nature of biases in county structures is mostly anecdotal.

COUNTIES AS THE TARGET OF REFORM

In recent years, county reformers have made substantial efforts to change government structures. Reformers urge shifts from the traditional county commission form, which they believe is significantly hampered by a lack of centralized executive authority (either appointed or elected). In the commission structure, voters separately elect a legislative body—usually called the board of county commissioners—that has limited policy-making power and a large number of executive department heads or row officers, such as county clerk, tax assessor, tax collector, sheriff, prosecutor or district attorney, coroner, and supervisor of elections.

This traditional form has been criticized for being highly fragmented and incapable of handling the new functional responsibilities of modern county governments. In its place, reformers advocate switching to a version of the commission–county administrator form (with an appointed executive similar to but typically less powerful than a city manager) or the county executive form (with an elected executive). Surveys by the International City/County Management Association (ICMA) indicate that proportionally, more changes have recently occurred in county government forms than in city government forms (Renner 1988a; DeSantis 1989; Boynton and DeSantis 1990). Vincent L. Marando and Mavis Mann Reeves (1991b), in a study of how state, region, and urbanization influence county reform initiatives, found that urbanized counties were most likely to change their government structure.

Little systematic evidence has been assembled, however, that assesses whether the form of county government makes a difference as to who gets elected or what public policies are pursued. Virtually all the existing literature on the effects of local government structures examines American municipalities. Some county research is indirectly useful in exploring county governments; however, its applicability is limited because of the uniqueness of counties' position in the American federal system and their peculiar traditional structures. Counties typically have less policy-making autonomy and are more fragmented internally than are other general-purpose local governments. More than 90 percent of America's 3,042 counties, for example, do not have home-rule charters, and a majority still retain the commission form of government (Salant 1991a).

Despite recent trends to the contrary, these patterns are expected, given the county's political origin. Counties were historically devised as convenient mechanisms for states to deliver a limited set of services within their geographic boundaries. As a result, their functional responsibilities differ from those of municipalities and, not surprisingly, so do their basic forms of government. There were few reasons for state legislatures to provide counties with substantial policy autonomy if their primary role was to administer state programs. It would also be unnecessary to provide counties with internal political structures designed to translate citizen demands into public policy or to promote policy-making leadership by county officials. Indeed, the political incentives of state legislatures would run in the opposite direction.

Progressive reformers at the turn of the twentieth century vigorously attacked the municipal mayor-council form and promoted the council-manager plan, presumably to combat corruption, increase efficiency, and effect economy in government. Reformers often sought to keep municipal government expenditures and activities to a minimum. As discussed above, however, the modern reform movement seeks to strengthen executive leadership to bring greater coordination and direction in carrying out a rapidly expanding number of government responsibilities. Nonetheless, with less policy-making flexibility, structure may have less importance in counties than in municipalities. It is possible that comparatively little within-state variation exists in the policies and expenditures of counties. Consequently, different rules or citizen demands may matter less in explaining the outputs of counties than in explaining those of cities.

DOES STRUCTURE MATTER?

The causes, characteristics, and consequences of local-government structures have interested political scientists for many years. Under the assumption that rules are never neutral, scholars have explored what types of cities adopt different structures (Alford and Scoble 1965; Dye and MacManus 1976; Farnham and Bryant 1985), how they function and change over time (Stillman 1974; Pressman 1972; Svara 1985a; Adrian 1988; Renner 1988a; DeSantis 1989; Boynton and DeSantis 1990), and their policy and representational consequences (Lineberry and Fowler 1967; Clark 1968; Lyons 1978; Dye and Garcia 1978; Morgan and Pelissero 1980; Morgan and Brudney 1985; Welch and Bledsoe 1988a; Schneider and Park 1989). The questions of consequences have been especially controversial and subject to considerable scrutiny in the academic literature.

Although the literature indicates which variables are closely associated with different forms of government and how those structures function, it is less definitive about the effects of different structures on the policy decisions made in American local governments. In their classic study of two hundred cities with more than fifty thousand people, Robert L. Lineberry and Edmund Fowler (1967) found that reformed governments (council-manager government, at-large and nonpartisan elections) taxed and spent at lower levels than unreformed governments (mayor-council government, district and partisan elections). The authors also concluded that political structure had a significant interactive impact on the relationship between the socioeconomic environment of municipalities and their public policies. Specifically, unreformed jurisdictions tended to be more responsive to the socioeconomic characteristics of their constituencies than reformed jurisdictions. A year later, however, Terry Clark (1968) reported that structural reforms were associated with higher levels of aggregate spending in American cities. Another researcher, Roland Liebert (1974), found that if one controlled for the functional inclusiveness of municipalities, the relationship between structure and policy disappeared altogether. The expenditure differences between mayor-council and council-manager cities appeared primarily because the former performed more policy functions. Although each of these studies used different samples and statistical techniques, all were cross-sectional in scope.

More recent studies by William E. Lyons (1978) and David Morgan and John Pelissero (1980) used longitudinal designs to investigate how government forms affected expenditures. These studies also appear to have produced contradictory results. Lyons found that between 1962 and 1972, unreformed cities increased expenditures more rapidly than reformed cities in response to increases in citizen demand and resource opportunities. Using a different longitudinal design, Morgan and Pelissero matched eleven jurisdictions that changed to reformed structures between 1948 and 1973 with eleven cities that retained their unreformed structures throughout this period. In contrast to Lyons, they found no significant differences in spending patterns between the control and experimental groups.

Two additional contributions do not appear to have sorted out the empirical confusion. Morgan and Jeffrey Brudney (1985) found a modest connection between reformed municipal structures and lower per capita spending after controlling for demographic characteristics and the functional inclusiveness of the jurisdictions. Susan Welch and Timothy Bledsoe (1988a) examined the attitudes of local elected officials toward the jurisdiction's level of spending. They found few statistically significant differences between the opinions of those representing reformed and unreformed municipalities.

Overall, the existing reform-consequences literature has tended to use fairly small samples and has focused almost exclusively on large central cities (fifty thousand or more inhabitants) in Metropolitan Statistical Areas (MSAs). This issue was raised forcefully by Paul Farnham and Stephen Bryant (1985) in their examination of the factors affecting community choices of government structures (part of the reform-causes literature). The authors analyzed a sample of 914 cities with populations exceeding ten thousand. A similar, more inclusive scope is necessary for the reform-consequences literature as well. It is certainly possible, if not probable, that the impact of government structure on policy outputs for the largest stratum does not represent all American municipalities or other units of local governments, including American counties.

Surprisingly, there are few studies that have ever attempted to systematically evaluate the policy or representational consequences of different forms of county governments. Such is the case despite the increasing policy and service responsibilities that counties are assuming in the American federal system (DeSantis 1989; Schneider and Park 1989; Salant 1991a), their substantial authority over controversial redistributive policies (Schneider and Park 1989), and the increasing diversification of county forms of government (DeSantis 1989; Salant 1991a).

A study by Mark Schneider and Kee Ok Park (1989) examined the total, developmental, and redistributive per capita expenditures and number of functions performed by 162 counties located in fifty of the largest MSAs using expenditure and form of government data from 1977. Controlling for the effects of region and population size, Schneider and Park concluded that county-executive jurisdictions spend the most and perform the most functions among the three basic forms of county government. County-administrator jurisdictions were consistently second, and the traditional commission counties were consistently last. The structural differences were more dramatic for per capita expenditures than for number of government functions performed. In fact, Schneider and Park's data indicated that county-executive forms spend more than twice as much per capita as county-commission systems.

The results of this data show that reformed county governments are associated with more expenditures and higher levels of government activism than are unreformed county governments. This should not be construed to contradict the conventional wisdom of reformed structures in American cities or the findings of Lineberry and Fowler, Lyons, or Morgan and Brudney. As discussed earlier, whereas the municipal reform movement was presumably aimed at economy and efficiency, contemporary reforms in American counties are promoted to increase professionalism and centralize executive leadership to more effectively control and manage their expanding service-delivery roles. County reformers seek to change political structures to handle an expanding government. In fact, the reformed county that had the highest expenditures (county-executive) follows the same basic blueprint as the unreformed city type (mayor-council). Consequently, there are clear reasons to expect that reformed county structures are correlated with policy outputs in the opposite direction of reformed municipal structures.

CAUSAL MODEL AND HYPOTHESES

Although the direction of the correlations might differ between cities and counties, the basic patterns of causality should be similar. Figure 5.1 presents a causal model relating county socioeconomic characteristics, political culture, political structure, and public policy outputs. The model is similar to that used by Lineberry and Fowler in their analysis of American cities.

There is certainly ample evidence that the socioeconomic characteristics of a county influence both political culture and political structure, which are also likely to be correlated. If we distinguish between political cultures using Daniel Elazar's (1966) classic categories, it is probable that traditionalist cultures have been the least likely to abandon the commission form. Moralist cultures would have been the most likely to modernize their county government structure, with individualist cultures falling between the two extremes.

The research reported in this chapter seeks to investigate the remaining causal linkages in the model. To what extent do a county's socioeconomic characteristics and political culture directly influence public policy outputs, and how are these relationships affected by political structures? The primary goal, therefore, is to explore the interactive effects of structure. The famous statement that

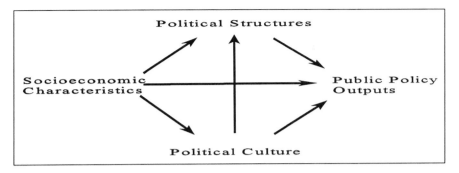

Fig. 5.1 A Causal Model of County Government Structure, Socioeconomic Characteristics, Political Culture, and Public-Policy Outputs

rules are not neutral does not necessarily imply that structure has a direct (or additive) effect on public policy outputs. It may be that rules merely facilitate (or hinder) the efforts of various groups or coalitions to get government to respond to their demands. In fact, a major criticism of the traditional unreformed model of county government is that it is less responsive to citizen demands and less capable of adapting to the changing demographic and social character of American counties.

Consequently, the hypothesis is advanced that the association between county political/socioeconomic characteristics and public policy outputs will be stronger in counties with reformed government structures than in those with unreformed structures. Given the comparative lack of county policy autonomy, however, it is possible that the impact of all of the variables in Lineberry and Fowler's model for cities are weaker in explaining county policy variations. With less independence from the state, county governments may be less able to respond to their citizens' needs and demands. To the extent that such is the case, lower correlations should be expected between county policy outputs and the jurisdiction's socioeconomic and political characteristics, regardless of political structure.

MEASUREMENT

Government structure data were obtained from the ICMA's "County Form of Government" survey conducted in 1988. The survey was sent to county clerks in all 3,042 counties in America. A second request was sent to those jurisdictions that did not initially respond. A total of 1,295 counties are included in this analysis (42.5 percent of the total). Financial and demographic information for each jurisdiction were obtained from U.S. Census Bureau.

The dependent variable (public-policy outputs) is measured using 1987–88 per capita expenditures. However, given the functional inclusiveness and other problems with this measure, several adjustments were made. First, educational expenditures are subtracted from the total. Although education is one of the most important and costly expenditure items for many counties, there are drastic interstate variations in the level of education expenditures that make it problematic to include this functional item in total per capita spending. In states such as Maryland, counties are responsible for and directly provide education. In other states, such as Texas and Florida, where independent school districts have their own taxing authority, counties have few, if any, links to education. In other states, such as California, counties generally operate special-service schools only, providing education to the disabled, to the mentally handicapped, and to those seeking vocational and technical training. Given this diversity in educational responsibility and the relatively high costs associated with this function, it is appropriate to consider only noneducation spending when comparing aggregate county spending patterns. [7]

In addition, given the methodological problems that others (Stipak 1991) have documented when modeling public expenditures, an alternative method is used as a measure of the dependent variable. We use the logarithm (base ten) of noneducation per capita expenditures. The use of a logarithm is widely employed by other researchers to take into account the argument that each dollar spent will have a diminishing marginal effect on overall city services.

Generalized-least-squares multiple regression is used to analyze differences in the counties' noneducational expenditures. This dependent variable is examined as a function of the following independent variables: form of government (commission, county administrator, county executive), 1985 population, metropolitan status (whether it is a county with an MSA central city, a suburban county in an MSA, or a rural non-MSA county), median per capita income, region (West, Northeast, North Central, and South), percentage of general fund revenues that are intergovernmental, and the 1988 Democratic presidential two-party vote percentage. In the situations above where dummy variables are used, the reference category is listed first.

The percentage of general fund revenues received from other governments is included as a measure of and a control for fiscal dependency. Total county expenditures might be expected to rise as intergovernmental revenues increase. The increases in expenditures, however, may not reflect a greater policy commitment to spend additional funds raised from within the jurisdiction. The fiscal impact of intergovernmental revenues can be stimulative, substitutive, or additive. The inclusion of this factor in the equation as an independent variable (as opposed to measuring the dependent variable as own-source revenue) permits the examination of the possibility that the relationship between fiscal dependency and total expenditures varies under different structural arrangements.

The two-party percentage for Michael Dukakis in 1988 is included as a proxy measure for political culture/ideology. The Democratic presidential vote in this election is assumed to be the weakest in traditionalist political cultures and the strongest in moralist political cultures. The individualist cultures should register vote totals between the two extremes. The 1988 Democratic presidential vote cut across the political culture types as no other recent national election has. As a result, it is preferable to using any combination of elections or index of Democratic party strength. In fact, we do not intend to distinguish counties on the basis of party competition. Rather, the goal is to rank counties with respect to voting behavior that reflects a more (or less) liberal political culture.

In the regression analysis, a pooled model for all respondents is estimated, including terms representing form of government as dummy variables with commission as the reference category. The models subsequently are separately reestimated by form of government to capture any differences that the structure variable may have on the other independent variables. This approach examines the relative impact of the independent variables across the three reestimated models and identifies any changes in sign, strength, or statistical significance. This process may appear somewhat more tedious than the conventional techniques for examining interactions and comparing regression equations; however, greater precision in individually evaluating the variables is necessary given the exploratory nature of research on county government structures.

DATA ANALYSIS

The multiple regression results are displayed in table 5.1. In examining the full pooled model, the R-square of .11 indicates that 11 percent of the variance in total noneducational per capita county expenditures (using the base ten logarithm) can be explained knowing all the independent variables in the equation. Despite the high proportion of unexplained variation in the dependent variable, the overall model is statistically significant ($p < .0001$), as are several individual factors.

The difference between the county administrator form of government and all others is positive (beta = .13) and statistically significant at the .0001 level. The difference between the county executive form and all others also is positive (beta = .04) but not statistically significant ($p = .19$). Reformed county structures appear to be associated with higher expenditures than unreformed ones, but the gap is not as great as expected. Each of the regional dummy variables are statistically significant at the .0001 level. North Central, northeastern and southern counties all spend significantly less than the reference category (western counties). Per capita income also has a significant independent effect on county expenditures (beta = .16). A county's ability to pay appears to be positively as-

Table 5.1 GLS Regression Results with Total Per Capita Expenditures as
Dependent Variable in Four Models

Variables in the model	Model 1: All Counties	Model 2: County Commission	Model 3: County Administrator	Model 4: County Executive
	Standardized Regression Coefficients			
County Administrator	0.13***	--	--	--
County Executive	0.04	--	--	--
1988 Presidential Vote	0.04	-0.01	0.13**	0.02
South	-0.38***	-0.33***	-0.35***	-0.52***
Northeast	-0.21***	-0.21***	-0.21***	-0.12
North Central	-0.23***	-0.23***	-0.23***	-0.30**
Rural	0.20***	0.32***	0.11	0.20*
Suburban	0.07*	0.12*	0.03	0.12
1985 Population	0.02	0.00	-0.02	0.07
Per Capita Income	0.16***	0.16***	0.19**	0.18*
Intergovernmental Revenue %	-0.03	-0.07	0.05	-0.09
Model Statistics				
Multiple R^2	.11	.15	.12	.15
F test value	14.55***	9.31***	6.50***	4.66***
N	1250	470	454	251

* = significant at the .05 level

** = significant at the .01 level

*** = significant at the .001 level

Sources: ICMA "County Form of Government" survey 1988 and U.S. Census Bureau.

sociated with service levels. As for metropolitan status, rural counties spend significantly more than the other categories and suburban jurisdictions have a beta
weight of .07 (probability = .05). This finding appears to contradict conventional
expectations regarding the increasing functions performed by the most urbanized counties. However, it is important to realize that this pattern is merely a
snapshot. It is not possible to determine from this data whether or not the rural-

urban gap has actually decreased over time. Neither population size nor the proportion of intergovernmental revenues is significantly correlated with the dependent variable. The same appears to be the case for the 1988 Democratic presidential vote.

Consistent with the above results, each of the individual models explains a small proportion of the total variance in the dependent variable. Perhaps more importantly for the hypothesis regarding the interactive effects of structure, the three models each explain approximately the same proportion of the variance. The counties with commission, county administrator and county executive forms produced R-squares of .15, .12 and .15, respectively.

The results from the three stratified models, however, suggest that several independent variables have differential impacts according to government structure. The 1988 Democratic presidential vote is not significantly correlated with county expenditures in either commission or county-executive structures but is for county-administrator forms, in which the average per capita expenditures increase along with the county's level of support for Dukakis. Although this finding only partially confirms expectations, it should be noted that the first two forms do not result in identical patterns. The vote for Dukakis in 1988 is negatively correlated with the dependent variable in commission counties and positively correlated with it in counties with an elected executive. The political-culture measure is most weakly correlated with policy outputs in unreformed jurisdictions.

The impact of county metropolitan status (county with a central city, suburban, or non-MSA) also appears to vary depending on government structure. Both dummy variables are significant in the commission model but not in the county-administrator model, and only the rural/nonrural distinction is significant in the county-executive model. Among the commission counties, rural jurisdictions have higher expenditures than nonrural areas. Suburban counties also appear to be associated with higher expenditures than nonsuburban counties. In county-executive jurisdictions, on the other hand, the suburban/nonsuburban difference is not statistically significant, but the rural/nonrural distinction is significant in the same direction as in commission counties. Given the cross-sectional nature of this data, it cannot be determined if the patterns above are a result of reformed structures enabling urban and suburban counties to close the gap with their rural counterparts, a plausible conclusion given the historically strong role of counties in rural areas.

Region appears to be significantly correlated with the dependent variable in all three forms of government. The South/non-South differences, in fact, produce betas with the highest absolute value in each of the three models. Regardless of government structure, Southern counties spend significantly less than counties in other regions of the country, perhaps because of the more powerful role of

Southern states vis-à-vis local governments. All of the other regional differences are statistically significant in each of the models, except the northeastern dummy variable for county-executive communities. Western counties (the reference category) spend more than counties in the other regions, regardless of government structure.

Per capita income also appears to have a significant effect on county expenditures, regardless of structure. Predictably, the correlation in each equation is positive. A county's ability to pay seems to increase county government activity in all models, reflecting conventional wisdom that more affluent jurisdictions can afford more services.

County population size and proportion of intergovernmental revenues apparently have no statistically significant impact on the dependent variable under any of the structures. Although this is the case, the direction of the relationships differ between the models. Increases in population are associated with increases in per capita county expenditures in each of the models except for county-administrator jurisdictions, where the correlation is negative. Alternatively, fiscal dependency is negatively correlated with expenditures in all but the county-administrator model. In none of these instances, however, can we reject the null hypothesis that the individual regression coefficients equal zero.

DISCUSSION

This chapter investigated the causal linkages between county government structure, political culture, socioeconomic environment, and public-policy outputs. Contrary to expectations for reformed versus unreformed cities, reformed counties were expected to spend more and be more responsive to population characteristics than unreformed counties. The findings are generally consistent with these assumptions and with the work of Schneider and Park. However, whereas Schneider and Park found higher spending levels associated with county executive jurisdictions, this research found significant differences only between the county-administrator and commission forms. The former tended to result in greater expenditures than the latter. County-executive forms outspent commission forms in the analysis as well, but this result was not statistically significant.

The findings from both the pooled and stratified models underscore regional differences in county governments and their operation. Because of the different historical patterns in the development of county governments, the roles that counties play in service delivery are somewhat different across regions. In many areas of the South, counties continue to play the more traditional role of state administrative subunits.

The 1988 Democratic presidential vote had a positive and significant effect on county expenditures only among county-administrator governments. The correlation in county executive jurisdictions was positive and in commission systems was negative, but neither was statistically significant.

Contrary to expectations, the socioeconomic characteristics of the jurisdictions were not more powerful determinants of expenditures in reformed counties than in unreformed counties. The R-square values indicate that additional variables explain a large portion of the variance in county expenditures. It is possible that county structures are less relevant than those of cities given the reduced policy-making autonomy of the former. It is also possible that other important variables have not been included in this analysis. Clearly, the linkage between forms of American county governments and public policies is complex.

Although the results of this inquiry are exploratory, they imply that county forms of government lack strong policy consequences. As modern American counties expand their policy responsibilities to adapt to a changing environment, they may not find it essential to alter their basic policy-making structures. It must be underscored, however, that these conclusions are tentative at best. We know very little about the consequences of county government structures because few researchers have systematically examined them. In light of the expanding role and salience of counties in the American federal system, it is critical that further research be conducted in this area.

FUTURE RESEARCH

Future research might include a more effective means of controlling for the variation in county functional inclusiveness (using noneducation expenditures is only a partial solution). Perhaps this problem can be avoided by examining different measures of policy outputs such as innovativeness within particular policy areas, proportionate expenditure changes over time, or differences in county bond ratings. In light of the probable mitigating influence of counties' comparatively limited political autonomy, it might also prove useful to examine separately those jurisdictions with and without home rule.

In addition, researchers should explore this area using different longitudinal designs. One variation might include analyzing the same counties before and after a change in structure and comparing the results to a control group of counties that did not change. It is also clear that additional demographic characteristics must be incorporated into future research. Regardless of the specific direction, however, it is critical that researchers not neglect American counties, including their governmental structures, so that counties do not remain academically forgotten governments.

6

County Conflict and Cooperation

Kenneth A. Klase, Jin W. Mok, and Gerald M. Pops

CONFLICT AND cooperation in and among American counties are important but neglected subjects of scholarly study. We know little of the causes, consequences, or conditions that foster conflict or cooperation at the county level. Equally neglected are how conflict is managed and how county officials secure cooperation from the many autonomous and semi-autonomous agencies that, collectively, share power. In contrast, the causes, consequences, and management of conflict within and among cities have received considerable attention (see Huelsberg and Lincoln 1985; Jenks 1994; Svara 1990b). That counties have been so ignored is somewhat surprising in light of the growing influence of counties on the daily lives of citizens (Menzel et al., 1992).

Moreover, due to the growth of state and federal government mandates (USACIR 1990a) and a surge of interjurisdictional issues, the number and complexity of conflicts facing county officials is expanding as well (Bingham 1986). Even in rural states with reasonably stable lifestyles, issues such as landfills for out-of-state garbage disposal and air and water pollution control are controversial and receive much debate.

This chapter provides a conceptual framework for exploring why conflicts arise in American county government and, by implication, how conflict might be resolved. Specifically, the kinds of conflict that arise in county government are examined with respect to their nature, intensity, and duration. Our analysis focuses on relevant variables affecting county governance and their likely influence in creating and conditioning conflict-management processes. The concept of conflict from a political and public-administration perspective is the basis for the development of the framework. The county conflict framework can also serve as an aid to understanding patterns of cooperation in county government.

CONFLICT DEFINED

The sine qua non of conflict is the presence of disagreement. Conflict typically arises when two or more parties fail to agree because of differing values, interests, resources, or—in the context of governing—approaches to analyzing or implementing public policy. Conflict is "a struggle over values and claims to scarce status, power and resources in which the aims of the opponents are to neutralize, injure or eliminate their rivals" (Coser 1956, 8). Significant conflict requires a manifestation of differences that exist between or among individuals and groups. Causes for these differences may be found in the conditions of and changes in the social and political structure rather than in marginal differences in styles, personalities, or methods of work. Moreover, significant conflict requires that differences be deep seated. In other words, for conflict of a significant nature, intensity, and duration, the differences must be important, not trivial.

Overt conflict also requires that different positions, values, and interests be purposefully asserted. It is not sufficient that these differences are opposed in principle; they must be articulated in such a way that they become overt, manifest. Conflict occurs then "when one sees the prospect of relative deprivation resulting from the actions of or in interacting with others" (Litterer 1966, 180). Even when the conflict appears to be resolved and agreement has been reached, particularly in policy development, the perceptions of parties to the conflict about these differences can continue to influence the implementation and eventual outcomes of public policy. Accordingly, the nature, intensity, and duration of conflict will differ depending on how the parties adjust to these differences (Pops and Mok 1991).

THE NATURE OF COUNTY CONFLICT

The perceptions of elected and appointed county officials about the origins of conflict and official and unofficial efforts to address conflict are important in understanding county government conflict. Official involvement is inevitable in agenda setting, policy formulation, and program implementation (Stephenson and Pops 1990). In numerous cases of day-to-day controversies involving public-policy matters, county officials are, in fact, the primary actors who define and mediate conflict and shape its outcomes. The kinds of conflict county officials perceive, how they understand conflict to have arisen, and how they perceive their role in addressing it are also central to understanding the approach taken by county leaders to manage conflict.

County-level conflict, like most public-sector conflict, possesses characteristics that are rarely, if ever, found in the private sector (Carpenter and Kennedy 1988, 4–11), largely because of the pluralistic foundations of American politics and public-policy making. There are other reasons as well. First, county disputes, like other public-sector conflicts, are frequently multilateral. For example, in the area of environmental disputes, the average number of parties to a dispute is four or more, and in some cases the number can be as high as forty (Bingham 1986, 100). Second, those who participate in conflict situations at the county level often do not possess a thorough understanding of legal and political processes, adequate knowledge of the issue, clarity regarding the scope of the conflict situation, or decision-making authority over goals and procedures. Thus, as new members join in a dispute or as original members withdraw, new issues can emerge that may either replace old issues or shift their focus. John Kingdon (1984), for example, argues that the policy-issue coalitions involved in conflicts cannot maintain their membership easily. Instead, they change as the locus and the focus of the issues change. Explicit and well-defined conflict-resolution procedures and structures may control conflict, but county-government conflict, like other public-sector conflict, often takes long periods of time for resolution and on occasion may become chaotic and even be beyond resolution (Carpenter and Kennedy 1988, 11–17).

Conflict at the county-government level occurs in many arenas. It can arise at the nexus between public and private sectors. For example, where public services are contracted out, conflict can often arise over such issues as legal restrictions, political accountability, and fiscal responsibilities (Redekop 1986). Furthermore, demands from one or more segments of the public for regulatory protection or new services can and often do force county governments into disputes with private-sector firms (e.g., rate setting by cable television companies). In this arena, the intensity of the conflict may depend on the extent to which the regulated firm views the role that government is asserting as legitimate. Demands might also be generated by citizen groups or special-interest groups, which likewise will affect the intensity, duration, and management of county conflict. Moreover, the nature of conflict can differ depending on whether the contracting entity is a not-for-profit or a for-profit organization. The resistance of regulated interests and individuals to compliance efforts by administrative agencies presents yet another arena of conflict.

The intergovernmental sector is also an important arena in which counties can and often do experience considerable buffeting and conflict (USACIR 1985). County governments often enter into agreements with other governments to provide public services, and those agreements can sometimes end in conflict. A recent trend contributing to intergovernmental conflict, especially characteristic of the Reagan-Bush administrations' brand of fend-for-yourself federalism, is the frequent use of mandates by higher-level governments. There is a clear perception by local-government officials that federal and state mandates create such conflict situations (Fix and Kenyon, eds., 1989). In addition, as federal and state fiscal aid dwindles, local governments often find themselves in competition with each other over issues such as economic development, taxation, and revenue enhancement (Menzel et al. 1992, 24).

In general, the attributes of local policies (goals, time dimensions, implementation procedures, perceived and actual impacts, and scope and type of targets) can significantly affect the occurrence, nature, and intensity of county conflict. The type and intensity of the conflict can also differ depending on the identity of the participants. As suggested, the parties in dispute with a county government could be other governments at the federal, state, and/or local levels. Thus, the relationships a county government forms and maintains with other levels of government can provide an important clue as to whether a dispute will occur at all and how significant it will be. Research indicates that if a federal or state agency exercises its authority in an illegitimate fashion or abuses its authority, subordinate-level agencies will object, and the potential for dispute between them grows (Blau 1964; Lorenco and Glinewell 1975).

Conflict in county government is thus applicable to a wide range of policy issues and jurisdictions. Indeed, county governments may be more susceptible than other governments to conflict situations. Their rapidly expanding roles as service providers have certainly propelled them into disputes with municipal governments and private-sector providers. Furthermore, the modernization movement that has transformed many counties from narrowly focused arms of the state to entities resembling full-service municipalities has been accompanied by stress, strain, and conflict. Moreover, the historic fragmentation of county government along with the proliferation of special districts and independent boards and authorities have fostered conflict conditions.

These fragmented mixes of authority and overlapping territories have resulted in complex interlocal governmental relationships and an environment rife with actual and potential conflict. In responding to these numerous changes, local governments, especially counties, have been subjected to severe fiscal constraints at the same time that state and federal mandates have been expanding without concomitant fiscal support. Taken as a whole, the environment of county government, with its multiple actors and wide-ranging dispute arenas, contributes to the nature, intensity, and duration of county conflict.

A CONCEPTUAL FRAMEWORK

A conceptual framework can be developed to understand the reasons why county governments experience conflict and, when they do, the differences in nature, intensity, and duration of that conflict. The literature on organization-environment relations (March and Simon 1958; Katz and Kahn 1982; James Thompson 1967) suggests that the county environment constitutes an open system subject to external influences. In this view, the external environment is composed of the broader, general arena in which all local governments function and the task environment, which is the more immediate and specific portion of the county environment that is relevant for such conflict.

The nature of the organizational environment is described by the specific components that compose it. This view considers the environment as a constraining phenomenon surrounding the organizational subsystem as well as the medium in which it must function. F. E. Kast and J. E. Rosenzweig (1979) describe such an environment in terms of the characteristics that constrain it. Other approaches identify major dimensions in relation to the allocation of resources in the task environment (Aldrich 1979) or in terms of the degree of complexity and instability present in the environment (Duncan 1972). Counties can most readily be described as subject to highly complex and dynamic environments as a result of high levels of perceived uncertainty and large numbers of components in the environment that are in the process of change.

Based on these general observations about county environments, a conceptual framework of county conflict can be specified along four major functional dimensions—economic, social, geographic, and political. The county's specific task environment is composed of several dimensional components: structural-functional variables (including developmental stage and organizational arrangements) and powers (legal autonomy and fiscal capacity). This framework focuses on conflict and why it occurs in county governments as they carry out their responsibilities.

Dimensions of the General Environment Affecting County Conflict

The major functional dimensions of the county-conflict framework include a number of external factors that are hypothesized to influence indirectly the onset of conflict and to affect how county government handles conflict when it occurs (see figure 6.1). These factors include general economic conditions, geographical uniqueness, social diversity, and political dimensions of the county, and they are treated as controlling factors in understanding county conflict. The relationship between the task-environment variables (fiscal capacity, legal autonomy, organizational arrangements, and developmental stage) depicted in figure 6.1 and the nature, intensity, and duration of county conflict—i.e., the primary independent and dependent variables in the framework—are affected by control variables in the general environment. These variables are considered likely to influence both the task-environment variables and the nature, intensity, and duration of county conflict. As such, these factors must be considered in the framework and taken into account in evaluating the incidence of conflict.

Economic Variables

Economic variables indicating the nature of the general economic environment of counties are hypothesized to be significant in setting the conditions of the general environment influencing county conflict. Examples of indicators that would measure the economic dimensions of the environment include economic

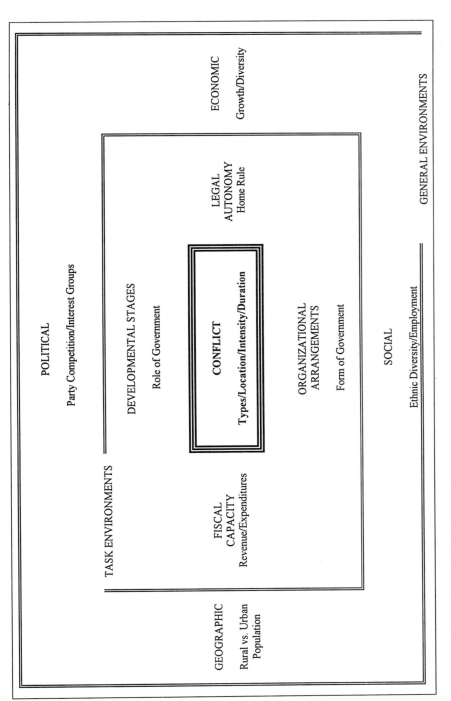

Fig. 6.1 County Conflict Framework

growth, per capita income, income spread (distribution of income by income class), assessed valuation of property, and diversity of industry and services. These specific measures represent the economic resources in the general environment of county government; they influence county governance and consequently the onset of conflict. In addition, these measures reflect the wealth and revenue base of the general environment and thus indicate the level of resources potentially available in facilitating policy outputs (Dye and Gray, eds., 1980; Lineberry and Sharkansky 1978; Dye 1984). A county's economic diversity may also reflect the likelihood of conflict among major economic interests in the county.

Geographic Variables

Geographical attributes of counties are significant because they determine certain aspects of the environment in which county conflict arises. Counties located in metropolitan areas—so-called urban or urbanizing counties—are most significantly affected by conflict-inducing needs and demands, while more rural counties have their own unique characteristics that affect the nature of conflict (Murphy and Rehfuss 1976; Duncombe 1977; Marando and Thomas 1977). The physical size of a county will affect conflict by creating the greater potential for cross-county differences to arise. The mobility of the population and the degree of access are also key factors in determining the nature of county conflicts because they often affect the homogeneity of the county population. The location of a county within the state, region, and nation can also affect the potential for higher levels of intergovernmental conflict. The following examples of geographic variables are thus hypothesized to be significant relative to task-environment variables and the nature, intensity, and duration of county conflict: whether the county is inside, adjacent to, or remote from a metropolitan area; physical size of the county; topography and obstacles to mobility; and distance from a state line or international border.

Social Variables

Social variables also affect the general context in which county conflicts arise. Perhaps the greatest social impact on that environment derives from the nature of the county population. Homogeneity instead of heterogeneity in the population is important in the development and maintenance of community lifestyles and values (noted with respect to metropolitan areas by Williams et al. 1965; Williams 1967; Simons 1968) and thus is a significant element in conditioning the general environment of county conflict. Not only is the level of diversity a factor, but other social factors either heighten or diminish the potential for conflicts to arise. Of particular importance in this regard is the relative stability of the social infrastructure in terms of employment levels and public assistance. The relative levels of collective bargaining and union activity are also social attributes of the environment that will affect the potential for conflict. Examples of social variables thus hypothesized to influence task-environment variables and the nature, intensity, and duration of county conflict include population diversity, social instability (percentage and number of unemployed people and of those on public assistance, rates of alcoholism and drug abuse), and unionization and other forms of collectivized activity.

Political Variables

Political variables likely to affect the general environment of county conflict and to influence the task environment variables as well as the nature, intensity, and duration of county conflict include the level of party competition within the county and within the state (Nice 1987), the presence or absence of cohesive political interest groups in the county, and the strength of political parties in the county. Political competition is indicated by the degree to which parties actively participate in county elections by nominating candidates for office and the degree to which they otherwise actively participate in the debate about county issues. These factors either heighten or diminish the potential for conflict to arise. The level of interest-group participation and pluralistic politics in a county will also predispose the general environment to varying levels of potential conflict.

Components of the Task Environment Directly Affecting County Conflict

Significant dimensional components of the task environment in the county-conflict framework include variables directly related to county governance that affect the nature, intensity, and duration of conflict, including structural-functional determinants and levels of power, stage of development (modernization), structural form of government, and degree of legal autonomy—especially home rule—and fiscal capacity.

Developmental Stage

The functional scope of counties affects the immediate environment in which conflict arises. Counties, although historically created by states to provide such services as law enforcement, relief to the poor, and roads and highways now provide many other services. The variety and magnitude of service roles result directly from the complexity of the modern intergovernmental system (Salant 1991a). The functional scope of county government reflects the level of development of the individual county, ranging from a stage of development in which more traditional functions predominate to higher stages of development where more modern functions are performed. This process of county modernization reflects the evolution of counties into more comprehensive units of government.

As administrative arms of the state, counties deliver services that are constitutionally mandated by the state as well as services required by statute and administrative regulation. Such services as law enforcement, property assessment, road maintenance, and tax collection are illustrative. At a higher stage of development, county governments provide many services similar to those provided by municipal governments, such as parks and recreation (separately or jointly with cities and towns through intergovernmental agreements) and planning and zoning services for residents of unincorporated areas.

Counties can also assume the role of regional government. At this stage, counties often take responsibility for transportation, air-quality management, resource conservation, creation and maintenance of landfill and toxic materials disposal sites, and economic development as well as regional-planning functions. In this role, counties may become dominant decision makers vis-à-vis cities within their borders and share responsibility with the state. Examples along these lines include the Baltimore, Maryland; Minneapolis–St. Paul, Minnesota; and Portland, Oregon, areas.

The variety of new roles that counties are assuming reflects an outgrowth of "urbanizing and suburbanizing trends and dwindling federal support to states and localities" (Salant 1991a, 6). As functional scope steadily increases and counties advance to higher stages of development, the lack of corresponding increases in resources inevitably puts them into a fiscal pressure cooker that is rife with conflict. As a result, it is plausible to hypothesize that the number of conflicts will increase and the nature and intensity of conflicts will change.

Organizational Arrangements

The traditional form of county government is a three- to five-member elected board of commissioners with power to oversee county operations. This form remains the most widely used in America, particularly in rural states. Other forms include the commission-administrator (manager) and the elected county executive forms, in which the chief executive has broad powers similar to those vested in a city manager in a council-manager municipality or a mayor in a strong mayor–council city. These forms are analogous to the traditional and reformed government structures frequently discussed in the literature on municipalities.

It was noted earlier that structural forms bear some relationship to the political environment. The council-manager form often takes root in communities with socially homogeneous values (with presumably reduced levels of conflict), while more political forms, including the elected-executive form, are found in socially heterogeneous communities with presumably higher levels of conflict (Kessel 1962). Robert C. Lineberry and Edmund Fowler (1967) note that reformed governments are often indicative of lower political responsiveness and lower taxing and spending, perhaps because decision makers are more insulated from potential conflicts and professional managers have more power in reformed governments (Lineberry and Sharkansky 1978). Mark Schneider and Kee Ok Park (1989) find that metropolitan counties with reformed structures (especially elected county executives) are more responsive, spend more, and provide more services than counties with the traditional commission form of government. Thus, a positive relationship exists between highly politicized forms of government, even if reformed in structure, and the level of spending and service provision.

Regarding cooperation, James H. Svara (1990b) notes that reformed municipal governments are more likely than traditional municipal governments to experience cooperative patterns. He attributes such cooperation to the greater degree of central authority, the relative insulation of elected officials from community conflicts, and the tendency for officials to share values in reformed municipal governments. As the level of professionalism in county government increases, counties would be expected to emphasize merit over political patronage, and the county administrator would be expected to have greater power to appoint department heads. A multitude of independent boards and commissions or numerous elected officials may also be in place, thus diluting the influence of county commissioners/legislators and administrators. The more highly politicized the county-government structure, as in traditional, unreformed locales, the more likely it is that conflict will arise. In reformed structures that include an elected county executive, the highly politicized environment often contributes to considerable conflict between the executive and the county council. Interactions among officials in counties with reformed and less politicized structures are likely to be characterized by cooperation because of the presence of central authority in the county commission, the integrated organizational authority of a professional manager, and the tendency for officials to share values.

Thus, the following are hypotheses concerning the relationship between county organizational arrangements such as form of government and the degree of central administrative leadership and conflict: (1) the form of county government influences the nature, intensity, and duration of conflicts—if county governments are reformed or less politicized, there will be a stronger tendency toward more cooperative patterns, while traditional or more politicized county governments will tend toward more conflictual patterns, controlling for the influence of other contextual variables such as developmental stage and legal autonomy; (2) the degree of central administrative leadership or fragmentation of authority will also affect the nature, intensity, and duration of conflicts—the more widely dispersed administrative authority is among political actors other than the county commissioners (other constitutional officers or independent boards and authorities), the more likely it is that conflict will increase.

Legal Autonomy

Thirty-eight states grant county home-rule authority, which is defined as "a grant of authority to counties through statutes or constitutions that allows local self-determination" (Jeffery, Salant, and Boroshok 1989, 4), and it effectively confers legal autonomy. Such powers can be granted by the state in structural, functional, and/or fiscal domains to allow for more reformed structures and to address the growing demands of county residents for a variety of services such as regional transportation and environmental protection (John P. Thomas 1982). Although the state will normally prevail in a legal sense whenever an issue is engaged, such as in the case of environmental law (Tarlock 1987), the home-rule provision is political and legal acknowledgment that "local governments are more cognizant of local needs and better suited to respond than are states" (Jeffery, Salant, and Boroshok 1989, 127).

Counties with home-rule authority have more flexibility to devise their own internal organizational structures, to utilize a wide variety of revenue sources, and to determine the scope of service provision. This flexibility presumably provides counties with the capability to respond to change in ways unavailable to counties without home rule. Such flexibility will affect patterns of conflict and cooperation, which may run in contradictory directions. On the one hand, counties with autonomy are likely to experience less conflict because they presumably can do a more effective job of problem solving. On the other hand, such counties may experience turf struggles that lead to heightened levels of conflict, especially between county-city, county-state, and county-federal governments.

On balance, however, organizational arrangements that increase professionalism, integrate administrative decision making, and minimize the fragmentation of authority are likely to foster cooperation. Thus, it can be hypothesized that the extent to which county governments are allowed to exercise self-governance in any domain (structural, functional, or fiscal) will influence the nature, intensity, and duration of conflicts. In other words, counties that have considerable legal autonomy will experience less conflict and will benefit from the flexibility to respond in a variety of ways to situations that result in conflict. Counties lacking significant decision-making autonomy and power will experience higher levels of conflict.

Fiscal Capacity

The ability of a county to generate its own source revenues is a crucial component of its power. In part, this ability is derived from legal authority granted by a state, but in large measure it also relates to the way a county organizes itself to seek revenue enhancement and to the political and economic situational variables that condition whether the county will seek home-rule powers. Generally speaking, the nature, intensity, and duration of conflict will vary with whether the county is revenue-rich or revenue-poor. If revenues are plentiful and within the capacity of the county to respond to community demands, a greater variety of such demands will be made. The county must then face conflict generated by such competition.

MANAGEMENT STRATEGIES

Management strategies adopted by counties to deal with conflict are generally consistent with typical patterns of organizational responses leading toward conflict resolution. The initial response by counties to conflictual situations may be avoidance, such as refusal to accept responsibility over a conflictual matter or determining that the costs of winning the conflict may outweigh the benefits, especially if the issue lacks significant relevance to community goals or values. If the issue cannot be avoided, the county may attempt to enhance its competitive position against others involved in the conflict by seeking wider political and material support.

If the county possesses resource superiority, county leaders may attempt suppression (or domination) of the conflict. However, if other participants demonstrate overwhelming power over the issue in conflict, a county may exercise accommodation (giving in and sacrificing its interests to that of the other party) to minimize losses. In some situations, county officials may react to conflict by compromise and bargaining, i.e., by willingly giving up something to get something of equal or greater value, particularly when other parties in the conflict possess relatively equal power over the conflict issue and the process. Counties may also attempt to resolve the conflict by finding ways to allow all parties to further their essential interests through collaboration or integration (K. W. Thomas 1976; Ury, Brett, and Goldbert 1988).

COOPERATIVE PATTERNS

This chapter has primarily sought to clarify the nature of county conflict and to delineate the factors that contribute to conflict. We would be remiss, however, if we did not focus some attention on cooperative patterns of interaction. After all, county governments are not universally subject to conflictual conditions, and cooperation is usually, but not always, more desirable.

Conflict and cooperation are often viewed as opposite ends of a continuum, but this view might not be the most theoretically correct. Indeed, it might be argued that conflict and cooperation have separate patterns of interaction that, under some circumstances, may be linked together. Svara (1990b), for example, views conflict and cooperation as two separate continua. The distinctions between the patterns are less obvious at intermediate points along the continua, where shifts between patterns may occur. In this view, the absence, containment, or resolution of conflict does not necessarily result in cooperation. Furthermore, this theoretical perspective provides an explanation of how conflict and cooperation can coexist.

In many respects, cooperative patterns of interaction correspond to the most positive aspects of the strategies for conflict resolution outlined earlier. Cooperative patterns, however, are based on trust resulting from compatible goals, consistent interests, and shared values. In such a situation, resources are used to secure agreement, and substantial trust is demonstrated by participants in the governmental process. The underlying assumption is that participants have common or compatible goals and values and engage in goal-directed behavior. Thus, cooperation rather than conflict prevails. This theory does not imply that disputes arise where patterns of cooperation are absent; however, when disputes occur, they are resolved by reference to common goals, interests, and values.

Even though patterns of conflictual interaction in counties are considered the result of the factors outlined in the county-conflict framework, the potential for patterns of cooperation is enhanced by reversing the effects hypothesized for the conflictual factors discussed. To shift from conflictual to cooperative patterns of interaction, county governments must establish organizational arrangements that clarify roles, enhance coordination, and assert central authority (Svara 1990b). Organizational arrangements that accomplish this shift result from the increased professionalism typically associated with reformed governments.

The developmental stage for a county can negatively affect role clarification and the level of coordination because higher levels of development often coincide with increasing complexity in organizational arrangements. In addition, increased legal autonomy and fiscal capacity can enhance the ability to take appropriate action. The basis for common action rests on including all parties in the discussion of the conflictual issue, in providing full access to information, and in keeping the lines of communication open (Svara 1990b). Addressing the underlying factors that contribute to conflict would strengthen relationships and enhance the prospects for shifting to cooperative patterns of interaction.

Conflict is rooted in the involved parties' values and interests, which although not fully compatible, may have essential overlapping elements. The shift to patterns of cooperation may be accomplished by discovering shared values or by the mutual desire to avoid inaction.

Successful management in county government requires an understanding of the complexity of the environment that gives rise to conflict (Gross 1964). The framework developed in this chapter identifies and clarifies the factors in the environment that are hypothesized to affect the nature, intensity, and duration of county conflict. Future validation of this framework will enhance the understanding of county conflict and cooperation and help county officials pursue goals by navigating successfully between circumstances and conditions that lead to conflict and/or cooperation.

PART III

Management Issues and Challenges

7

Leadership and Professionalism in County Government

James H. Svara

ADVANCING LEADERSHIP and professionalism have been central to the debate and deliberations concerning local-government reform in the twentieth century. Counties have not been excluded from that debate, but they have largely remained on the sidelines. The structural conditions in counties (the prevalence of the traditional plural executive, commission form of government and fragmentation) have impeded strengthening leadership. Political partisanship has also served as an obstacle to greater professionalism in county government.

The discussion of governmental reform in counties started later than in municipal government, and change in county government structure is less common. In the late 1980s, for example, only one of every four American counties had a commission-administrator form of government, and 12 percent had an elected executive (Jeffery, Salant, and Boroshok 1989). Perhaps because of these prevailing attitudes and practices, the roles and behavior of officials in county government have attracted little scholarly attention. Consequently, there is a tremendous imbalance between the material available on leadership and professionalism in cities and in counties.

Addressing these topics in the county setting must begin, therefore, with an examination of the presumed obstacles to leadership and professionalism. Until the stereotypes that cause counties to be ignored are challenged, the slighting of counties is likely to continue.

To examine what is known and not known about leadership and professionalism in county government, this chapter will first categorize the relevant topics. Next, the existing literature on the subject is reviewed. Finally, the kind of inquiry needed to deal with the gaps in knowledge is suggested.

OBSTACLES TO LEADERSHIP AND PROFESSIONALISM

There are a number of features that could plausibly impede county officials from attaining the same kind of leadership or degree of professionalism achieved by their counterparts in cities. As county administrator Claude D. Malone (1986, 5) puts it, "Some counties still suffer from *tism*'s and *ism*'s—nepotism, favoritism, junketism, pork barrelism, perkism, patronism. However, with time, close media attention, a more knowledgeable population, and federal and state laws to the contrary, *tism*'s and *ism*'s are disappearing."

Despite the decline in these particular problems and the high quality of officials in counties described later in this chapter, the municipal-reform literature would identify the following conditions found in counties as antithetical to effective leadership and professionalism.

First, the most common form of government—the county commission—is a plural executive body. As one student of county government described the situation in the mid-1960s, "We suspect that the only way we can maintain our headless county structure is to insist that all other levels of government abandon the executive plan and share our handicaps by being made to adopt the county multiple leadership, committee system" (Bernard N. Hillenbrand, quoted in Cape 1967, 23).

As noted earlier, forms of government with elected or appointed executives are used in only 37 percent of all U.S. counties. Still, the use of the executive and administrator forms is more common in urban areas than in rural areas. As of 1979, only 42 percent of the U.S. population lived in counties with the traditional commission form (USACIR 1982). Furthermore, some states use the commissioner-manager form extensively. In nine states, a majority of counties use managers, and seven additional states have more than twenty county managers each.

Second, commissioners are typically elected in partisan elections. Eighty-two percent of commission elections are partisan, whereas three-quarters of city councils are elected on a nonpartisan ballot (Sokolow 1993a, 31). The type of ballot and the typical concurrence of county elections with state and national elections increase the likelihood that commissioners will have a partisan outlook.

This characteristic has potential consequences for leadership and professionalism. County government may be dominated by an elected official who exerts power beyond the office occupied (e.g., the sheriff), or the entire county electoral process may be dominated by "a county political machine, party organization, or political leader or boss" (Bollens 1969, 23). In addition, patronage is likely to be deeply entrenched. Moreover, the party majority may be more likely to shift on a county commission than a city council because state and national forces as well as local ones can affect election outcomes. In a survey of county executives and administrators, Gregory Streib and William L. Waugh, Jr., (1991c) found widespread sentiment that frequent shifts in political leadership are a limiting factor in improving the management capacity of county government.

Third, commissioners may retain residual authority over certain management functions. Consequently, the organizational authority of the county manager is often ambiguous. For example, the formal position of all managers in North Carolina is the same in that they assure that the policies of the governing board are executed and direct and supervise the administration of all offices under the control of the governing board (Bell 1989). All managers have the power to prepare and submit the annual budget and capital program to the governing board. Whereas the city manager has complete authority over personnel appointments, the county manager must secure the approval of the county commission for appointments unless this authority is delegated to the manager by resolution. In addition, the county commission appoints a clerk, county attorney, county assessor, and tax collector. Both city and county managers have the authority to dismiss staff, but the county manager shares administrative authority with the commission and lacks direct administrative control over department heads.

Fourth, the county organization is more fragmented than the typical city organization, especially when the council and commissioner or manager form of government is used. There are elected officials with line authority, most importantly the sheriff, who is usually responsible for law enforcement and management of the jail. These elected line officials have the power to hire and discharge staff. Streib and Waugh (1991c) found that the high number of elected department heads is widely viewed as a hindrance to strengthening the management capacity of county government.

In addition, there are often quasi-independent agencies in county government that are responsible for major human-service functions. The boards and commissions in these agencies have a formal role in policy making, budgeting, and selection of the director. In both situations, these subordinate officials may operate in the county governmental process according to different standards, ignore the organizational authority of the executive or the county manager, explicitly mobilize political supporters, and directly lobby the county commission. In these circumstances, the executive leadership of the manager is likely to be impeded.

Fifth, county officials may be more inclined to engage in conflict with each other because of the factors already discussed. Partisan elections, uncertainty over the limits of the commissioners' administrative authority, and fragmentation of authority are likely to generate conflict among officials. Conflict between elected and appointed county officials was commonly cited as another factor that impedes the improvement of management capacity (Streib and Waugh 1991a).

Sixth, in varying degrees, counties function as administrative arms of the state government that manage federal programs. Commissioners and administrators spend a great deal of time and resources implementing programs mandated by the state and federal governments. As a consequence, commissioners, elected executives, and county managers may have less opportunity to exercise leadership.

Considering these features, it could be misleading to assume that county executives or commission chairpersons and managers are identical to mayors and city managers in how they handle their duties. County officials must be able to adapt to greater complexity and ambiguity in the governmental structure and political process. In this respect, Vincent L. Marando and Mavis Mann Reeves (1991a, 46) are correct in warning that the tendency to transfer theories of city government to counties may be a "misapplication of theory." For example, the relationship between fragmentation and professionalism may need to be reexamined with regard to counties. Still, the conditions are not so radically different that the roles and behaviors of county and city officials cannot be compared at all. Indeed, several empirical studies show that there is substantial similarity between city and county officials.

Furthermore, it is often argued that the same institutional practices that contribute to the centralization of authority and improvement in management practices in cities can be applied to counties. First issued in 1956, the National Civic League model county charter advocates use of the (municipal) council-manager form, with the county executive form presented as an alternative reform strategy (National Civic League 1990). The recommended features are virtually the same for counties as for cities. The directly elected chairperson of the county commission is not advocated as strongly as is the direct election of mayors; selection of the chairperson from within the commission is the first alternative listed in the county charter. In addition, some limitation of the manager's control of appointments is accepted for officials whose appointment, removal, and supervision are covered by constitutional or statutory provisions, such as the county clerk. Thus, counties have been viewed as more resistant to reform but nonetheless as candidates for the same kinds of change that have occurred in cities.

LITERATURE REVIEW

To review what is known and should be known about leadership and professionalism in county government, it is useful to identify major topics that could be studied based on research conducted on city governments. These topics are as follows: (1) chief elected officials (leadership models and behavior; styles, roles, and types of leadership; and comparison of chief elected officers with and without executive powers); (2) governing board roles and functions; (3) commission-manager relations; and (4) manager roles and values.

Current knowledge can be summarized quite simply. There are a few studies on these topics in counties with the county-manager form of government and virtually no prior research on counties with the traditional commission or the elected-executive forms.

Chief Elected Officials

The innovator and facilitator models can be used to study the roles and contributions of local chief elected officials. The innovator model, based on studies in mayor-council cities, has been the norm for mayoral leadership (Dahl 1961; George 1968; Cunningham 1970). The innovator sets goals, builds coalitions, and influences the council, bureaucracy, and public to act in accordance with the mayor's preferences. Although formal resources help to establish this type of leadership, mayors must also pyramid resources from informal sources to gain leverage over other actors. Because conflict is common in city government, mayors face obstacles in establishing their position and must contend with challengers, including the council and entrenched department heads. The central thrust of this approach is that mayoral leadership is necessary to overcome the "considerable fragmentation of authority and dispersal of power characteristic of the formal governmental structure" of American cities (George 1968, 1196). To do so, Ferman (1985, 10) argues that "formal tools and informal resources must be manipulated in such a way that the mayor establishes the conditions for increasing executive power."

The facilitator model is derived from studies of mayoral leadership in council-manager governments. Facilitative mayors do not execute or directly promote the accomplishment of tasks because city managers head the municipal organizations. Rather, such mayors lead by empowering others, in particular councils and managers, rather than seeking power themselves. They contribute to the coordination of effort among officials, raise the level of communication within the government and with the public, and provide guidance in the formation of policy. Facilitative mayors accomplish objectives by enhancing the performance of others (Svara 1990b, 87).

These models are applicable to county government and to understanding the differences between the elected executive and the county-commission chairperson in the commissioner-manager form of government. The concept of pyramiding resources from the innovator model is certainly relevant to the county executive, who cannot rely on direct formal control over diverse units of county government.

Research on mayors has identified several types of leadership depending on the mayor's resource strength and effectiveness in policy initiation. The caretaker is weak in both dimensions, the reformer is strong in policy initiation but weak in resources, the broker emphasizes manipulation of resources over policy initiation, and the innovator is strong in both dimensions. Because authority is more fragmented in counties than in strong-mayor cities, one would expect that county executives would most often manifest the broker style of leadership. How county executives portray this style, however, is likely to differ from how mayors behave. County executives must be particularly skillful at adapting to the ambiguities of the formal position they occupy. A corollary proposition is that innovator-type leaders in counties will be particularly strong at coalition building.

There are no systematic studies of the elected county executive, but those who have received media attention in recent years can be seen as examples of the innovator type of leader in county government. William N. Norris, elected in 1978 as mayor of Shelby County, Tennessee, initiated a $200 million "Culture of Poverty" program to improve the quality of life for poor residents of the county, helped to expand Memphis as a distribution center, and fostered substantial job creation ("All-Pro Government Team" 1988). Parris N. Glendening, elected in 1982 as county executive in Prince George's County, Maryland, has engineered the renaissance of a county that was on the edge of collapse by improving the fiscal condition, business climate, environmental programs, and the educational system (Perlman 1990). (Glendening was elected governor of Maryland in 1994.) Edward H. McNamara, elected in 1986 as county executive in Wayne County, Michigan, faced severe economic difficulties and a $200 million deficit. He reorganized county government, made management changes, took measures to control health and child-care costs for indigents, and fostered economic-development initiatives (Shubart 1992). What is missing from these accounts is a detailed analysis of *how* the executives utilized formal and informal resources to accomplish these results.

The facilitative model can be applied to the chairperson in counties that use the commission-manager form of government. Like the mayor, the chairperson fills a range of roles (Svara and Associates 1994). These roles are listed in figure 7.1. The first set of roles is traditional in the sense that it is built into the office, and all mayors and chairpersons are likely to fill them unless an effort is made to avoid them. The second set of roles involve active coordination and communication—active in the sense that the mayor or chairperson must choose to fill them. In the coordination and communication roles, there will likely be differences between the approach and effectiveness of the activist chief elected official and the passive one. Finally, there are three policy and organizing roles that some mayors and chairpersons fill. Chief elected officials who are effective in these roles help define goals as well as create a sense of direction or a climate for change, help shape the relationships among governmental officials and with the public, and set the policy agenda.

The leadership provided by an incumbent depends on which roles are filled and how well they are handled. Some general conclusions have emerged from observing how mayors and chairpersons combine the three dimensions. The mayor or chairperson fills the traditional roles in the first dimension but few others

Traditional/"Automatic" Roles
1. Ceremonial Tasks: speeches, greetings, ribbon cuttings, etc.

2. Link to Public: acting as spokesperson for the council; announcing and explaining positions taken by the council; receiving comments and complaints from citizens; making government more accessible to citizens; media relations.

3. Presiding officer: facilitating discussion and resolution of business in council meetings; may help to determine agenda for meetings.

4. Representative/Promoter: liaison with local, state, and federal government; promoting intergovernmental cooperation; representative before outside agencies; promoting the city/county; creating a positive image; attracting development.

Active Coordination and Communication
5. Articulator/Mobilizer: educating the council, manager, and/or public; articulating issues; promoting understanding of problems; instilling awareness of the need for action; building support for projects.

6. Liaison and Partnership with Manager: providing liaison with the manager for the council; increasing communication and understanding between the council and the manager; teamwork—sharing tasks with manager in complementary way.

7. Team Relations and Network Builder: coalescing the council; establishing a positive tone for the council; developing a communication and support network inside and outside government; helping others accomplish their goals; actively involving the community in governmental affairs.

Policy and Organizing Roles
8. Goal Setter: setting goals and objectives; identifying problems; lining up a majority on the council; building consensus; creating a sense of direction, a climate for change.

9. Delegator/Organizer: assigning tasks for coordinated effort; assisting the council and manager in maintaining their roles; helping council members recognize their responsibilities; defining and adjusting the relationship between the council and the manager; defending the values of council-manager government.

10. Policy Initiator: developing programs and policies to address problems; shaping the policy agenda.

Fig. 7.1 Roles for Mayors and County Chairpersons. From Svara and Associates 1994, pp. 224–25.

can be called the symbolic head of government. If the next set of roles is performed as well, the mayor or chairperson becomes a coordinator. The coordinator is a team leader and helps the manager and council communicate effectively. Coordinators help achieve high levels of shared information but are weak in policy initiation.

Directors contribute to the smooth functioning of government and provide a general sense of leadership. They enhance the influence of elected officials by unifying the council, filling the policy vacuum that can exist on that body, and guiding policy makers toward goals that meet the needs of the community. Furthermore, directors are actively involved in monitoring and adjusting relationships within local government to maintain balance, cooperation, and high standards. They do not supplant managers' prerogatives or diminish their leadership.

These leadership role styles represent the revision of an earlier model (see Svara 1987) based on analysis of case studies of successful local elected officials, including two county commission chairpersons. The model of facilitative leadership is useful in studying the county commission chairperson as the mayor. Moreover, two case studies have focused on county chairpersons: Carla DuPuy served as chairperson of Mecklenburg County, North Carolina, from 1985 to 1990 (Mead 1994), and Paula MacIlwaine served as a member of the Montgomery County, Ohio, commission from 1976 to 1991, including eight years as chairperson (Mazey 1994).

Both DuPuy and MacIlwaine were effective leaders, and they illustrate the distinction between the coordinator and the director. Each created an atmosphere that promoted cohesion and communication among officials and strengthened the capacity of the commission to identify problems and make decisions. As a coordinator, DuPuy was not strongly associated with a policy agenda of her own, even though she contributed to fashioning and acting on an agenda. As a director, MacIlwaine had her own policy agenda, although it reflected the views of other officials. This is a subtle distinction in the sense that neither was a solitary leader and both had broad goals for their counties.

DuPuy was highly effective in developing cohesion and purpose but was not herself an active policy initiator except in a couple of areas. In part, this strategy resulted from her view that the chairperson should address issues that no one else wanted to handle, for example, a landfill problem. Like other coordinators, she was oriented more toward process than toward policy. She made substantial contributions, however, by communicating the work of county government to the public, strengthening interaction between the commission and the manager, and increasing the cohesiveness of the commission itself.

MacIlwaine, as a director-type chairperson, created an agenda in the sense that she originated it and put her imprint on it. She was recognized by other officials and the public for this contribution. Moreover, she developed all aspects of the office and provided traditional, coordinative, and policy leadership. She worked diligently to increase communication and team-building, not only among commissioner colleagues but also among elected officials in the county, including the treasurer, county engineer, auditor, prosecutor, and sheriff. She used task forces, experts, and skilled facilitators to develop policy initiatives. By practicing participatory leadership, MacIlwaine developed a policy action agenda that was supported by elected and appointed officials of both parties, the public, and the business community. Her initiatives included working to put in place a professional form of county government, expanding the number of females and minorities in government, launching strategic planning initiatives, mustering a sales-tax increase linked to an economic-development initiative that created a tax-sharing program among local jurisdictions, creating incentives for a wide range of cultural-arts groups to coordinate their activities, and promoting welfare reform.

There are no published studies on the leadership of the chairperson in traditional commission forms of government, and it would appear that these officials can be understood by using an amalgam of the two models. The absence of a professional administrator confounds the utilization of the facilitative style in pure form. The chairperson cannot rely on an appointed executive to support the policy-making activities of the commission and to handle administrative and management tasks. The chairperson directly performs some of these tasks, delegates some to other commissioners, and seeks to oversee and coordinate their performance. Obviously, the chairperson cannot rely on formal power to bring other officials into alignment with an agenda or compel them to act. The effective chairperson must combine the pyramiding of resources from the innovator model with the empowering and coordination of the facilitative model.

Some research has directly compared mayors and county-commission chairpersons in governments that use the council-manager form of government. In a study of North Carolina managers, Svara (1988a) reports that county managers gave the chairperson essentially the same rating as city managers gave the mayor in handling ceremonial and coordinative roles, but the chairperson received lower ratings in the policy guidance dimension of the position.[1] For example, in both groups, more than 70 percent were considered to be highly effective as presiding officers, and more than 40 percent received this rating as liaison with the manager and team builder. The proportion of chairpersons who were rated as highly effective was substantially lower in the goal-setting, delegator/organizer, and policy-advocate roles, however. Whereas approximately two mayors in five were given this rating by city managers, only one chairperson in four received a similar rating from county managers.

Still, the findings provide evidence that the offices are enough alike to support a common leadership model and transferring information about performance between the two. The findings suggest that the chairperson should be considered a potentially important leader in county government, although there are shortcomings in the performance of most chairpersons, particularly in policy (as opposed to coordinative) leadership.

Governing-Board Roles

As noted, most county commissions are plural executive bodies. Commissioners exercise those executive functions not assigned to other elected officials or to boards, or they delegate functions to an appointed administrator. The commission does not retain residual executive authority when the true county-executive form is utilized (Wilson 1966). In the other forms, it would be expected that commissioners would be more involved in administrative and management decisions than the councils in cities that use the council-manager form of government.

There is evidence that county commissioners are heavily involved in administration and relatively uninvolved in policy formation. In their study of counties in Florida and Georgia, Marando and Robert D. Thomas (1977) found that half of the commissioners were active in administrative matters pertaining to finance and that 44 percent were involved in the administration of roads. In comparison to these two traditional functions, only 15–30 percent were active in the administration of nontraditional functions such as solid-waste management (27 percent), planning and zoning (27 percent), recreation development (29 percent), welfare (18 percent), water problems (18 percent), and law enforcement (15 percent).

Observations by Alvin D. Sokolow reinforce these findings (1993a, 33–35). In meetings of four county commissions in Illinois and California, administrative matters—as opposed to policy and regulatory decisions—consumed more than 80 percent of the total meeting time in Illinois and 56 percent and 69 percent, respectively, in the two California counties.

What is surprising, in view of the formal role of the commission as the governing board for the county, is its low involvement in legislative activity—establishing what should be done with regard to a problem. Just over two-fifths of the commissioners surveyed were involved in policy making for finance and roads, but a higher proportion were involved in administrative activities in these functions. In the six nontraditional functions, the proportions ranged from 25 percent to 34 percent. The proportions were always higher than the level of administrative activity in the respective functions. Marando and Thomas (1977, 89) argue that this higher level of legislative involvement is understandable "because nontraditional functions are performed primarily in response to citizen demands rather than to administrative requirements established by the state."[2] Still, the finding that only one-third of the commissioners saw themselves as participants in legislative activities raises the question of whether county commissioners are sufficiently involved in policy making to fulfill their responsibilities as a governing board or are involved in policy at the level of specific decisions about service delivery.

Several factors may contribute to the low level of commission involvement in policy making. First, the status of counties as administrative subdivisions of the state and the growing imposition of state mandates limit the extent of local discretion and draw attention to the administrative details of service delivery and program implementation. Second, numerous autonomous officials (constitutional offers) and boards that often share responsibility for supporting the state-court system in the county preempt county commissioners from making policy in the areas covered by these officials and agencies. Third, the population served affects the behavior of commissioners (Sokolow 1993a). In rural counties, the tradition of limited government remains, and the mixtures of rural, suburban, and urban constituencies common to urbanized counties often constrains the ability of commissioners to take policy initiatives.

North Carolina county managers surveyed in 1987 provide a mixed but generally positive rating of the commission's performance in counties with the commissioner-manager form (Svara 1988b). More than 80 percent of the county managers believe that the governing board provides sufficient direction and overall leadership to government. There are, however, a number of shortcomings as well. Despite good provision of overall direction, 71 percent of the commissions focus excessively on short-term problems and neglect long-term concerns, and a slight majority are viewed more as reviewing and vetoing agencies than as leaders in policy making. Governing boards make important contributions to the administrative dimension of the governmental process, particularly by overseeing the implementation and evaluation of policies. In the opinion of county managers, however, almost half of the commissions deal too much with administrative matters and not enough with policy issues and do not understand their role in administration. Moreover, county managers claim that more than one-third are too involved in administrative activities. When county and city manager responses are compared, county commissions are rated higher or the same in policy-making activities. They are, however, more inclined to get involved in administrative matters.

The contributions of commissioners in counties with the commissioner-manager form of government gradually recede from a high level in the formulation of the mission of local government—determining its goals and purposes—to a low level in management.[3] The level of involvement in middle-range policy decisions (e.g., the budget) are greater than in administration (implementation and service delivery), but both fall in between the levels of involvement found in the mission and management dimensions (Svara 1988b). When county managers were asked to indicate how involved the commission should be, the managers indicated that they would prefer the commission to be much more active in mission formulation and somewhat more involved in policy. The governing board should continue the same overall level of activity in administration—although this position reflects a desire for increased involvement in evaluating programs and much less involvement in investigating citizen complaints. In management, the involvement level is generally satisfactory, except that the managers would like the commissioners to be less involved in personnel matters.

There are a few differences in county decision-making patterns related to size. Commissioners' roles in planning and zoning and the policy dimension generally are positively related to population size—i.e., there is more involvement in larger counties. On the other hand, commissioners' roles in service decisions, hiring, and the management dimension are greater in less-populated counties.

Commission–County Manager Relations

In commission-manager governments, the climate is typically favorable for cooperative relationships between elected officials and staff. There is no separation of powers that causes the governing board and manager to struggle for control. Several measures of the interactions between the commission and the manager and within the commission indicate that this potential for cooperation is being realized, according to North Carolina county managers who responded to a 1987 survey (Svara 1988b). Virtually all managers report that they have a good working relationship with the governing board. Half of the county commissions, however, do not provide appraisals of the manager's performance that are satisfactory in depth and frequency in the opinion of the managers. In relations with each other, more than 80 percent of the managers believe that the commissioners have a good relationship with each other and that the chairperson works well with the rest of the board. The overall relationship among all officials in most of these counties is positive; it is rated good or very good in 74 percent of the counties. A negative pattern is rare, occurring in only 4 percent of the counties. In the remainder, the relationship is satisfactory but could be improved.

Even though officials may relate positively, they may have trouble dealing with certain kinds of tasks or decisions. According to the North Carolina county managers, however, their governments rarely experience a high level of conflict between the commission and the manager over who should handle any specific activities. Only in reviewing the budget do as many as 10 percent of the managers report substantial conflict. A moderate amount of conflict often arises between the commission and the manager, however. In more than half of the counties, hiring staff other than department heads produces some conflict, and some conflict arises in more than 40 percent of the counties concerning development strategies, reviewing the budget, operational decisions about the provision of services, citizen complaints, hiring department heads, and changing management practices.

Manager Roles

The governmental structure and political process of counties differ sufficiently from those of cities using the council-manager form of government that it is appropriate to ask whether county managers can be professionals in the same broad sense as city managers. Using the characteristics of city managers as the frame of reference for assessing the professionalism of county managers, the latter measure up well based on analysis of the data from city and county managers in North Carolina (Svara 1989). In North Carolina, one finds few consistent differences between city and county managers. Among respondents to the 1987 survey, county managers have higher education attainment on average than do city managers. The length of time that managers have spent in their current position indicates, however, that counties have higher turnover rates than cities: the average tenure of city managers was 5.6 years, compared to 4.2 years among county managers. More than twice as many county managers are in their first year and fewer than half as many have been in their current position ten years or more. The longer tenure for city managers probably reflects the fact that the council-manager plan has been established in cities longer than it has been in counties.[4]

City and county managers make similar contributions to the governmental process. Both are highly involved in initiating consideration of problems, recommending solutions, and/or taking action on their own—as indicated in table 7.1. Their level of activity is virtually the same except in appointing department heads, where city managers have greater latitude than do county managers. This discrepancy reflects the difference in the two positions' formal authority in this area. Still, city and county managers appear to carry out their duties in a similarly active way.

When comparing actual and preferred involvement, both sets of managers are generally satisfied with their contributions, although county managers identify more areas in which they would like to play a greater role.[5] City managers would like substantially more control over appointing department heads and more involvement in shaping strategies for development, service decisions, hiring staff, and contracting. County managers are more dissatisfied, preferring substantially more involvement in changing institutions, evaluating programs, and appointing department heads. They would like a somewhat larger role in six activities—determining strategies, determining purpose and scope of government, developing annual program goals, service decisions, hiring other staff, and changing management practices.

The values of the local government managers reflect a commitment to active leadership. They generally agree that managers should advocate changes

Table 7.1 Involvement by Managers in Specific Decisions in Cities and Counties

| | Manager's Involvement* | | | |
| | Actual | | Preferred | |
	CI	CO	CI	CO
Mission**				
Analyzing future needs	3.8	3.9	3.9	3.9
Strategies for development	3.7	3.7	3.9	3.9
Changing institutions	3.1	3.2	3.2	3.5
Initiating/cancelling	3.5	3.5	3.6	3.6
Purpose and scope	3.7	3.6	3.7	3.8
Average	**3.6**	**3.6**	**3.7**	**3.7**
Policy***				
Annual program goals	3.8	3.8	3.8	4.0
Planning and zoning	3.5	3.4	3.5	3.5
Formulating budget	4.3	4.3	4.3	4.4
Reviewing budget	3.7	3.6	3.7	3.5
Average	**3.8**	**3.8**	**3.8**	**3.9**
Administration[†]				
Service decisions	4.0	3.9	4.2	4.1
Citizen complaints	4.1	4.0	4.1	4.1
Project decisions	3.7	3.8	3.8	3.9
Evaluating programs	3.8	3.7	3.7	4.0
Average	**3.9**	**3.8**	**4.0**	**4.0**
Management[‡]				
Hiring department heads	4.2	3.9	4.0	4.0
Hiring other staff	4.1	4.0	4.3	4.2
Contracts/purchasing	4.0	4.1	4.2	4.2
Change management	3.9	3.9	4.0	4.1
Average	**4.1**	**4.0**	**4.2**	**4.2**

Involvement is measured on a five-point scale. Interpretation of each point is as follows: 1=very low—not involved; 2=low—minimum review or reaction; 3=moderate—advising or reviewing; 4=high—leading, guiding, or pressuring; 5=very high—handled entirely.

**Mission* refers to the determination of the purpose, goals, and constitutional structure of local government.

***Policy* entails adopting the projects and programs to achieve the mission.

[†]*Administration* entails service delivery and implementation.

[‡]*Managment* is the coordination and control of the resources of government.

N = 131 city and 58 county managers in North Carolina surveyed in 1987.
Source: Svara 1989.

in policy when necessary, assume leadership in shaping policies, and advocate new services to promote equity and fairness. All the managers agreed that they should actively promote equity and fairness in the distribution of existing services. Managers accept an obligation to promote openness and to take stands on controversial matters. A commitment to citizen participation is reflected in the widespread belief that the manager should facilitate the expression of citizen opinions even if they are contrary to council views. Three-quarters of the city managers and two-thirds of the county managers took this position. There are limits, however, in counties. Whereas three-fifths of city managers agreed that they should advocate policies in the face of opposition, only 28 percent of the county managers felt this way. Among managers in the largest cities and counties, however, 61 percent agreed that such advocacy is necessary.

In dealing with the governing board, managers generally favored a consultative approach in formulating the budget, especially in counties. The managers of the largest jurisdictions were most supportive of consultation. Managers believe that they should assert their prerogatives in administration and management. More than 80 percent feel that the manager should make it clear when the board is intruding in administrative matters and insist on a free hand in directing internal operations.

The political and structural characteristics of counties apparently affect the extent to which managers undertake efforts to improve productivity. Based on a national survey of county managers, Edward B. Lewis (1993) found that the managers with high productivity improvement are more likely than those with low productivity improvement to work in a stable and predictable environment in which the public is more accepting of government action. A supportive county commission that uses staff well and pushes the manager for change also contributes to high productivity improvement. Although home rule and the cooperativeness of elected row officials are not related to productivity improvement, greater administrative authority by the manager over the budget, appointments, and internal investigations are connected. The most important factors are the levels of professionalism and involvement by the manager. These personal factors contribute to a pattern of innovative behavior in management practices, policy development, and resource expansion. Thus, the county government environment does not preclude professionalism but interacts with personal characteristics to influence how actively managers seek to innovate.

What is not clear from these findings is how county managers view their situation and deal with the presumed impediments to professionalism. In view of the structural and political differences in counties, it is important to know how they function in their positions. Svara (1993b) conducted in-depth interviews with four county managers to examine how they perceive their circumstances and deal with presumed impediments to professionalism. The partisan orientation of commissioners has been a minor factor in most cases, but it can produce intense conflict. The impact of parties is usually seen only at election time, if at all. In a politically competitive county, disagreements during the campaign can produce attacks on the administrative staff, even if not intended. For example, a criticism by a commissioner from the minority party may appear to be an attack on the county manager and staff. In counties dominated by one-party, partisan divisions are largely neutralized. It can be hard, however, to avoid a partisan image in a two-party county.

In general, commissioners have transferred or abandoned their authority over personnel matters to the managers interviewed. In most cases, there was a gradual shift in transferring personnel authority to the manager. It appears that these managers interact directly and influentially with their elected superiors on a full range of programs and services offered by their government and set the tone and direction for their organizations. It is sometimes difficult to establish support for basic principles of professional management with new commissioners, and county managers must integrate their organizational structure through communication, persuasion, negotiation, and skillful use of resources.

In practice, these county governments do not appear to be highly fragmented despite their structure. The managers have major assets to support their influence over all the departments of county government, both those that are under their direct authority and those that are not. The assets are proximity to the board of commissioners, commissioners' respect for the professional criteria used by the manager to make recommendations, and the managers' budget authority. The managers also rely on persuasion, communication, and collaborative leadership to overcome structural fragmentation. The end result is the creation of a negotiated structure that operates in an integrated way. Although county managers cannot rely as fully as their city counterparts on formal authority, they operate as professionals by effectively communicating with elected superiors, officials not under their direct control, and subordinates. As Claude D. Malone (1986, 5) puts it, county managers have been "working all along with horizontal structures rather than vertical ones."

Svara and Malone conclude that county managers are adept at people skills and consensus building, perhaps even more so than city managers. Rather than using the traditional city manager dictatorial style—the county manager's stereotypical view of the municipal manager—county managers must be collaborative leaders. Effective communication is particularly important to county managers. Malone argues that county managers were "shifting to networking and people-style management before cities knew what it meant" (1986, 5). County managers believe that city managers will have to become more like them to respond to current and future challenges.

FUTURE RESEARCH DIRECTIONS

There are significant gaps in our knowledge of county governments. What is known about one form should be matched with other forms. Studies in one state need to be replicated in others or conducted nationally. This discussion about leadership and professionalism suggests several questions and interesting research issues.

It is important to know more about the behavior of county executives. The special structural conditions with which they deal make it more difficult to achieve the broker and innovator types of leadership. Their experience would be instructive to executive mayors. As has been the case in important works on mayors, case studies of individuals or small samples of county executives would be a useful starting point in this research.

A start has been made in studying the chairperson in the county manager form of government, but this work needs to be expanded with additional case studies and surveys. We need to know about their roles, attitudes, and behavior and whether institutional arrangements like method of selection, appointment authority, or staff support are related to performance.

The traditional commission form, although still the most common among American counties, has been largely ignored. Methods of organizing work, relationships of commissioners with each other and with staff, leadership roles, and factors that contribute to innovation are topics that should be explored. The chairperson deserves special attention in this form. Expanded understanding of factors that contribute to effective performance among the chairpersons in these governments would be instructive for weak mayors, particularly those in small cities that use the mayor-council form of government.

More knowledge is also needed about the formal powers of the commission(ers) in the three forms of county government. How involved is the commission in governmental activities pertaining to mission, policy, administration, and management depending on the form of government, charter characteristics, region, size, and so forth? What is the variety in arrangements regarding formal control of elected department heads, boards, and commissions?

The legal basis for county government is another issue. Do home rule charters promote greater stability and longer job tenure for managers? Do formal personnel and organizational controls that reduce fragmentation of authority affect the behavior of county executives and managers? For example, does the greater leverage provided by formal resources promote risk taking or produce a more authoritarian management style?

There are a number of questions regarding the position of county managers. Is the tenure of county managers shorter if controls are established for the length of time the particular form of government has been established? Are county managers more likely to be forced out of their positions than city managers? What is the relationship between partisan shifts on commissions and manager turnover? The conditions that reinforce professionalism in county management should be examined—e.g., when the manager form was established in the county, characteristics of commissioners, number and percentage of jurisdictions in the state that use the manager form of government, and background characteristics of the manager? The methods used by county managers to create an informally integrated organization should be studied as well. Do the internal management styles of city and county managers differ? If so, how can the practices of facilitative and collaborative leadership in fragmented organizations be used in formally integrated organizations? What are the ethical issues faced by city and county managers, and how are these officials alike or different in handling them?

CHALLENGES AND OPPORTUNITIES

In considering county leadership and professionalism, there is a tremendous gap between research that has been conducted and the potential for theoretically important and practically useful work, as is often the case with other aspects of county government. The behavioral revolution in political science moved scholarly inquiry beyond the legal and structural aspects of government to explore informal resources and the processes of government, organizations, and community politics. The county offers unique opportunities to study the interaction between structure and process, because most structures are complex. Chief elected officials are usually not chosen through a jurisdictionwide electoral mechanism that serves to promote recognition and the generation of a mandate, and even county executives who are elected countywide are probably eclipsed in the public's view by mayors occupying political space in the same jurisdictions. Elected and administrative leaders in counties must necessarily rely more heavily on personal and informal resources than on formal resources in performing their duties. Because formal integration is limited, organizational activity beyond the department depends more extensively on channels that are created and sustained by behavior of officials. County governments do not relate to a coherent polity or constituency but rather must fashion one from a variety of jurisdictions and unincorporated areas.

How county officials cope with these conditions and develop effective leadership are important issues worthy of further exploration. The lessons from effective elected officials and managers should be highly instructive to officials who operate in the often less-complex realm of city government. Counties should move from the shadows to the forefront of inquiries about local-government leadership and professionalism. This step, if taken, will surely advance the knowledge frontier of the American county.

NOTES

1. The questionnaire was mailed in July 1987 to all cities and counties in North Carolina with a manager or administrator. When jurisdictions with a vacancy in the position were omitted, 216 cities and 94 counties were surveyed. Responses were received from 131 cities and 58 counties, a response rate of 61 percent and 62 percent, respectively.

2. Marando and Thomas (1977, 89–91) found no significant relationship between the level of commissioner administrative or legislative activity and the presence of a county administrator.

3. In contrast to Georgia and Florida, North Carolina counties are not involved in road construction and maintenance, functions in which Marando and Thomas found extensive commissioner administrative activity. Responsibility for roads in North Carolina's rural areas was taken over by the state during the Great Depression.

4. In 1978, ten years prior to this survey, there were only forty-two appointed administrators in North Carolina, according to ICMA in 1978; by 1987, the number had risen to ninety-four.

5. The managers indicated separate ratings for actual and preferred involvement in a range of specific activities. The ratings they assign to themselves are virtually identical (plus or minus .1 on the rating scale) in most cases and were interpreted as an indicator of satisfaction.

8

Strengthening County Management

Gregory Streib

COUNTY GOVERNMENTS have experienced dramatic changes over the past two decades. While they once struggled for acceptance as legitimate members of the governmental community, they now frequently sit at the center of a complex web of local, state, national, and international interests. There are some parallels between the changes in county government and the developmental history of municipalities, but counties are doing more than merely following along in municipal footsteps. Counties have been forced to deal with a massive array of problems more or less at the same time, while municipalities have gradually increased their management capacity over a much longer period. As they struggle to cope, many counties must also come to grips with rapidly escalating demands for urban-type services, the continued devolution of federal domestic policy responsibilities, and the growing interdependencies of city, county, regional, national, and international economies (Luke 1991, 1992).

In response to their changing responsibilities, American counties have been adopting more modern governmental structures, exchanging political bosses for merit appointments, and attempting to deliver a wider mix of services in a more effective manner. Like municipal governments, counties are finding it necessary to recruit professionally trained administrators who are expected to play important leadership roles (Stone, Price, and Stone 1940; Robert Denhardt 1985; Green 1989; Nalbandian 1990). But county governments are more likely to need administrators with the strong bargaining and integrative skills that municipal governments have only started to emphasize (Svara, ed., 1993). County managers are more apt to encounter elected officials with strong partisan orientations, they cannot draw on the same heritage of professionalism, and they seldom possess the same grants of authority (Svara 1993b). Their success is more likely to depend on their powers of persuasion and their ability to develop coalitions of like-minded individuals and groups. These types of shared-power relationships are becoming increasingly common in the public sector (Bryson and Crosby 1992), but this is one area where there is a notable divergence between city and county managers.

Successful leaders in today's urban counties must be able to find ways to thrive in an increasingly complex political environment. Merely mastering the nuts and bolts of service delivery will not be enough; they must also become masters at gathering information, such as the "get it all together" generalist managers described by Harlan Cleveland (1985). County leaders must be able to acquire knowledge and wisdom that can only come from absorbing and interpreting information from a variety of sources. Once acquired, such skills will enable officials to connect with key external actors, whether across the street at city hall or far away, and to work effectively with professional colleagues and elected officials throughout the intergovernmental system. Although managers of small, rural counties may still depend heavily on traditional management and technical skills, they too must address an ever-changing kaleidoscope of issues and interact with an increasing number of citizens, neighborhood groups, and special-interest lobbyists.

This chapter develops and discusses an agenda that might be drawn upon to strengthen the management of the American county. Although the discussion focuses primarily on urban counties experiencing managerial stress, some suggestions should benefit rural counties as well. The agenda sketched out in this chapter seeks to generate debate and discussion in the practitioner and academic communities concerning the management skills and knowledge needed in American counties.

AN AGENDA FOR REFORM

Although counties have made considerable progress over the past two decades in strengthening their management capacity, the pace of change will be difficult to maintain. We are entering an era when slow incremental change is unlikely to yield worthwhile benefits. The necessary level of management excellence can only come from sustained, collaborative efforts by a host of persons, groups, and organizations. The complex problems facing counties require thorough analysis, specialized knowledge, and multiple perspectives or worldviews. No single official or county can be expected to develop comprehensive solutions to a wide range of complex problems. Help will be needed from a variety of external sources, including federal agencies, state governments, municipal governments, professional associations such as the International City/ County Management Association (ICMA), consultants, universities, and academic researchers. The resources and talent of these diverse groups, if tapped, could produce the following benefits:

An Improved County Government Support Network. Such a network will develop from linkages with those institutions and groups that take an ongoing interest in fostering the continued development of county governments. An example of the type of contribution an external actor can make can be seen in the historical relationship between municipal governments and the ICMA (Stillman 1974). Involvement by a number of different actors could create a level of synergy that would greatly amplify any individual contributions. Researchers could aid the development of this support network by examining current educational and training programs and the needs of county government leaders.

Improved County Leadership Capacity. Better leadership will require a greater understanding of the relationship between county governmental structures and management effectiveness. For example, more needs to be known about the leadership potential of county managers (Svara 1993b). It seems likely that significant improvements in this area will require further expansion of county home-rule authority and increased use of alternate governmental forms. General knowledge about the leadership skills and strategies that would be most effective in the political environment of counties would also be useful.

Improved Knowledge of Management Tools. Practical knowledge is needed of the management tools that are most useful to county leaders. Researchers, professional associations, consultants, and county leaders must work together to learn more about this subject and disseminate new knowledge.

Although this agenda consists of three separate items, real progress likely will require simultaneous action, partly because the support network must serve as an incubator for the development of leadership capacity and knowledge of management tools. Also, it is presumed that there is considerable overlap between leadership capacity and knowledge of management tools. The exact mix of skills needed will depend to some extent on the circumstances of individual county leaders, but further development of county government capacity clearly requires progress in both areas. On the whole, failure in any one facet could jeopardize the entire agenda. Figure 8.1 displays the relationships among the three areas.

IMPROVED MANAGEMENT REQUIRES STRONGER SUPPORT STRUCTURES

County management skill levels will not increase or develop spontaneously. Strong linkages with support structures will be necessary to achieve and maintain a high level of performance. To some extent, county governments can rely on the traditional support structures of municipal governments, but it cannot be assumed that these sources can meet all county needs, which include formal classroom instruction, educational materials, training programs, and technical assistance. Likely components of this support network include academic researchers, universities, professional associations, and consultants. The following efforts could help meet county government needs:

Formal Education. Universities could help develop and maintain county-

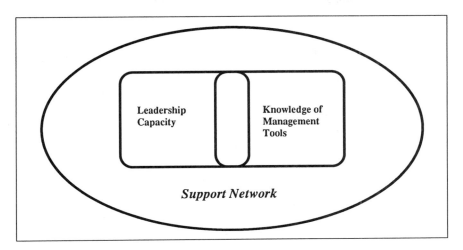

Fig. 8.1 Key Components of County Management Skill

government-management skills by informing students about the importance of
county government and the positive and negative aspects of careers in this field.
They could provide detailed information about county-government structure
and operation, insights into appropriate management tools, and an understanding of the political environment. Formal education programs could also provide
internship opportunities that support professional growth and development.

Educational Materials. University faculty could play a role in developing
educational materials, including course textbooks, scholarly articles, course syl-
labi, and perhaps even videos and films. Professional associations and consultants
could also play an important role in these areas.

Training Programs. Training programs could help fill the gap where formal
education ends and professional careers begin and continue. State departments,
universities, professional associations, and consultants could offer special programs for county leaders. Cooperative action among these groups would be
ideal.

Technical Support. Many issues facing county governments require basic
technical knowledge. This type of assistance requires the help of a wide range of
specialists and materials. State departments or professional associations could
take the lead in developing and distributing needed materials. Consultants could
also play an important role.

Although many observers might believe that counties can receive a great
deal of support from the nation's colleges and universities, there is reason to
doubt whether this is really the case, in part because the educational needs of
municipal and county governments have attracted little scholarly interest. Only

a minority of masters of public administration programs have developed a strong local-government focus (Stillman 1974; NASPAA 1990; Streib 1995). It is little wonder that a committee jointly sponsored by the National Association of Schools of Public Affairs and Administration (NASPAA) and the International City/County Management Association (ICMA) maintains that local-government education is often the "accidental by-product of other professional education programs" (Banovetz, ed., 1989, 2). Similar criticism has been proffered by a longtime city manager who argues that city managers suffer from "dysfunctional education" (Kirchhoff 1990, 2).

To a great extent, public-administration programs and faculty have clung to a generalist perspective (Schott 1976; Mosher 1968; Robert Denhardt 1982; Golembiewski 1983) that has done little to foster the development of specialized skills in most public-administration subfields. This lack of specialized knowledge obviously limits the ability of university faculty to develop educational materials, offer training programs, or supply technical support. Peter Szanton's (1981) findings that universities typically fail to serve urban needs remain largely valid in the 1990s. Szanton found that academics prioritized teaching and research and had little interest in providing practical advice to front-line managers. Although Szanton concluded that many university failings stemmed from the general difficulty of aiding urban governments, additional research by Roy E. Green (1989) shows that city managers prefer training by ICMA specialists or state association staff rather than by university faculty. Also, D. D. Dunn, F. K. Gibson, and J. Whorton (1985) report that local governments are more likely to turn to consulting firms for technical assistance than they are to regional or state universities. Although it is easy to point out universities that excel at local-government-management education or community service, such institutions appear to constitute noteworthy exceptions.

Without strong support from colleges and universities, county governments must rely on the help provided by professional associations, state agencies, and/or consulting firms. Although county governments have lacked a national association dedicated to supporting the programmatic development of management training skills, the International City Management Association's recent change to the International City/County Management Association is an encouraging development. In some cases, state governments may be able to offer substantial assistance, but the evidence strongly suggests that county leaders prefer to manage their own affairs (Streib and Waugh 1991b, 1991c). Consultants can be a good resource for well-defined problems or issues, but they cannot offer the broad-based assistance that a professional association might provide. Professional associations are also more likely to view themselves as information providers than as salespersons for particular products or services.

County leaders can help themselves by continuing to develop their advocacy skills. Either as individual governments or as part of larger associations they must continually bring attention to their needs, which will require the development of an improved understanding of their own strengths and weaknesses. Researchers can make a valuable contribution by focusing effort on the types of relationships that exist between county governments and support providers, paying close attention to whether these efforts fulfil existing needs. In time, they also need to examine the support needs of the entire county workforce. Such efforts might expand on the work that David Hinton and John Kerrigan (1980, 1989) and James D. Slack (1990a, 1990b) have done on the support needs of municipal governments.

LEADERSHIP CAPACITY IS CRITICAL TO FURTHER PROGRESS

External support is important, but the fate of individual counties is likely to rest with the quality of their leaders. Many are large service organizations and are extremely dependent on the motivation of their workforces. Good leadership can help to give county workers a sense of purpose and direction (Bennis and Nanus 1985; Kouzes and Posner 1987; Kotter 1990), and provide the level of integration (Hosmer 1982; August U. Smith 1989; Streib 1992) needed to keep counties operating smoothly. County governments require individuals, elected and appointed, who can provide a meaningful vision of the future; communicate that vision effectively; bring friends, competitors, and opponents together through bargaining, negotiation, and mediation; and display the appropriate values that will assure enduring public benefits. These "get it all together" skills will be essential to county leaders.

Of course, management strategies that stress worker empowerment will require these types of leadership skills throughout the management hierarchy, regardless of governmental form or structure. As Robert Denhardt (1993, 133) has noted, many public leaders are committed to "deepened involvement of lower level participants in organizational decision making." Developing this broad base of leadership talent will obviously strain support structures to their limits, but failure to develop these skills is likely to have a negative impact on a wide variety of county activities.

Structure as an Obstacle to Leadership Development

Attaining effective leadership in county governments is especially challenging because of the dominance of the commission form of government (DeSantis 1989; Streib and Waugh 1991b, 1991c). Although there is little solid evidence that some governmental forms are superior to others, the commission form of government has been a lightning rod for criticism since the early stages of the municipal-reform movement (Gilbertson 1917). This governmental form generally consists of a three- or five-person elected board whose members share authority and operational responsibility. Critics charge that this arrangement suffers from fragmentation of authority and the lack of a politically accountable chief executive. As Richard S. Childs commented more than sixty years ago, "As a form of government—if indeed so formless and ramshackle a thing can be said to be a form—it is distinguished from customary practice in other jurisdictions by the lack of a chief executive" (1925, 3). This statement still echoes in the 1990s.

Many counties have replaced the commission form of government with either an appointed administrator or an elected executive, but the commission form still dominates the county landscape (Jeffery, Salant, and Boroshok 1989). Researchers could help by illuminating the relationship between county-government performance and governmental forms. Also, more information about the relative leadership effectiveness of appointed administrators and elected executives is needed.

It should not be assumed, however, that simply increasing the number of county administrators or executives will bring immediate improvements in leadership capacity. Apart from the partisan nature of county politics, county officials commonly share authority with a variety of elected constitutional officers. This practice can be traced back to the colonial period and is a widely recognized management constraint (Childs 1925; Snider 1952; Cape 1967; Zeller 1975). Although their research did not directly address the issue of leadership capacity, Gregory Streib and William L. Waugh, Jr., (1991c) recently found 63 percent of the county administrators and 57 percent of the county executives who responded to a survey cited the high number of elected department heads as a major concern.

Essential Leadership Skills

Whether or not they experience structural reforms, it is still important for county leaders to cultivate the kinds of skills that will help them to develop support for their ideas and motivate others. A model developed by Mark A. Abramson (1989) and illustrated in figure 8.2 provides a useful starting point for discussing those skills that will be most important.

Vision. Leadership requires vision, defined as "an alternative future to the status quo" (Abramson 1989, 563). Warren Bennis and B. Nanus (1985) found that the ability to define and pursue an attractive organizational future was a key component of effective leadership. Furthermore, J. M. Kouzes and B. Posner found that articulating a vision is one important aspect of motivating organizations to do extraordinary things (1987). County leaders can use their sense of

L=VCH

Where L is LEADERSHIP

V is VISION

C is COMMUNICATION

H is HARD WORK

Fig. 8.2 Critical Leadership Components

vision to build a high level of commitment among other members of the management team and other county employees (Cayer 1993). It could also help them focus the efforts of diverse constituencies toward specific tasks.

Communication. Effective leaders must be able to articulate their visions in a way that attracts the attention and captures the imagination of others (Abramson 1990; Peters 1988; Kouzes and Posner 1988). Presentation, writing, and general communication skills are important elements of effective communication and can be used to persuade others to accept ideas.

Hard Work. Hard work by county leaders sets an example for the workforce, which may help morale in counties that are struggling with pressures to produce high-quality services with inadequate resources.

Of all the leadership components detailed by Abramson, vision is the most important for county leaders. They must be able to assess the critical dimensions of their environment and chart directions that energize and inspire others to share their views. Such cooperation is impossible unless leaders are able to develop a vision from the latent and often unfocused desires of relevant actors and groups. Robert Denhardt and Kevin Prelgovisk use the term *social development* to describe this type of leadership. It "gives priority to the needs and desires of the members of the group rather than the power wielder" (1992, 37). This facilitative approach could help county leaders establish clear priorities while resolving conflict.

Apart from a sense of vision, county leaders also need interpersonal skills that will help them win support for their ideas (Svara, ed., 1993). For example, socially outgoing leaders would be able to make the most of opportunities to communicate their ideas to others. It is also helpful if leaders possess the skills necessary to collaborate with others, foster cooperation, support negotiation, and manage conflict (Herrman 1994). At a practical level, however, it should be noted that these efforts entail some risk. Appointed county administrators must walk a fine line between their administrative duties and responsibilities and involvement in what are essentially political activities. It should come as some comfort, though, that many writers have long argued that municipal managers play an important political role (Bosworth 1958; Kammerer et al. 1964; Wright 1969; Ammons and Newell 1988). More recently, John Nalbandian has argued that "city management has become a politically active profession" (1989, 183). County managers will have to cultivate the ability to facilitate the growth and development of others without becoming intimately involved in overtly partisan political affairs and activities.

Values Constitute an Essential Part of Effective Leadership

The values of county leaders are especially important because they must work closely with a diverse set of internal and external constituents and politically powerful friends and opponents. Moreover, values offer guidance when reconciling competing perspectives on policy decisions and imagining alternative futures. They can help county leaders cope with the disorder and ambiguity that inevitably occur when attempting to serve multiple masters or sovereigns (Peters 1988; Robert Denhardt 1993). Given that county leaders are typically in an environment of confusion and conflict, they must place great reliance on their own value systems.

The types of values that will be important are just as likely to come from our national political heritage as from traditional management theory. As Nalbandian (1990) points out, the single-minded pursuit of efficiency is no longer enough. The most desirable values for county leaders are those that stress enduring social and democratic principles such as openness, participation, and fairness rather than administrative expediency or short-term fixes that may be politically attractive. Nalbandian argues for values such as representation, individual rights, and social equity. Other writers suggest "regime values" (Rohr 1989), democratic ideals (Kathryn Denhardt 1989), and civic duty (Newland 1985). Decisions consistent with these values would help to strengthen and invigorate our society as a laboratory of democracy.

Apart from the values they apply, county leaders also need to develop longer time horizons. They need to consider the effects of their actions over the long term (Luke 1991, 1992). Many decisions made by county leaders may affect future generations or residents not involved in current decision-making processes. Seeking to maintain intergenerational equity should be an important ethical concern. County leaders must adopt an ethic of stewardship acknowledging that "people are the custodians and stewards of a precious natural order and have a creative role in enhancing it as well as being among its participants" (Attfield 1983, 63).

A final value is the way that county leaders conduct themselves. They must be approachable and open to new ideas (Robert Denhardt 1993). They should not become so myopic that they lose respect for the ideas of others. Cleveland expressed support for personal openness when he argued that generalists must show "a genuine interest in what other people think and what makes them tick" (1985, 161). The challenge for county leaders will be to maintain personal openness in the conflict-laden environments that often characterize county governments, especially in urban and urbanizing regions.

KNOWLEDGE OF EFFECTIVE MANAGEMENT TOOLS IS ESSENTIAL FOR SUCCESS

Leadership is important, but county leaders also must use appropriate management tools to solve problems. They can rely on trained staff members to some extent, but they must possess knowledge about how to get the job done. Academic researchers, professional associations, and consultants can help guide county leaders to the management tools and techniques that are most effective. Although the exact needs of county leaders need to be cataloged, experience with municipal governments suggests that a thorough knowledge of housekeeping tools, strategic decision making, management control, and evaluation methods is needed.

Housekeeping Tools

Apart from whatever new challenges may be over the horizon, all counties must perform a number of basic functions, and county leaders need the requisite management and technical skills to assure that these tasks are carried out in a professional manner. These functions include financial management (payroll, accounting, inventory, purchasing, and so forth); personnel management (recruitment and selection, job classification, performance appraisal, benefits administration, and so on); risk management; contract management; basic services, such as voter registration, tax assessment and collection, law enforcement, and road construction; and facilities maintenance.

These areas are more critical than they may seem because they absorb the lion's share of county budgets. Also, if not handled correctly, any one of these functional areas could cause major problems. Poor performance-appraisal systems can result in expensive lawsuits, overassessment of residential property can cause citizen outrage, and mistakes in important contracts can lead to wasted public funds. Also, in a service-oriented economy, the public has begun to set higher standards for service provision. Unsatisfactory government services are likely to produce negative publicity and disgruntled citizens. Such problems diminish the image of county government and waste scarce time and energy. When county governments become bogged down in routine tasks, their capacity to deal creatively with problems and exploit opportunities is diminished significantly.

Strategic Decision Making

Good county housekeeping may once have sufficed for good management, but such is no longer the case. Modern county governments must find solutions to complex and perplexing problems. County leaders must be able to identify critical issues and direct the search for solutions. Tools for strategic decision making, management control, and evaluation can provide valuable support. As figure 8.3 shows, there is a strong relationship between housekeeping tools and those that focus mainly on problem-solving activities. Housekeeping activities keep routine processes stable so that counties can proceed through the cyclical process of strategic decision making, implementation, management control, and evaluation. Strategic decision making is critical to this cyclical process because it can help counties respond quickly and effectively to external threats and opportunities (Eadie 1986, 1989; John Maxwell 1990). There are many different approaches to strategic decision making (Sorkin, Ferris, and Hudak 1984; Streib 1991); however, all begin with development of a mission statement, an assessment of organizational strengths and weakness, and an understanding of the external environment (Eadie 1983; Bryson 1988).

Although little is known about the current usage of strategic decision making in county governments, there is ample evidence that it is common in municipal governments (Streib and Poister 1990; Streib 1991). Strategic decision making will likely become commonplace in counties, but many questions remain about how to use it most effectively. Future research and practical experience should provide some answers. Many authors have argued that early approaches to strategic decision making such as strategic planning have not been useful for government activities because they frequently produce thorough and insightful plans that are not used (Eadie 1989; Gray 1986). Research on municipal govern-

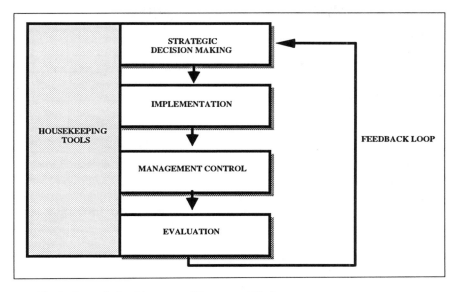

Fig. 8.3 Interrelationships among Management Tools

ments suggests that few local governments have developed the level of management sophistication needed to make full use of strategic decision making (Streib and Poister 1990; Streib 1992).

The literature suggests that county leaders can make the most immediate use of strategic-decision-making techniques by developing their environmental-assessment skills. To do so will require county leaders to use their intuition and information about the history of their county, available assets, citizen desires, and external social, economic, and political factors. Although this process involves some data gathering, county leaders also need to develop a more humanistic perspective on county activities, which means that they will have to seek out knowledgeable individuals and groups and involve them in assessment processes (Bryson and Crosby 1992). The information gathered and the networks established should help county leaders develop practical solutions to complex problems. However, officials should be careful not to develop elaborate strategic-decision-making processes that will be difficult to maintain. Beyond developing environmental-assessment skills, leaders can work closely within the networks they have developed to set strategies and goals for county activities (Streib 1991; Gabris 1989, 1992).

County leaders should be forewarned, however, that setting goals is not likely to be easy (Olsen and Eadie 1982; Bryson and Roering 1988; Klay 1989). Goal setting is a political process because it determines what issues will receive the greatest concentration of resources. County leaders may find it hard to focus fragmented county governments on a specific agenda. In this area, the leadership skills of county leaders will have great importance. If they cannot manage to negotiate the goal-setting process, it is unlikely that they will find solutions to county problems. Of course, even after county leaders establish goals, there will be many opportunities for others to derail their plans.

Management-Control Tools

The purpose of management control is to assure that implementation of policies and programs is consistent with goals and objectives. Control processes begin with the establishment of meaningful performance indicators. Sources of data can include internal records, accounting data, observational counts and physical inspections, and customer surveys. The usefulness of this information can vary greatly according to the type of indicators used, the type of measurements made, and the type of analysis. Participants in the county support network can help identify the most useful measures and the most effective analytical approaches.

Full utilization of performance data will require a management system that links performance levels and goals and objectives. An effective management system will modify goals and objectives in response to environmental changes (Steiss 1982, 1985). Research on municipal governments by Theodore H. Poister and Streib (1989) found that the use of system-oriented tools such as zero-based budgeting, planning-programming-budgeting (PPB), and management by objectives (MBO) increased dramatically between 1976 and 1987. Also, respondents to their study report that these tools are most effective when used citywide. These findings illustrate the growing need for mechanisms to monitor and control the problem-solving activities of local governments. Moreover these tools can help county governments remain focused on critical tasks, solve problems effectively, and contain rising costs.

PPB and MBO are apt to aid the development of effective management control systems for modern counties and can effectively support efforts to develop strategic decision making. PPB provides a top-down perspective on the relationship between resource allocations and the accomplishment of program tasks, which would support the development of clear linkages between expenditures and the goals and objectives developed by county leaders as a part of strategic-decision-making exercises.

Even though PPB is a powerful management tool, county leaders must realize they will need to employ many management tools if they expect to meet all of their needs. Poister and Streib (1989) have documented that municipal managers employ a wide variety of different tools. For example, PPB can focus attention on program objectives, but it does little to assure that the activities of individual county employees are consistent with these objectives. MBO can help in this area. Recent survey findings reported by Poister and Streib found that MBO was used by 50 percent of the responding municipalities, with 30 percent using it citywide and 20 percent in selected areas. MBO was rated very effective by 28 percent of those who used it and somewhat effective by 68 percent. It was viewed as most effective for keeping a focus on priorities, coordinating goals, and maintaining control. The stronger relationships between managers and employees fostered by MBO could help county leaders emphasize the importance of specific objectives and maintain quality service provision.

County governments may also find that a well-designed management information system (MIS) (a formal network to provide management information for decision making) can aid management-control efforts. "The goal of MIS is to get correct information to the appropriate manager at the right time, in a useful form" (Dock and Wetherbe 1988, 85–86). Although it would clearly be useful for county leaders to have current information readily available about critical county activities, such easy access can be difficult to attain. Modern computer technology has greatly increased the ability to collect and store data, but organizing this data into useful formats has proven a daunting challenge. A number of authors have noted disillusionment with MIS (Mintzberg 1990; Klay 1989).

One possible goal would be for county governments to develop decision support systems, which would be flexible and lend themselves to examining a number of different types of issues. Such systems would access and combine data from a number of different sources and could also contain a number of standardized routines for analyzing county issues. Unfortunately, such systems remain largely in the conceptual stages of development (Swain and White 1992), and their true value remains uncertain.

Despite the promise of high-tech decision-making systems, it may be that the greatest contribution of computer technology to county government will be in communication. "With the advent of desk-top publishing, electronic mail, electronic bulletin boards, closed circuit television, satellite hook-up, and tele-conferencing, chief executive officers can reach almost every employee directly" (Halachmi 1991, 242). This technology can greatly influence the ability of county leaders to communicate their vision and values to county employees and influence their behavior. A possible negative aspect of this technology is that it may further diffuse communication within county governments. "With computer communication, such as electronic and voice mail, and with the use of networks and bulletin boards, a worker can seek assistance and advice from other members of the organization, other members of his or her profession, or any other interested party" (245). Although there are many benefits to be derived from these types of improved communication, it will increase the difficulty of maintaining management control, because employees will be receiving information and direction from a variety of sources.

Evaluation Methods

Management information systems and other tools such as MBO and PPB can offer many insights into the efficiency and effectiveness of county activities. For example, management information systems can identify sources of waste in service provision and MBO can help supervisors gain a better understanding of the problems that employees encounter when performing their jobs. Similar insights can come from the budget process. However, a formal evaluation process can help assure that information from all of these sources receives the attention of appropriate officials.

Most county leaders probably understand that evaluation can be useful in making decisions to expand, contract, or continue existing programs, but they should also know that it can aid program implementation. These formative evaluations can help assure that programs get off to a good start. Because such assessments take place before programs are fully developed, they can catch problems before they become serious. Summative evaluations, which take place after programs have been in operation for a substantial period of time, can help by examining "what took place and how it contributed to the alleged results" (Halachmi 1992, 216), but formative evaluations can help to assure that serious problems are avoided.

Whether the information used in evaluation processes comes from the control process, a formative evaluation, or a sophisticated summative evaluation, it is important that the findings be incorporated into the strategic-decision-making process. These sources will provide valuable information about county problem-solving strategies.

County Governments and Total Quality Management

One of the most important trends in public management is the flourishing interest in total quality management (TQM), a management philosophy that "1) identifies and corrects problems by means of data, not opinions or emotions; 2) empowers employees and uses teams to identify and solve problems; and 3) continuously seeks to improve the entire organization's ability to meet or exceed the demands of internal and external customers" (Kline 1992, 7). There can be little doubt that TQM is a hot topic in public-management circles. It almost seems a requirement that every major journal issue now feature at least one article about TQM. Terms such as *quality, customer service, teamwork, continuous improvement, empowerment,* and *employee involvement* have become passwords that allow managers, in both the private and public sectors, membership into a kind of elite corps dedicated to changing the nature of work in the United States.

Recent survey findings reported by Streib and Poister (1994), show that TQM has made strong headway into municipal governments with populations between twenty-five thousand and one million. Twenty-seven percent of the respondents reported that they used TQM in selected areas, and 12 percent indicated citywide use. Slightly more than 25 percent of the respondents agreed that TQM was very effective, and the vast majority of the respondents agreed that it was somewhat effective. The ratings were considerably more positive among the citywide users. Although neither the level of use of TQM nor the effectiveness ratings compared well with other more established management tools, Streib and Poister believe that TQM is well on its way toward fuller acceptance in the municipal environment. Given these findings, it is likely that county officials have also developed an interest in TQM.

Even though we can assume that county government officials are experimenting with TQM, we do not know how great an impact TQM will have on traditional county-management processes. To some extent, the rush to TQM might be a result of the entire government revitalization movement, supported by authors such as David Osborne and Ted Gaebler (1992) and by Vice President Al Gore's National Performance Review (1993), rather than of a genuine embrace of valuable management tool. If this is true, then TQM might remain in use for a long time, but it would not likely leave a substantial legacy.

One major reason for questioning the value of TQM for county applications is the ongoing debate over how to define the customers of publicly provided services or programs. Some scholars have argued that it is undemocratic to focus on the needs of those who use a service rather than those taxpayers and citizens who really pay for it (Swiss 1992). Who are the customers of a county sheriff, for example? Customers may be easy for production-based industries to identify, but it could be inconsistent with the public purposes of government agencies, "which demand attention not only to doing things right (the goal of TQM) but to do the right things" (Robert Denhardt 1993, 73–74). At the very least, the need to effectively define a valid customer is a major challenge to any public organization that intends to use TQM (West, Berman, and Milakovich 1993).

Even if conceptual problems concerning the definition of customers can be overcome, additional questions remain about how far to go in pursuing a TQM system. For example, TQM stresses the importance of management processes, as opposed to individual performance. "Quality is achieved when workers . . . cooperate with each other, not compete, and rely on customer feedback as the best measure of whether the system is working effectively" (Hyde 1990–91, 4). If one accepts the logic of this argument, then the next step is the abolishment of individual performance appraisals (James Bowman 1994). Clearly, it is hard to imagine counties taking such a step at any point in the near future.

TQM should, at the very least, promote an enhanced appreciation for citizens as customers (however defined), teamwork, quality, empowerment, and doing the job right the first time. Such developments would fall short of trumpeting a new era of TQM, but they might well produce some positive benefits. Interest in TQM is great enough, however, that a number of counties might move toward full-fledged TQM systems, and the outcomes of these efforts would be more difficult to predict. The fragmented nature of county governance would seem to represent added hindrance for the successful development of any comprehensive management system, and the unique characteristics of TQM are likely to create some formidable challenges.

CONCLUSION

This chapter presented an agenda for strengthening county-government management. These recommendations are not meant to imply that county government management is a failure or that county officials and other interested parties are not doing an adequate job. The central point of the agenda is that individual effort, even if diligent and sincere, will not have an across-the-board impact on the quality of county management. Counties will always possess talented individuals who transform individual county processes or extraordinary individuals who direct entire counties to a high level of management skill. Unfortunately, however, major changes will not come to county government as a whole without cooperative efforts. County governments will not achieve managerial excellence in a vacuum.

Above all, county leaders must realize that they are in a startling period of change and that they will need fresh approaches to solving the many problems confronting counties. Elected leaders must strive to understand the complexities of county governance, and appointed administrators must become more involved in policy making. Although there will never be a complete substitute for effective political leadership, administrators must look for ways to bridge the gaps that often develop between political and administrative processes. In many cases, leaders will have to become the architects of new decision-making systems that provide elected officials with the amount and quality of information needed to deal with multifaceted problems.

However, county leaders should not let the pursuit of management excellence turn them into management (tool) junkies. The road to management excellence is not paved with best-sellers. Management tools are important, but they must be under the control of individuals who possess leadership abilities, or they will likely have minimal impact. Also, management tools will accomplish little unless county employees are able to work together toward commonly defined and accepted goals and objectives.

Finally, progress toward improving county-management skills will require considerable outside support. Enlightened state leadership would be a good place to start. Also, universities and academic researchers could work closely with state governments and professional associations to provide county governments with important information and services. If counties are not able to develop and maintain an appropriate level of management skill, important segments of our population are likely to suffer. From the managerial perspective, the knowledge frontier of the American county from a managerial perspective is much too important to ignore as the twenty-first century approaches.

PART IV

Fiscal Issues and Policies

9

Fiscal Aid and Mandates
The County Experience

J. Edwin Benton

THE GROWTH of fiscal grants-in-aid from one level of government to another has revolutionized the American federal system. In 1902, federal aid to state and local governments amounted to $3 million and accounted for less than 1 percent of all state and local revenue (Dye 1981, 50; Vines 1976, 21). State aid to local governments in 1902 amounted to $52 million and accounted for only 6 percent of total local revenue (Maxwell and Aronson 1977, 85). By 1991, federal grants to states and local governments exceeded $150 billion and accounted for 20 percent of all state and local revenue (USACIR 1992b, 60). State grants to local governments in 1990 exceeded $170 billion and provided for nearly 30 percent of all local revenue (USACIR 1992b, 90).

Federal and state fiscal aid to local governments has had both positive and negative consequences. On one hand, the infusion of outside money into local government budgets has permitted local officials to provide an array of services and programs that would not otherwise have been possible. Conversely, intergovernmental fiscal aid has, in the opinion of some observers, distorted local government spending priorities, prompted greater (sometimes unrealistic) citizen expectations of government's ability to solve problems, confounded fiscal and political accountability, and produced fiscal dependencies. As a result, local officials have developed a love-hate attitude toward federal and state fiscal assistance, attempting to maximize the positive outcomes while minimizing or even avoiding the negative ones.

Unwanted, burdensome mandates often present other challenges to city and county officials, including how to absorb the costs and how to discourage or prevent state and federal governments from heaping new (unfunded) mandates upon them. The mandate issue, unlike the fiscal-aid issue, which can be traced to the 1950s–60s, did not emerge nationally until the 1970s. A 1984 U.S. Advisory Commission on Intergovernmental Relations (USACIR) report, *Regulatory Federalism: Policy, Process, Impact, and Reform* identified thirty-six federal mandates affecting state and local governments as of 1980. Applying the same definition of mandates used in the 1984 USACIR report, Timothy J. Conlan and David R. Beam (1992, 7), count an additional twenty-seven mandates passed by Congress between 1981 and 1990. Although there is no precise accounting of the total number of state mandates, it is safe to say that the number can be placed in the thousands. In Florida alone, the state legislature enacted 362 mandates between 1981 and 1990 (Florida Advisory Council on Intergovernmental Relations 1991, 17).

Many local officials regard federal and state mandates as a principal irritant in federal-local and state-local relations. Over the past two decades, the imposition of costly and complex mandates by the federal and state governments discouraged intergovernmental cooperation while increasing conflict among the various levels of government. Mandates are viewed as an intrusion into local home rule and suggest that higher level authorities lack respect for local self-governance. Furthermore, mandates are associated with the spiraling cost of local-government operations and the increasing inability of city and county officials to spend dwindling revenues effectively and efficiently.

The mandate issue has taken on such significance that some states have held referenda (usually spearheaded by city and county associations) aimed at preventing their legislatures from enacting unfunded mandates. Moreover, at the national level, the mandate revolt reached such proportions that the first ever NUMDay (National Unfunded Mandates Day) was held on October 27, 1993.

This chapter will examine two significant fiscal issues confronting American counties—federal fiscal aid to states and unfunded federal and state mandates—and will provide suggestions for future research in this area.

INTERGOVERNMENTAL AID AS A FISCAL ISSUE

The 1960s was characterized by a significant increase in the number of scholarly studies that documented the growth and impact of intergovernmental aid.[1] These works focused primarily on the impact of federal aid on recipient governments and communities. While many studies examined the effects of federal aid on states and municipalities, no study focused primarily on counties. Still, the intergovernmental aid literature is instructive for understanding the fiscal condition of the American county in the 1990s and can be drawn upon to highlight the need for further inquiry. There are four categories of intergovernmental aid effects: fiscal, geographic, policy choice, and institutional.

Fiscal Impacts

Much of the research on intergovernmental grants has focused on the spending priorities of grant recipients. This set of studies has attempted to document how federal grants alter or distort local government expenditures. For instance, do grants with matching requirements entice jurisdictions to divert funds from other programs? Although state and local officials often express the view that federal aid skews state and local government priorities, analyzing these effects is difficult (see Gramlich 1977, 219, 227–28). Indeed, there are not unqualified conclusions about the fiscal effect of grants on recipients.

In question form, are federal grants stimulative, additive, or substitutive? Studies by Seymour Sachs and Robert Harris (1964), Roy Bahl and Robert J. Saunders (1965), Thomas R. Dye (1966), Russell Harrison (1975), Edward Gramlich (1977), Susan B. Hanson and Patrick Cooper (1980), George Break (1980), and J. Edwin Benton (1992a) suggest that any of these effects are possible, depending on the recipient unit, the function or program supported, and the grant.

Other studies examining the economic effects of federal and state aid (Pelissero 1984, 1985, 1986; Marando 1981; Robert D. Thomas 1981; Stephens and Olson 1981; Ward 1981; Stein 1981b; Dye and Hurley 1978) have focused on its redistributive nature, asking whether national or state government is better at targeting aid outlays (that is, directing grant monies to needy places and/or people). No clear answer has been reached.

Much of the research on economic impacts of federal aid assumes a supply model of resource distribution. In this scenario, the national government establishes a federal program and supplies financial assistance to some or all intended recipients. Such a perspective implies that recipient governments play a passive role. This depiction, however, does not conform to reality.

As an alternative to this scenario, Robert M. Stein (1981a) suggests an integrated demand-supply model whereby political and economic need factors, which resemble demand forces in a market-type setting, prompt state and local jurisdictions to hunt for federal aid. According to his model, demand varies across the range of possible recipients. A test of this model with data from cities with populations above twenty-five thousand in the federal aid system in 1967, 1972, and 1977 found that applications for and acquisition of federal aid increased greatly among cities over that period. More importantly, Stein found that entry into the aid system was inversely related to the socioeconomic status of cities. In other words, cities that entered the aid arena before 1977 were more affluent and relied more on administrative capacity (grantsmanship skills) and strategic political factors than those cities seeking federal aid after 1977.

As noted above, some studies have demonstrated that federal grants received by a state or a local government can alter or even distort expenditure patterns. Some studies have found that grants are stimulative (that is, the recipient raises its financial support by more than the required amount), while other research has shown that grants have a substitutive effect, indicating that recipients shifted their own funds away from a program receiving intergovernmental aid.

Most studies, however, show that grants have an additive effect, meaning that expenditure increases from grants are equal to the amount of the grant plus any matching funds supplied by the recipient.

Little research on this subject, however, has examined fiscal aid in the 1980s and the 1990s. Moreover, no study has exclusively examined the impact of federal grants on county expenditure patterns. What effect (stimulative, substitutive, or additive) have federal grants had on county expenditures in the 1980s and 1990s? In addition, how do these effects compare with those produced by federal aid prior to the cut in federal funds that occurred in 1982? Answers to these questions, however, must take into consideration the possible mediating impact of economic conditions (i.e., recessions and inflation).

In addition, no investigator has looked at how state aid affects local (county) government expenditure decisions. Two basic questions remain unanswered: has state aid to county governments increased or decreased in the wake of Reagan-Bush administration policies designed to decrease federal aid, and has state aid had a stimulative, substitutive, or additive effect on county government spending? Moreover, it would be useful to know if state aid has supported counties in providing services as a political subdivision of a state or as municipal-type or regional governments (see Salant 1988).

A related topic dealing with fiscal impacts is targeting. Previous research on the targeting of federal and state aid and the fiscal impacts provides few answers about counties as recipients of such grants. For example, does national or state government do a better job of targeting aid to counties? Similarly, in what program areas has federal or state aid been targeted to counties? Are federal and state aid directed primarily to places or to people? And if targeted to places, which types of counties benefit more—urban or rural, small or large?

Finally, no study has investigated the possibility that Stein's integrated demand-supply model also can assist in explaining the circumstances under which counties pursue federal and state grants. Do counties resemble newer or older municipal entrants in the quest for federal and state aid? Do counties display the same kind of grantsmanship skill and political prowess as do municipalities when it comes to the pursuit of federal and state grants?

Geographic Impacts

Another line of research has traced the geographic impacts of grants. Deil Wright (1988, 254–58), for example, has sought to determine whether some states or regions have benefitted more from grants than others. To what extent do state and local governments depend on federal or state money as a share of their general revenue? Is there a systematic bias present in the per capita distribution of federal and state aid among the states and local governments? Does the amount of federal aid relative to personal income vary among the states? (See also Markusen, Saxenian, and Weiss 1981; Bahl 1984.)

During the 1960s and 1970s, the federal grant-in-aid system grew enormously. Subsequently, intense competition occurred for federal grants among state governments, among local governments, and even between state and local governments. By the 1980s and 1990s, where federal aid began to shrink, competition intensified further. A number of studies have attempted to determine if certain states or regions (when examining combined state and local expenditures) have been more or less successful at securing federal funds than others.

These studies, enlightening as they may be, leave many unanswered questions about geographical impacts from a county perspective. In short, no known study has examined the receipt of federal aid by disaggregating state and local combined receipts or even by disaggregating receipts of local units of governments. There is no reliable information on the relative success of different types of counties (urban versus rural) or of various regions of the country in securing federal funds. In addition, little is known about those counties that win and those that lose state aid. Finally, there is no descriptive information pertinent to county dependency on federal and state aid and those factors related to dependency.

Policy Choices

An impressionistic field of research pertinent to grant effects concerns how policy choices made by state and local officials are affected by federal aid (Hale and Palley 1981; Anton 1984; Hedge 1983; Peterson, Rabe, and Wong, 1986; Nathan and Doolittle 1987; Wright 1988, 264–67). Wright underscores this point when he says, "Although no single broad-scale and validated hypothesis has yet been made or confirmed, several hypotheses of narrower scope seem promising, and some are accepted by many IGR practitioners and scholars" (1988, 265). One hypothesis predicts that state and local officials change their agendas because programs that receive federal aid can be pursued with less fiscal sacrifice than other programs. Aid can also influence the preferences of state and local officials with respect to goods or services whose price can be lowered as a result of federal assistance. In short, federal aid can alter priorities of decision makers when choosing among programs or policies.

If federal aid influences state and local fiscal behavior, can state and local officials also help shape the federal aid system? State and local officials frequently lobby Congress by contacting members of their congressional delegation and by working through a myriad of professional associations. In addition, state and local officials frequently enlist the support of federal agencies as a means of influencing the shape and direction of the specific federal aid programs. However, little research has been done on this subject.

Other studies indicate that federal aid can transform the decision-making hierarchy in state and local governments. That is, aid can create potent forces that propel program specialists toward greater autonomy from legislators, executives, and the like. Moreover, this process could result in expanded federal bureaucratic power to review, oversee, and approve decisions made by state and local officials. Finally, Thomas J. Anton (1984) suggests that because federal funds are a mechanism for transporting power and influence across political boundaries, they raise the likelihood of direct confrontation between national and state and local officials.

Intergovernmental aid, as noted above, can act as a magnet, drawing state and local officials toward certain policies and programs and away from others. Efforts to detect these practices means that different kinds of research questions must be raised and different kind of data must be used. Previous research on policy-choice impacts relied on impressions, perceptions, and views of state and local officials rather than on expenditure data to test relevant hypotheses. However, researchers must also focus on the policy choices made by county officials when they receive both federal and state aid.

County expenditure data could be utilized to examine several assumptions implicit in the literature. For example, this kind of data could be employed to investigate the supposition that intergovernmental fiscal assistance is responsible for reordering county policy priorities. In short, such studies could provide answers to questions such as whether county officials are more likely to initiate programs (especially those not deemed feasible prior to the availability of federal or state aid) once intergovernmental funds become available and whether county officials are more likely to support programs or policies when the cost of providing services associated with them is reduced as a result of receiving federal or state aid? It is also important to know if these tendencies have changed in the aftermath of the Reagan-Bush administrations' efforts to curtail federal outlays.

In addition, county expenditure data could assist in tracking the behavior of public officials involved in programs receiving intergovernmental fiscal assistance. One hypothesis, for instance, is that county program specialists exercise less autonomy from local legislative and executive officials when federal and state aid is in the form of block grants and revenue sharing. These data also could be instrumental in determining if county government responses to federal and state aid cutbacks vary according to the degree of prior county involvement in the aided programs, fiscal condition of the county government, or the socioeconomic profile of the county.

Expenditure data, however, can provide only limited insight into the intergovernmental dynamics involved in the process of implementing programs receiving federal and state aid. Therefore, information derived from these studies must be augmented with surveys of county, state, and federal officials. In particular, county officials' perceptions, views, and impressions about the process of implementing programs partially funded by federal and state aid could be employed to document the effects of counties pursuing various kinds of aided programs. Specifically, these types of data could demonstrate whether the implementation process is characterized by conflict, tension, competition, or cooperation. Finally, it is also important to determine if these characteristics of the implementation process vary according to whether federal and state aid is increasing or decreasing.

Institutional Impacts

Some studies have examined the institutional impacts of intergovernmental aid. Stein (1984) and John E. Chubb (1985), for example, have documented that grants significantly affect state and local employment. A much broader set of studies has focused on the quasi-hierarchical networks of authority produced by grant funds and the resulting conditions that, as Anton (1984) suggests, make national administrative leadership and influence problematic. More specifically, these studies (Derthick 1970; Ingram 1977; Weissert 1981; Nathan and Doolittle 1987; Hedge 1983; Joel A. Thompson 1987) have identified a number of strategies (i.e., organizational structure, colonization, agenda setting, and bargaining) that federal aid program administrators use to sustain, enhance, or extend their influence over and effects on aid recipients. Greater attention should be devoted to these strategies and how federal and state administrators employ them to shape authority relations with county officials and agencies and to implement policy. Two questions that deserve closer scrutiny are whether the results of the strategies employed by federal officials and administrators differ from the results obtained by their state counterparts and whether a cutback in federal (or state) aid changes the way in which these strategies are utilized and, more importantly, the results of intergovernmental interactions.

Knowledge of the institutional impacts of intergovernmental aid could also be enhanced by determining if federal and state aid affects the size of county bureaucracies in the same manner as it affects the level of municipal employment. It is also important to determine whether the impact of federal aid differs from that of state aid. Moreover, it would be helpful to compare the impact of federal and state aid on the size of the county workforce before and after 1982 (when federal aid was reduced in actual dollars) or 1978 (the year in which federal aid peaked when viewed in constant dollars). Finally, a comparison of these numbers with those for municipalities would be instructive.

It would also be useful to know if these hypothesized relationships exist when the focus narrows to specific program areas. For example, does the size of the county workforce employed in transportation change with increases (or decreases) in federal, state, or combined federal and state aid? Does the number of persons employed in various county social-service and health-care agencies fluctuate with the receipt of federal or state aid?

MANDATES AS A FISCAL ISSUE

Academic studies of mandates first began to appear in the late 1970s. Examples include Catherine Lovell et al. (1979), Lovell and Charles A. Tobin (1981), USACIR (1984), and Joseph F. Zimmerman (1987). Initial studies focused primarily on federal mandates, with state officials the major complainants. Following the devolution of many governmental responsibilities in the Reagan administration, scholarly attention shifted to state mandates. Recent studies of state mandates include Susan A. MacManus, J. Edwin Benton, and Donald C. Menzel (1993), MacManus (1991a), and Zimmerman (1990). Not surprisingly, the primary complainants are local officials.

Five recent reports also focus on the mandate issue. The U.S. General Accounting Office (GAO) (1988) surveyed all fifty states to solicit information on state programs for estimating and reimbursing the cost of mandates imposed on local governments. A second study was prepared by the Task Force on State-Local Relations of the National Conference of State Legislatures (Gold 1989). This study examined a wide array of state policies toward local governments and made recommendations about how states should reconsider these policies in light of the fundamental changes taking place in the federal system.

A study carried out by the Urban Institute identified mandates as one of the most important current state and local policy issues (Fix and Kenyon, eds., 1989). The ensuing report traces the history of the mandate issue, describes the cost-impact techniques of the Congressional Budget Office, summarizes the results of the GAO study, and analyzes specific state experiences with mandate reimbursement. A study conducted by the USACIR (1990a) focused on seven states—Connecticut, Florida, New York, Massachusetts, Ohio, Rhode Island, and South Carolina—and identified strategies that have been employed to reduce state-local tensions. Finally, the USACIR (1993) cataloged the most important mandates enacted by the Congress during the previous ten years, produced a rough approximation of their cumulative costs, and surveyed the efforts of the executive branch to control intergovernmental regulation during the 1980s.

The few academic and government studies examining the impact of mandates, however, have focused almost exclusively on cities (Muller and Fix 1980) or on local governments in general (USACIR 1978; Lovell et al. 1979; Zimmerman 1987, 1990). Moreover, these studies differ greatly in their scope and methodology and raise more questions than they answer, although they do represent an excellent beginning. Indeed, they suggest the need to explore several important issues related to federal and state mandates imposed on local governments in general and on county governments in particular. These areas are precise costs, political ramifications, and future trends.

Precise Costs

The few studies that have attempted to estimate the costs of federal and state mandates (Lovell et al. 1979; Fix and Kenyon, eds., 1989) suggest that mandates have had a significant fiscal impact on local governments. According to the USACIR (1984), however, heavy reliance should not be placed on the results of these and other studies. Several obstacles make it difficult to measure accurately the costs of mandates. First, it is difficult to compile reliable data. Local officials are frequently unable to provide estimates, or the estimates they give are suspect. Second, only rough estimates can be given for the indirect costs associated with mandates. Third, it is difficult to determine the locally preferred service levels that would exist in the absence of a mandate. Such estimates are usually arbitrary and difficult to assess without a thorough awareness of local conditions. In addition to the estimate problems, it is not advisable to compare mandate cost data from these studies because they employ different definitions of mandates, estimate costs differently, and utilize small samples.

In spite of these warnings, it should be noted that much of what is known about mandate costs is derived from these earlier studies. After all, they do, for better or worse, represent a starting point for research seeking to estimate the costs of federal and state mandates imposed on counties. The study by Lovell et al. (1979, 162–67), for instance, reported that the five counties extensively used own-source revenues to pay for state mandates, although not as extensively as cities. Nearly 65 percent of all state mandates imposed on counties were paid for completely or partially by county own-source revenue. The percentage for federal mandates was much smaller, 27 percent. Thus, these data tend to support the view held by many county officials that mandates have added to the cost of county governments, altering their budgets markedly.[2]

Although these findings provide an important assessment of the fiscal impacts of mandates, they do not provide detailed or precise estimates of the degree to which mandates are a fiscal burden on county governments. The preliminary nature of these findings is attributable directly to the type of information obtained. More specifically, county officials in the five counties studied by Lovell et al. were asked to indicate the percentage of mandate-induced costs paid for by five different sources (general fund, special fund, user fee, federal government, and state government). As a result, the authors indicate that the qualitative nature of their findings leads them to suggest that mandates produced fiscal impacts in the form of additional costs to county governments.

The tentative nature of these findings, as well as the USACIR's admonitions about reliance on these data, suggests the need for further research on the subject of the precise costs of mandates. Are per capita mandate costs and the percentage of a county's budget devoted to mandate costs increasing over time, and do county officials view these costs as substantial or as forcing the alteration of spending priorities?[3] Moreover, do mandate-related costs vary according to a county's size, socioeconomic makeup, fiscal condition, and home-rule status? Do county officials perceive that the overall effects of mandates are cumulative, worsening over time, and eroding local autonomy? Do county officials view certain kinds of mandates (for example, personnel related) as more offensive than others? Finally, do the costs associated with mandates differ significantly from one functional area to another (public safety, transportation, recreation) or by type of mandate?

Political Ramifications

The literature suggests that mandated activities replace locally preferred activities and force local governments, including counties, to reorder their priorities. Mandates, in short, play an increasingly important role in determining what county governments do and how they spend their money. For all local governments, mandating has developed into a significant national concern. For them, the mandate issue is represented by several political-institutional issues.

The first is an intergovernmental issue. Tension between the federal government and state and local governments and also between states and local governments has always existed. This tension has been exacerbated by growth of federal and state laws and executive and administrative regulations designed to force local governments to carry out state and national policies. In short, accumulated state- and nationally defined needs and demands have superseded local autonomy. The pervasiveness of mandating has substituted prescription and compulsion for the negotiating relationship among various governmental bodies that federalist defenders insist is a significant touchstone of the American political system.

Another political-institutional issue is standardization versus particularization. Although the growth of mandates would indicate that an increasing number of problems necessitate national or state policy prescriptions, local governments, including counties, must implement solutions. Counties therefore must contend with universal rules and adapt to specific circumstances. Sometimes these rules are counterproductive or, at worst, unworkable. Mandates are less adaptable to particular situations of each community. The ensuing mismatch of many mandates to communities therefore contributes to the problem.

The third political-institutional consideration is political accountability. In a complex, interdependent, intergovernmental setting, where as many as half of the actions of county governments are undertaken as a result of mandates from the state or federal governments, the means for realizing accountability are not easy to identify. Indeed, it is hard for citizens to hold county officials responsible for the variety of services or the allocation of resources in a budget where mandates abound.

The situation described here is similar to the issue confronting what Burchall et al. (1984) labeled the intergovernmental city. If a majority of the county budget is mandated, who does the public hold accountable for the actions of that county? How does the public distinguish among the activities the county carries out on orders from the state, Congress, or federal administrative agencies, and what it does on its own initiative? In sum, political accountability is difficult to achieve in an intergovernmental system where mandating is commonplace.

These trends and concerns are likely to have a number of political consequences. For the most part, they should significantly impact the character of intergovernmental relations, principally state-local and federal-local ones. At this point, one only can speculate about these consequences. It might be hypothesized, for example, that the political fallout from unfunded state mandates will be heavier for county officials than for state officials, particularly if counties must raise taxes. Furthermore, unfunded mandates (particularly from states) will erode local autonomy (especially for home-rule counties), and federal and state priorities will subsequently replace county spending priorities.

There is a very different perspective on the political ramifications of mandates that also should be considered: it is quite possible that mandates may sometimes cause county officials to do things that they want to do. Therefore, the federal or state government may provide county officials with political protection. In short, the political forces that pushed for the creation of a mandate at the state or federal level are likely to have originated at the county level. At any rate, additional research is warranted to explore this possibility.

Future Trends

The mandate literature documents a substantial increase in the number of federal mandates—broadly defined as crosscutting requirements, partial preemptions, crossover sanctions, and direct orders—during the 1960s, 1970s, and 1980s.[4] Whereas fourteen federal mandates were in existence by the end of the 1960s, twenty-two and twenty-seven new mandates were enacted during the 1970s and 1980s, respectively (USACIR 1993). The growth in federal mandates during the 1960s and 1970s was buoyed primarily by the increase in the number of the direct orders and crossover sanctions, while the number of crosscutting regulations and partial preemptions increased significantly during the 1980s. According to Conlan and Beam (1992), this measurable growth in the intergovernmental regulatory activity of the federal government during the past two decades is surprising given the overall decline in legislative output (that is, Congress passed fewer public bills per legislative session during the 1980s than the 1960s and 1970s) and the concerted deregulation efforts of the Reagan and Bush administrations.

Two caveats about these findings, however, are in order. First, several regulatory relief efforts were enacted by Congress during the 1980s (e.g., bilingual-education requirements were relaxed and a series of new block grants was established), but these are not reflected in the USACIR's inventory of twenty-seven new mandates. It is also important to note that the new mandates listed in the 1993 USACIR report do not include several costly conditions that were added to existing grants-in-aid (new requirements attached to the Medicaid program, workfare requirements added to Aid to Families with Dependent Children, and legislation raising local-government contributions for federal water projects). Although these omissions make it difficult to make comparisons with mandate figures reported in the 1984 USACIR report, it is reasonable to speculate that the inventory in the more recent report probably understates the extent to which the regulatory activities of the federal government expanded during the 1980s.

Current knowledge about trends in state mandates is less impressive. No known study has sought to estimate the number of mandates that the fifty states impose on local governments, although advisory councils on intergovernmental relations in four states (Florida, South Carolina, New York, and Virginia) have inventoried mandates in their respective states. The general impression among local officials and students of state-local relations, however, is that the number of state mandates is substantial (rough estimates place the number in the thousands) and has been increasing significantly over the past three decades. Because counties and municipalities are creatures of the state, it is not surprising that Lovell et al. (1979) found that an overwhelming number of state mandates are of the direct-order variety.[5]

There is a need to know whether federal and state mandates relevant to counties are continuing to increase or decrease. It is reasonable to speculate that the initiatives of the Reagan and Bush administrations, which were designed to return significant administrative and oversight responsibilities to the states and local governments, would significantly affect the trend in mandates. In short, one could hypothesize that state mandates were increasing while federal mandates were decreasing. Perceptions of local officials and observers of state regulatory activity suggest that state mandates did increase in the 1980s. However, the results of the latest USACIR study (1993) indicate that the 1980s witnessed a continued increase in federal mandates. Indeed, Lovell's (1983, 186) seven-state study of mandates concluded that the new block grants to the states do not necessarily mean less regulation or more flexibility for local governments because state regulations have replaced federal requirements. Moreover, one observer noted that federal mandates have by no means decreased and no full-scale legislative program for reducing federal intergovernmental regulations was ever formulated (see Walker 1986, 2). This point is reinforced by Margaret Wrightson, former staff director of the Senate Subcommittee on Intergovernmental Relations, who concluded that the Reagan administration was far less successful in reducing intergovernmental regulatory burdens and in some cases actually increased them (1986, 5). In sum, according to Conlan and Beam (1992, 8), the 1980s remained an era of regulatory expansion rather than contraction.

What about the 1990s? Several scenarios are possible and therefore suggest the need for investigation. The deregulatory efforts of the Reagan and Bush administrations may have a lagged effect, thus producing a decline in federal mandates imposed on counties in the 1990s. A second possibility is that the intergovernmental policy of the Clinton administration may increase the number of federal mandates applicable to counties. A continuation of the devolution of administrative responsibility in fend-for-yourself federalism may result in a further increase in state mandates imposed on counties under both scenarios. Given these and other possible changes in the character of intergovernmental relations, it is important to monitor overall trends in federal and state mandates as well as trends in various types of mandates as the twenty-first century approaches.

A related subject that warrants scrutiny is local reaction to the continuing wave of federal and state mandates. Based on the belief that state legislators are not cognizant of the fiscal burden placed on local governments by mandates, associations of local governments have pressured nearly half of the state legislatures to adopt a policy requiring that a fiscal note be added to all bills with spending implications for local governments. Efforts to persuade Congress to attach notes to federal legislation have been largely unsuccessful. According to Zimmerman (1992, 180–81), experience with state notes revealed that they had little impact in curtailing the number of new mandates. As a consequence, are counties (as well other local governments) now more likely to seek partial or full reimbursement of mandated costs or transfers of responsibility to either the federal or state government? Moreover, to what extent are federal and state mandates being ignored?

INTEGRATING MANDATE AND INTERGOVERNMENTAL FISCAL AID RESEARCH

The fiscal issues of intergovernmental aid and costly mandates have been considered separately. The review of the literature on these subjects has led to the development of two discrete research agendas on county government fiscal issues, one for intergovernmental fiscal aid and one for mandates. However, the most promising agenda for future research on county fiscal issues may be one that integrates what is known about each of these issues and tests hypotheses and designs models pertinent to the joint impact of mandates and intergovernmental aid on the budgetary decisions of American counties.

In the mid-1970s, local governments, including counties, began to experience significant fiscal stress. A number of factors, including but not limited to the poor performance of the economy (i.e., recessions and inflation), rising citizen service expectations, declining revenues, and increasing service costs, contributed to the woes of local governments. The increase in federal and state mandates and the subsequent decline in federal aid aggravated this situation. Therefore, students of county-government fiscal constraints should focus on the ways and the extent to which these joint effects have affected counties. For instance, the dual impact of increasing mandates and decreasing federal aid could result in an increase in both short- and long-term bonded indebtedness. Conversely, it might lead to decisions by county officials to postpone needed capital improvement, thus resulting in the decay of infrastructure. Moreover, the proliferation of mandates and the decline in federal fiscal assistance may result in tax increases (particularly property taxes), the initiation of new taxes (e.g., sales or payroll taxes), or charges for services. Furthermore, there is a need to know if the fiscal stress resulting from the increase in mandates and the decrease in federal aid has been greater for smaller, less affluent, and snowbelt counties.

It can be hypothesized that the increase in mandates and the decline in federal aid would lead to a decrease in county expenditures for and the number of county employees allocated to nonmandated functions. But does this trend represent a change from the pattern that existed prior to the decrease in federal aid (in constant dollars in 1978 or in actual dollars in 1982) and the increase in mandates? In addition, have increases in state aid offset potential decreases in county expenditures and employment and been used to augment expenditures and the size of county workforces? Similarly, how do these trends compare to the pattern of municipal expenditures for and the number of city employees allotted to nonmandated functions?

Finally, scholarly attention should be directed to the joint impact that mandates and intergovernmental aid have on the content and character of state-county and federal-county relations. In short, hierarchical arrangements can be sustained, modified, or altered completely as a result of changes in intergovernmental aid or mandates. Have these practices changed in the wake of a proliferation of mandates and a decline in federal aid and/or an increase in state aid? Are federal-county and state-county relations characterized by conflict, cooperation, or bargaining as a consequence of changes in intergovernmental aid and federal and state mandates?

RESEARCH ON COUNTY FISCAL ISSUES

As the previous discussion indicates, research on county fiscal issues in general and on the intergovernmental fiscal aid and mandate issues in particular has been limited. Although there are numerous studies of local-government fiscal issues, no single study focuses on county governments, and very few single out counties for separate discussion and analysis. In fact, much of what is known about this subject relates to local governments in general rather than to county governments specifically. Moreover, the findings of existing literature serve only to remind us of the rudimentary nature of our knowledge and the lack of a solid base of theory upon which to conduct additional research. In short, too little scholarly research has been devoted to fiscal issues confronting counties, particularly given the rapidly escalating amount of attention these concerns demand of county officials.

This review of the literature on the intergovernmental aid and mandate issues has underscored the wisdom—indeed, the necessity—of paying greater attention to the research design of future studies. Simply put, the databases assembled and utilized in many early studies on intergovernmental aid and mandates were adequate only for exploratory research, and the conclusions were therefore limited in scope. These studies, nevertheless, laid the groundwork for future research and permitted researchers to be more ambitious. As a preliminary task, scholars conducting research on county fiscal issues (including the mandate and intergovernmental-aid issues) should consider what kinds of theories and hypotheses are relevant for these research concerns and what kinds of data are needed.

The first, and perhaps primary, concern therefore should be the nature and structure of the databases. The cases of the intergovernmental-aid and mandate issues present good examples of the neglect of county government as an object of scholarly study. Because counties are administrative arms of state government, the subject of county government as a topic for research has all too frequently been ignored or assumed to be an inconsequential part of local government. Consequently, most studies and discussions of fiscal issues have analyzed data for cities or have looked at a mix of data for cities and counties. When employing the latter type of database, researchers typically gave little consideration to the possibility that findings for cities and counties might differ. The first suggestion for improving the research design of future studies should be obvious: county government should be the exclusive focus of study.

Other considerations about the nature of databases for future research point to a second suggestion. The exclusive focus on counties as units of analysis would permit and should encourage researchers to collect data from a wider variety of counties. That is, future databases should represent the universe of counties according to size, socioeconomic composition, government structure, legal status, fiscal condition, geography, and history. Thus, a more diverse set of cross-sectional studies could be employed to test hypotheses and reassess the current body of theory. Up to this point, attention has been directed primarily at large counties. As a result, research findings and implications must be couched in tentative language, attempts to generalize or make inferences to other research settings must be tempered with caution, and significant advances in theory must be postponed.

A third suggestion relates to the type of data that is required to test hypotheses. It would appear that the necessary data would come from two primary sources, government documents and surveys. A great deal of the fiscal data are readily available in federal, state, and county budgets, and on occasion, from surveys of governments conducted by the U.S. Bureau of the Census, USACIR, and the National Association of Counties. Data on social, political, and economic characteristics typically are available from publications by the U.S. Bureau of the Census and from state statistical reports. Very little attitudinal data, however, exist for testing hypotheses related to perceptions and views about policy impacts, state-local relations, and policy preferences (see Wright 1988). Therefore, future studies should collect attitudinal data from federal, state, and county elected and nonelected officials, county residents, and county government associations.

A fourth suggestion relates to augmenting cross-sectional studies with case studies and longitudinal analyses. Case studies permit intensive examinations of policy subissues that are normally beyond the scope and purpose of cross-sectional studies. Longitudinal studies allow the same jurisdiction(s) and research issue(s) to be examined over a period of time, thus enhancing the likelihood for detecting trends. Both types of studies are necessary to build theory.

THE VIEW AHEAD

A number of vexing fiscal issues will challenge the creativity and ingenuity of county officials in the next decade. Dealing with federal and state mandates and adjusting to changes in intergovernmental fiscal aid will rank high on the list. Searching for viable alternative sources of revenue and responding to citizen demands to promote economic development also will rank near the top of the list. Other problem areas, perhaps not as intense, also will be on this list of pressing concerns. These lesser issues will nonetheless compete for the attention of county officials and subsequently will present a test of their problem-solving skills.

A corresponding challenge awaits those in the academic community who seek to advance the understanding and knowledge of how county officials deal with these issues. Other fruitful areas of research will focus on fiscal-policy determination and revenue and expenditure forecasting. Those more interested in a policy prescription approach may focus on what policies seem to work best, are the most efficient and cost effective, are the most politically acceptable or desirable, and are most likely to achieve policy goals. The knowledge frontier of the American county, although now better known, remains a challenge for those who study and work in the arena of county government.

NOTES

1. For earlier studies on intergovernmental aid, see Anderson and Durfee 1957; Graves 1964. In addition, the Kestenbaum Commission published a number of scholarly studies on grants-in-aid and other fiscal matters as part of its report (Commission on Intergovernmental Relations 1955).

2. These costs may be greater than what some studies have estimated because much of the implementation literature indicates that it is risky to assume that all mandates are followed.

3. This is the same misplaced-priorities issue that typically has been associated with the receipt of federal grants-in-aid. According to this idea, federal grants alter or distort the recipient's expenditure patterns. Stated differently, federal grants with matching requirements lead jurisdictions to pull money away from programs that might otherwise be funded to raise the matching amount and obtain the grant.

4. Although other studies (Lovell et al. 1979; Zimmerman 1991) have suggested different typologies for identifying federal mandates, they have come to the same conclusion: there was a significant increase in the number of federal mandates imposed on counties and cities during the past three decades. Lovell et al. defined mandates either as direct orders or as conditions of grants-in-aid. Zimmerman classified federal mandates according to the following types: civil rights, good neighbor, personnel, public health, public safety, service level, tax, worker safety, and voting rights.

5. Although he provides no numbers for each, Zimmerman (1992, 180–81) has identified thirteen types of state mandates: due process, entitlement, environmental, equal treatment, ethical, good neighbor, informational, membership, personnel, record keeping, structural service level, and tax.

10

Revenue Diversification among American Counties

Beverly A. Cigler

A COUNTY'S FISCAL capacity and flexibility depend on the appropriateness, variety, and productivity of its revenue sources. Flexibility results from having authority over revenue sources that can be varied in response to new and changing demands for services. Extensive use of earmarked taxes, charges, or special assessments and tightly drawn tax bases reduce fiscal flexibility (Cigler 1993d). Whether counties need more revenues—or should have more revenue flexibility—is less an issue than are questions about the appropriate mix of revenues for financing services and meeting policy-making responsibilities in an equitable manner. Questions about who pays what and how, to which level of government, and for what services are fundamental to determining fairness in the cost of public-service provision.

This chapter reviews county revenue sources, commonly called revenue streams, such as those derived from traditional sources like the property tax; examines state-county revenue diversification options and their policy effects; and summarizes the factors related to county finance that influence fiscal capacity and flexibility. Where appropriate, research findings are noted, although research on county finance is sparse. A case in point is a recent volume on counties (Berman, ed., 1993) that devotes substantial attention to spending patterns but includes no chapter on county finance.

COUNTY REVENUES

Intergovernmental fiscal transfers are an important source of county revenues (see figure 10.1), although, as indicated in chapter 9, such transfers have declined in recent years. Intergovernmental funding between counties and state or national agencies either requires a percentage match by the county or is formula based, in theory increasing funding as the demand for mandated services increases. In practice, funding is often capped by appropriation, so that an increase in required services is not always accompanied by greater funding. Mandates to

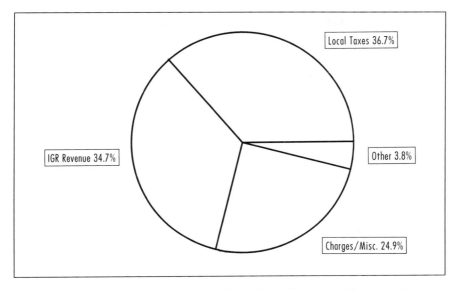

Fig. 10.1 County Revenue Sources, 1990. From *County Government Finances: 1989–90*, U.S. Department of Commerce, Economics and Statistics Administration, United States Government Printing Office, Washington, D.C., January 1992, p. 1.

provide service on demand strain county delivery systems and consume additional county revenues. Many counties aggressively and often successfully pursue court remedies to recoup tax dollars spent in support of mandates. In the process, however, the county loses interest earnings and the ability to use funds for other purposes.

Until national general revenue sharing was abolished in 1986, counties received extensive national funding. Counties continue to receive block and categorical grants that must be spent for specific purposes and usually require a matching contribution. Smaller counties, for example, are eligible for community development block grants, used primarily to expand economic opportunities for low- or moderate-income persons.

State aid for counties varies widely and can be used for general or specific purposes. Some states assume funding responsibility for functions formerly handled by counties, and counties have responsibility for education in several states (e.g., North Carolina, Maryland, and Tennessee). Counties are the leading human-services providers, but some states do not mandate county involvement in providing public health, hospitals, corrections, or public welfare.

As a result of varying responsibilities accorded to counties, there are wide variations in state transfers of funds to counties. Vincent L. Marando and C. Douglas Baker (1993) contend that, on average, states provide counties with ten times the revenue provided by the national government. According to John P. Thomas (1987), roughly 80 percent of counties do not receive any direct financial assistance from the national government. Lillian Rymarowicz and Dennis Zimmerman (1988) found that both urban and rural counties experienced a 73 percent decrease in direct federal aid as a percentage of total revenues between 1980 and 1990.

Property taxes, both real and personal, comprise the largest single source of county own-source revenue (see figure 10.2) and will likely continue to be the largest source of funding for county operations. The tax limitation movement of the late 1970s and 1980s and state and local actions resulted in a diversification of local revenue bases. Some scholars argued that property tax use was declining (Bland 1989). Property taxes, however, constituted almost three-quarters of all local tax revenues in 1991, a dependence virtually unchanged from 1980, which is interesting given the enactment of California's Proposition 13 in 1978, Massachusetts's Proposition $2^1/_2$ in 1981, and the general public aversion for property taxes. It may be that the continued strength of property taxes is the result of improved assessment practices and the use of circuit breakers to make the tax less regressive. Philip M. Dearborn (1993), for example, points to the use of split tax rates, with land taxed at higher rates than improvement, and renewed court challenges to assessment practices in the 1990s.

The use of property taxes varies widely by type of government. In 1991, for example, independent school districts received 97.5 percent of their tax revenues from property taxes, municipalities received only 52.1 percent from that source, and counties received 74 percent. There is wide variation among states in the use of local property taxes. Most low-use states are in the South and West and high-use states tend to be in the North and Northeast (Dearborn 1993).

Despite its drawbacks, the property tax has many advantages. It provides a stable source of revenue; taxes nonresident property owners who benefit from local services; finances property-related services such as police and fire protection and the construction of infrastructure such as streets, curbs, sidewalks, and storm drainage systems; is difficult to evade, making collection and enforcement relatively easy; and enables local governments to achieve autonomy from the national and state governments (Bland 1989).

County revenue is also derived from user charges at airports, recreation, and rental facilities; fees (e.g., via courts, wills, sheriffs); miscellaneous receipts; and national and state grants and reimbursement for county expenditures for some mandated social services (for example, for programs for the mentally disabled, controlled substance abusers, neglected and abused children, and the chronically ill and elderly). County fees in the judicial and criminal justice area are basically established by state legislative authority, with any increases requiring legislative approval. Licenses, permits, fines, and forfeitures are fairly static revenues and

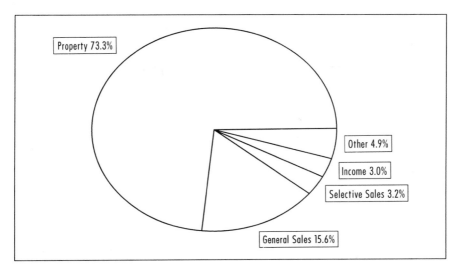

Fig. 10.2 County Tax Revenue, 1990. From *County Government Finances: 1989–90*, U.S. Department of Commerce, Economics and Statistics Administration, United States Government Printing Office, Washington, D.C., January 1992, p. 1.

change only through state legislation. Miscellaneous receipts are usually one-time-only or minor revenues. Counties can also receive interest earnings. User charges comprised just 16 percent of the total county revenue in 1976–77 but accounted for nearly one-quarter of the total county revenues in 1985–86 (DeSantis 1989; DeSantis and Renner 1993; U.S. Bureau of the Census 1990b).

REGIONAL SPRAWL AND COUNTY FINANCES

Sprawl, a land-use pattern characterized by low-density or uneven physical development occurring at the fringe of an urbanized area, has placed metropolitan counties in a pivotal role. Counties are the primary unit of local government for many citizens, with increasingly important service-delivery and policy-making responsibilities (Streib and Waugh 1990, 1991; Benton and Menzel 1991; Menzel and Benton 1991b; Ebel 1991; Schneider and Park 1989). Regional sprawl results from individual, business, and community land-use decisions—generally supported by public subsidies for roads, sewers, water lines, mortgages, and tax breaks as well as by a facilitative transportation system that includes affordable personal vehicles, low fuel prices, excellent roads, and free parking at work and shopping destinations. The urban fringe attracts development due to the widespread availability of and access to open space, lower-density development that permits higher return on investment, quality education in school districts in developing areas that are financially advantaged by the new tax base, and perceptions of a better quality of life than in higher-density urban areas.

With the exception of Baker (1992), who examined the relationship between governmental fragmentation and metropolitan county expenditures, and David Morgan and Michael Hirlinger (1992), who examined the effects of reorganized county government on revenue and employment, little research has focused explicitly on urban counties. The explicit revenue implications of the linkage between the property tax and sprawl are vague, but public finance plays a significant role in shaping metropolitan growth patterns, primarily because use of the property tax by assorted jurisdictions represents the dominant factor in a region's public financial structure, local government fragmentation, and the fact that much of the growth that occurs in a region—especially one that is slow growing—is actually an intraregional redistribution of households and commercial/industrial development.

Reliance on the property tax results in a service-delivery system that depends heavily on a community's tax base. Developing communities must aggressively seek growth, especially commercial and industrial growth that requires fewer community services than residential development, to ensure the resources necessary for service provision. Tax-base competition gives jurisdictions strong financial incentives to try to zone out poor people. When fringe growth occurs simultaneously with the abandonment of older urban communities, the revenue bases of the older communities shrink, thus causing service cuts and making older communities even less able to compete for the growth and development necessary to support essential services.

The movement of residents and businesses outward within a metropolitan area drains its economic vitality and results in additional disinvestment. The resulting tax-base shrinkage reduces the ability of older communities to repair, maintain, and operate existing infrastructure, such as storm-water and sanitary sewers. At the same time, continued outward growth means that the region must keep investing public funds in construction of new infrastructure even though the existing infrastructure is underutilized.

Since the late 1970s, grants, loans, and revenue-sharing assistance from the national and state governments to help underwrite infrastructure costs have either been eliminated or have dwindled, as have targeted resources to older communities (for housing, education, transportation, job training, etc.) to help adjust for regional inequities. In addition, new rules and regulations applied to local governments often place new responsibilities on them without providing funds for implementation. The Environmental Protection Agency (EPA), for example, has mandated the elimination of combined sewer overflow systems, a major source of water pollution.

INCREASING COUNTY REVENUE FLEXIBILITY

The subsidizing of outward development and redevelopment in older communities places metropolitan counties in a major regional finance role. Growing state and county interest in and the increased use of alternative revenue sources have also been spurred by the decentralization of fiscal federalism since the late 1970s. This trend was fueled by the mix of such factors as federal disengagement, the tax-limitation movement, recessions, deficits, and demographic trends. In addition, state laws generally require that county budgets be balanced, making county budgeting processes largely revenue driven: available revenues determine the level of spending for any given year (Bland 1989; Gosling 1992).

Counties share fiscal, service-delivery, and policy-making responsibilities with states and other local governments. The alternatives available to counties in meeting their responsibilities are difficult: expenditure reduction, which reduces the level and/or type of services provided to citizens; increasing tax rates on current sources of revenue at a time when citizens have expressed dissatisfaction with the property and other taxes; borrowing, at a time when county debt is already high (Bahl and Duncombe 1993); and/or finding new sources of revenue, including the adoption of new taxes or charges for service, as well as tax-base changes. The last category is the most difficult to accomplish because some type of state action is generally required. The state role in empowering counties for diversifying their revenues is crucial.

States can draw on five broad options to increase the revenue flexibility of counties: (1) changing the level or pattern of intergovernmental assistance; (2) altering county tax options; (3) revising the property-tax laws and their administration; (4) altering user charges or fees; and (5) encouraging or mandating a fundamental restructuring of the system of local governance, which includes linking planning and land-use powers to opportunities for intergovernmental cooperation that ultimately enhance county revenues.

Intergovernmental Assistance

In the 1980s, counties became more reliant on state intergovernmental assistance, primarily from state shared-revenue programs. In the 1990s, however, many state revenue structures are themselves weak. In the short run, this phenomenon results from a national recession, but it is primarily the effect of increases in Medicaid, corrections spending, and rising school enrollments that have helped produce structural state deficits (Cigler 1993a 1993d).

It is unlikely that hard-pressed states will allocate significantly greater resources to their local governments (Gold 1992). States are reexamining their patterns of aid and making attempts to provide more targeted assistance by changing distribution formulas and/or the conditions of assistance as well as monitoring state aid (Cigler 1993b). Other sources of state revenue—gasoline taxes, so-called sin taxes on tobacco products and alcohol, a sales tax on selected services, and/or lottery proceeds—can be shared with general-purpose local governments. And, if the sorting-out issues in the federal system are seriously addressed, states could assume increased financial responsibility for courts and poverty-related activities (e.g., indigent health care and cash welfare assistance).

The targeting of county support for urban redevelopment affects county revenues. Enterprise zones were adopted by state and local officials after 1980 and some 1,400 zones now exist in thirty-seven states to spur investment and job creation in specified geographic areas by means of relaxed government controls and tax incentives. Eligibility requirements, selection processes, and incentives vary by state but include tax credits; reductions or abatements on sales, materials, inventory, or property taxes; job-training or employer tax credits; management and technical assistance and related earmarked services; and increased public services in the zones.

Little research documents the successes and failures of enterprise zones, thereby making it difficult to judge success against the stated purpose of spurring investment and employment in depressed areas. John F. McDonald's 1992 study of fourteen downstate counties in Illinois found strong evidence that enterprise-zone counties outside of metropolitan Chicago and Cook County experienced growth in the distribution sector that was considerably greater than counties in similar areas. The enterprise zones may have attracted new economic activity, but there was no evidence that these programs stimulated total private employment. McDonald also found that the state did not keep records concerning the cost of the enterprise-zone program (e.g., sales-tax exemptions and state income-tax deductions and credits earned by participating firms), and the responses of firms could not be related to the magnitudes of the tax-expenditure incentives in the program.

County Tax Options

Increased local taxation authority through statutory constitutional provision offers the greatest prospect for achieving county revenue flexibility. "Good taxes" commonly raise the desired amount of revenue; are considered fair, based on equity standards; have reasonable administrative and compliance costs; and do not create economic inefficiency by causing serious distortions in markets (Aronson 1985; Musgrave and Musgrave 1984).

A general thrust for tax reform is toward a broader base and lower, less intrusive rates. County option sales taxes were in place in thirty-one states by 1987

(USACIR 1989) and are used by one-third of all counties—including all counties in ten states (Todd 1991). Virginia and California are the only states with a universal local sales tax at a mandated rate—in effect, a state tax that is shared with localities based on point of sale, thus minimizing distortions in locational choice within those states and lowering governmental administrative costs as well as retailers' compliance costs. Florida's 1986 attempt to expand the base of its sales tax highlights a problem: Florida tried to include consumer and business services, such as legal and advertising services, but legal and legislative challenges resulted in a repeal of the new law.

The major source of untapped local tax revenue is a local-option income tax, which is usually allowable if no local-option sales tax is in effect. Three types of local income taxes can be authorized: a full-fledged tax such as a state income tax administered by local units; a local income tax piggybacked on a state income tax and collected by a state; and a locally administered payroll tax (Charles D. Liner 1992). Such a payroll tax, levied at a single flat rate, is the major local income-tax option. This tax is usually collected by payroll withholding, with no exemptions, deductions, or filing of tax returns, thereby affording ease of government administration and low taxpayer compliance costs. However, the cost to employers, especially small businesses, can be high.

Local income taxes are used in eleven states but are more common among municipalities. Counties use a sales tax in just four states (USACIR 1988a). Pennsylvania's municipal (not county) governments are the leading users, although there is interest in extending the option to counties. Maryland's local income tax is based on the percentage of state income tax liability, and Indiana uses a flat rate of federal adjusted gross income.

The local-option sales and income taxes have some negative features, such as large rate differentials and differences in base definition. Local-option taxes can be collected by the county but are often collected by the state (to circumvent problems of uneven administration and enforcement) and disbursed to the counties after some portion of the amount collected is paid to the state to defray the costs of administration. The U.S. Advisory Commission on Intergovernmental Relations (USACIR) (1988a) favors state administration but cautions about delays in county receipt of funds. County officials sometimes complain that the distribution agreements are inequitable because population changes are not always accompanied by provisions for updated or renegotiated agreements related to state administration (Weeks and Campbell 1993).

When a state piggybacks county sales taxes, it can distribute revenues to the county in which they are collected. Urban counties with regional shopping or employment centers, for example, receive revenues from those living in other counties. A second type of state distribution method is to give some portion of the piggyback sales tax (e.g., 0.5 percent) to the county not on the basis of collection but on the basis of a county's share of population. In this case, a portion of the county-option sales tax is less a county tax and more like a type of state revenue sharing. The county-option sales tax is regressive—i.e., lower-income taxpayers pay proportionately more of their income than do higher-income taxpayers.

The piggyback income tax is based on either adjusted gross income or state tax liability, minimizing the administrative costs to the locality and the compliance costs to taxpayers. The piggyback income tax, in addition, uses a broader income base than the payroll type of income tax and can allow for exemptions and deductions (Knapp and Fox 1992). Charles D. Liner (1992) argues that a piggyback local income tax could be made to have the same degree of progressivity as the most progressive state income tax and that it is paid only by residents of the county that levies the tax. This conforms to the benefits-received principle of taxation: those who benefit from a public service should bear the costs, and the burden of supporting a public service should be distributed in proportion to the amount of use or benefit received from the service.

On the other hand, as Liner points out, a payroll tax is regressive because it is derived solely from wages, the key or only source of a low-income taxpayer's earnings. Payroll taxes also violate another commonly accepted principle of tax fairness and equity, the ability-to-pay principle, which asserts that taxes should be levied in accordance with taxpayers' ability to pay. Specifically, the payroll tax violates the subordinate concept of horizontal equity—i.e., those with the same ability to pay should pay the same amount in taxes. Families that receive all of their income from wages are taxed on all of their income via a payroll tax. Families that receive all of their income from interest or dividends for example, bear no tax burden (Charles D. Liner 1992).

Other alternative county taxes include alcoholic-beverage excise taxes, tobacco-products taxes, severance taxes, insurance-premium taxes, business and occupation taxes, hotel-motel or occupancy taxes, and real-estate transfer taxes. In some places, these taxes can only be applied in unincorporated areas of a county, and they often have restrictions on use of the revenues and how the levies must occur. For example, a percentage of the revenue from a hotel-motel tax might be earmarked for promoting tourism, conventions, and trade shows. Depending on design and earmarking principles, in addition, these taxes may violate the benefits-received and ability-to-pay principles of tax fairness.

County-option taxes are generally earmarked for specific purposes and require voter approval. Both factors limit flexibility. Most states continue to specify which jurisdictions can levy a tax, what the taxes can be used for, and how the levies must occur. The USACIR routinely recommends several safeguards when designing and implementing local nonproperty taxes: a uniform tax base, state administration, universal or widespread coverage, a constrained rate option, and state equalization. Basic information on the status of state and county attentiveness to these safeguards is lacking. The latter safeguard, it must be noted, is most suitable to discussions of tax sharing and state aid, discussed elsewhere in this chapter.

Counties in some states are constrained in the use of nonproperty taxes by laws that give incorporated towns the right to preempt certain nonproperty taxes. While such laws provide municipalities with stable and predictable sources of revenue and guard against excessive taxation of residents and businesses, county governments are hurt.

Property Tax Revisions and Improved Administration

County revenue must be maintained at a steady flow to support the continuous and uninterrupted provision of public services. Sales and income taxes are elastic. A recession, for example, would decrease revenue yields. Elastic revenues are important to include in a county tax system, but stable revenue sources, such as the property tax and user charges and fees that do not fluctuate automatically with changes in the economy, are fundamental. Yields from stable revenue sources change primarily when the rate is altered, although population growth and zoning changes from residential to commercial affects tax yields. Also, user charges and fees vary with the usage of a facility or activity (e.g., zoo visitations and building permits). An appropriate mix of stable and elastic revenue sources maintains the necessary balance in the public-finance system to adequately support county operations.

The property tax remains the most important county tax (Aronson and Hilley 1986). Real property is immobile, and property taxes are productive. It has been argued that property taxes are less regressive than previously thought and less regressive than some of the alternative taxes that are promoted (Bowman, MacManus, and Mikesell 1992). Some economists even claim that the property tax is a progressive tax (see, for example, Aaron 1975). Nonetheless, property taxes are unpopular although not widely perceived as unfair. As Liner (1992) suggests, factors related to the payment of the property tax may account for its unpopularity. Payment is due in a lump sum (although people with mortgages usually make monthly payments to an escrow account). Tax liabilities are not tied to income, so retired residents on fixed incomes are liable for increased taxes. Reassessments can increase the tax liability suddenly and substantially.

John H. Bowman, Susan H. MacManus, and John L. Mikesell (1992) reviewed research that found that increased access to diversified revenue may have some negative effects. An overall increase in tax effort in a metropolitan area may negatively affect overall employment growth. The authors argue that sophisticated research on the locational decisions of firms shows that tax uniformity or neutrality tends to promote efficiency, suggesting that more research is needed to examine the degree to which activity is affected and the sensitivity of the effect to different tax provisions. Helen F. Ladd (1992) confirmed the presence of tax mimicking for total local-tax burdens and for property-tax burdens in a study of large U.S. counties: local governments take into account the tax burdens in other jurisdictions when making their own tax decisions.

A number of changes geared toward broadening the property tax base are available for generating additional county revenues. New criteria for identifying and exempting from taxation property used for purely charitable purposes can be developed. John P. Thomas (1991) notes that it is not unusual in some counties to find that more than 60 percent of the property-tax base has been exempted. In the search for new revenues, counties and municipalities are now challenging the tax-exempt status of nonprofit hospitals, educational institutions, and similar organizations. State constitutions and assessment laws generally do not include a comprehensive definition of a purely public charity, so these cases are being decided by the courts. States can also remove restrictions that exempt state property from local property taxes, including the provision of in-lieu-of-tax payments provided by the state to local jurisdictions.

The ability to use tax-increment financing (TIF), a common municipal financing tool, may be given to a county also. TIF districts, in which specified funds are raised to finance public improvements, are created by earmarking part of the regularly assessed property taxes. No additional fees are collected from property owners, and the TIF districts remain part of the county government. TIF offers a visible link between those who pay for infrastructure and the construction, but it depends on potential development and uses the same millage rates for an entire jurisdiction.

Serious problems in administering the property tax persist (Mields 1993). Counties often fail to meet statutory requirements to maintain current market values through timely property reassessments. Some counties fail to implement improvements in administration, valuation, and collection and computer technology that would help achieve progressivity (Rourk 1993).

To improve the fairness of property taxes, some states have established grant programs for counties to reassess valuations of real property, and some states require annual valuations. States can provide assistance to counties in establishing assessment standards, in maintaining data for county assessors, in training assessors, and in updating and computerizing county assessment systems. A state can correct unfairness in tax laws by separating the appeals function from the local tax-administration function.

States can also permit taxing jurisdictions to target property-tax relief, which can affect exclusively homeowners (i.e., a homestead exclusion) or all property owners (i.e., a universal exclusion) through reductions of a given amount in the market value of the property. Circuit-breaker laws can protect the elderly or others from having to pay more than a set percentage of their income in property taxes.

User Charges and Fees

Nontax revenues are moving toward a greater variety in the types of user charges and fees imposed by counties for services. The use of service charges and fees allows a relatively tight linkage between service provision and the costs of the service—i.e., the benefits principle is upheld. If the demand for a particular service is not widespread and/or if the beneficiaries can be identified and given benefits denied to nonpayers, user-charge financing is desirable.

Services for which user fees can be charged include water, sewage disposal, parking fees, bridge and highway tolls, garbage collection, and recreation. Care must be taken so that low-income persons are not adversely affected by user-charge systems. Counties in many states charge building-permit and inspection fees to help defray the cost of building-code enforcement. Traffic and parking fines, forfeitures of money posted to guarantee appearance in court, and court fees and costs also provide revenue to counties, as do license fees to cover the cost of regulation. User fees enhance access to capital markets because a flow of revenue is guaranteed. It is typical for a city, notes Thomas (1991) to generate 70 percent of its revenue from non-property-tax sources. To obtain parity in the unincorporated areas, Thomas argues that counties need more municipal-type revenue sources such as user-oriented fees and charges rather than taxes.

An administrative challenge associated with user charges is the difficulty of true pricing of public services. Counties use two types of proprietary funds—enterprise funds and internal service funds (ISFs). The former account for the financing of self-supporting activities that sell services to the general public; the latter account for the financing of services (e.g., data processing, vehicle maintenance) provided by one county agency to another county agency and supplied on a cost-reimbursement or charge-back basis (Chang and Freeman 1991).

There is an important relationship between efficient provision of internal services and the quality of the services delivered to the public (Ukeles 1982), but little is known about the use and operation of ISFs in the public sector, especially counties (Coe and O'Sullivan 1993; Chang and Freeman 1991). ISFs can form the basis for the accurate pricing of user fees and service fees (Downing 1992; Netzer 1992). Charles K. Coe and Elizabethann O'Sullivan (1993) found that cities used ISFs for pricing services, facilitating equipment replacement, and for making contracting-out decisions. Stanley Y. Chang (1987) found that governments may not be fully recovering depreciation through user fees. Herman B. Leonard (1986) argues that a major contributor to undermaintenance of infrastructure is that government entities do not recognize ongoing depreciation expense.

An emerging public finance trend relating to urban sprawl concerns the true cost of development. In the past, governments at all levels subsidized development through public construction and ignored the fact that all taxpayers supported growth. Resource scarcity in the public sector heightens the awareness that two costs are associated with development: the private costs for those who occupy new homes and buildings and the public costs to those who pay taxes and who do not use or benefit from the development.

In the dawning era of public financing by user fee, the costs of supporting fringe growth are perceived to require user fees on an enormous scale. These development-impact fees are an example of a benefits-received approach to financing the public facilities needed to serve new growth and development. Florida has the most rigid judicial and legislative guidelines regarding the use and implementation of impact fees. A wide variety of literature, especially in the field of planning, examines the calculation and application of impact fees, related court cases, and their effects (Bridges 1991). Impact fees do not substitute for other sources of infrastructure financing, but they are becoming an important source of financing infrastructure necessitated by new development (Campbell and Giertz 1990).

A related development is the passage of concurrency legislation in several states to deal with negative effects of urban sprawl. Florida's 1985 Growth Management Act includes concurrency—no development can take place unless services such as roads, water, sewer, solid waste, parks and recreation, education, and health are provided at the same time as the development. Local governments are empowered to set standards for each service and to prohibit development unless these requirements are met. Communities can agree to provide the services, or developers can provide them or post bonds to ensure that necessary infrastructure and services are provided as development takes place. Florida's Department of Community Affairs coordinates and regulates the implementation of the law. Planning/zoning regulations must be coordinated on a regional and statewide basis by the local governments. If coordination is inadequate, a moratorium can be placed by the state on local development. Washington state's Growth Management Act of 1990 seeks to insure concurrency via provisions relating to land use and capital facilities planning, transportation planning, and subdivision plat approvals linked to open space, drainage, street, sewer, water, recreation, school, and sidewalk needs.

Concurrency, often called pay as you grow, helps to manage growth. It has many advantages in comparison to traditional "pay later" approaches. The obstacles to passage and implementation are extensive, however. As such, concurrency demands municipal-county fiscal collaboration and can be categorized as a strategy within the local-government-restructuring option, discussed next.

Restructuring the System of Local Government

The greatest likelihood for dramatic change in the county fiscal situation may lie in restructuring local government. Three approaches are receiving close attention: (1) the alteration of relationships between and among jurisdictions and their revenue bases within a region by creating special districts; (2) tax-base sharing among jurisdictions; and (3) transferral of powers among governments (e.g., city-county consolidations, state assumption of poverty-related responsibilities from counties, interlocal agreements, some types of privatization).

Public Authorities and Special Districts

Public authorities are the fastest growing type of government (Perlman 1993) and account for approximately one-third of local government financing in the United States. EPA regulations for solid-waste management, water and sewer systems, and other problems of a regional nature are increasingly handled through the creation of public authorities. Many states, for example, have formed solid-waste-management districts. In 1990, Indiana gave its ninety-two counties the option of forming multicounty districts or establishing themselves as a single county district. Sixty-two solid-waste-management districts were formed: ten were multicounty (with forty counties) and the other fifty-two counties formed single-county districts. Larry DeBoer (1992) found that smaller counties were somewhat more likely to join multicounty districts than were larger counties. The districts are new units of government with the responsibility of developing twenty-year solid-waste-management plans to achieve waste reductions. The districts can contract for collection, recycling, and disposal facilities as well as raise revenues via assessment of fees or property taxes.

A growing literature argues the advantages and disadvantages of public authorities (Mitchell 1992; Axelrod 1992). However, systematic data on authorities in general, or aspects of financing is yet to be generated. Public authorities can be created by several counties, and they often operate with voter approval. They receive the power to raise revenues for both capital and operating purposes through the assessment of fees or taxes or the issuance of bonds, although many do not have taxing authority. They may also receive interest income and can apply for grants. In effect, the creation of multicounty regional authorities is a revenue-diversification strategy used by cities to transfer responsibilities to the county level. Rather than directly providing the new service, however, the counties create public authorities, with county responsibility ending after appointment of the board of commissioners.

Tax-Base Sharing

This strategy offers a possible solution to the imbalance between public service needs and financial resources in older communities. Under such systems, a portion of all new development fees (usually limited to nonresidential development) are paid into a regional pool and redistributed by a population formula. In that way, a portion of new growth on the urban fringe is shared by the communities abandoned in the process of fueling sprawling growth. Tax-base sharing can not only reduce the incentives that drive urban sprawl but it can also support the channeling of additional resources to older communities as they seek to redevelop their abandoned space. In addition, tax-base sharing can promote more orderly growth in developing jurisdictions by adding service-provision resources from the shared pool.

Jurisdictions throughout the seven-county Minneapolis–St. Paul area have been sharing the region's commercial/industrial base since 1971 via the Minnesota Fiscal Disparities Program, which provides for a regionwide pooling of 40 percent of all commercial/industrial tax-base growth. The regional pool is distributed annually to the local jurisdictions based on a formula that uses the jurisdiction's population and the market value of taxable real property as variables. In 1991 metropolitan area communities shared nearly 31 percent of the region's commercial/industrial base. The program has significantly reduced tax-base disparities. Sam Staley (1990) summarized the literature on tax-base sharing and completed research on several Ohio counties. A more recent review was published by William J. Pammer, Jr., and Jack L. Dustin (1993), who report on cases of voluntary tax sharing in Ohio. The literature on the topic overall, however, is sparse on empirical analysis and is primarily theoretical.

Case studies by Alvin D. Sokolow (1993b) in three counties in California's most productive and diverse agricultural area provide insight on still another type of tax-base sharing. His research demonstrates that California's tax limitation movement and the state's fiscal, programmatic, and boundary rules all constrain county finances. However, they also provide intergovernmental opportunities that enhance county finances. Specifically, the counties successfully initiated intergovernmental agreements in which affluent municipalities agreed to share their revenues with the counties. Sokolow found that county governments initiated the efforts to gain a share of municipal revenues from the reluctant municipalities. The negotiating tool possessed by the counties was the ability to thwart municipal growth plans, especially blocking city annexations. In return for some portion of municipal revenues, the cities received county support for growth actions. As Sokolow points out, state constraints on counties are ever present, but they can also be used to empower counties in their search for alternative revenues.

Transfer of Powers and Intergovernmental Agreements

Robert D. Thomas and Suphapong Boonyapratuang's (1993) study of fourteen Texas counties demonstrates that within the broad constraints set by a state, county residents shape their own patterns of governance by working within a network of government types and numbers within their region. Often, the county is not a central player, leading the authors to caution that the much-discussed prospect of reshaping of county government to emerge as a new form of metropolitan government (e.g., Fosler 1991) is buttressed by little empirical evidence.

The structural and financial reshaping of counties to be leaders in metropolitan governance is unlikely, given the requirements of amended state constitutions and statutes needing local approval. However, counties may emerge as leaders in regional governance for rural areas (Cigler 1993c, 1994; Koven and Hadwiger 1992). There has been a substantial increase in rural county use of functional service consolidations, especially in the public-safety and solid-waste-management areas.

Counties can participate in intergovernmental service contracts, joint service agreements for planning, financing, or delivering a service, and intergovernmental service transfers (i.e., the transfer of service responsibility from one government to another), although the last option is not widely authorized (USACIR 1985). Intergovernmental service contracts and joint service agreements, on the other hand, are widely used (USACIR 1985). City-county consolidation, which calls for the merger of a city into the county government to create a consolidated government with all powers and responsibilities is another option, although it is used infrequently (Benton and Gamble 1984; Fuller 1991).

Privatization of public facilities is an alternative to public ownership. The private sector can provide services under contract or franchise by the government or, in some cases, the private investor owns a specific public-works facility through purchasing certificates of participation or equipment trust certificates. The most commonly used type of privatization by counties, however, is the contracting-out of service delivery (Cigler 1990).

TRENDS INTERACTING WITH
REVENUE DIVERSIFICATION

Counties in the 1990s will continue to work with states and other local governments to find alternative revenue sources. A number of events, trends, and

processes—often with contradictory effects—will interact with revenue diversification efforts to affect county revenues. These overlapping factors include:

(1) New county budgeting processes that incorporate the strategic-planning
process with the budgeting process as well as other productivity improvements (e.g., Carr 1991) that enable some cost savings.

(2) County expenditure-reduction efforts of all types.

(3) County efforts to persuade states and the national government to provide funding for mandated programs, especially human-services programs
for which counties are experiencing net reductions in state and national support at a time of rising service demand.

(4) Court decisions that have required state assumption of costs for mandated programs. Counties in several states are pursuing legal actions as
funds for costly mandated services are not reimbursed. Court decisions on
school financing will affect counties as jurisdictions within a metropolitan
area compete for the same tax base.

(5) Declining interest rates due to a slow-growth national economy.

(6) Demands for new, often costly, county programs. Such demands are
often driven by demographic changes, such as the aging of the U.S. population, which results in the need for increased health care and hospitals, transportation, recreation, and so forth (Cigler, 1993a, 1993d).

(7) Outcomes of capital budget decisions.

(8) The use of alternative service-delivery systems (e.g., functional consolidation of services, contracting out, and so on) by all types of governments
within a region.

(9) The potential for a new tax-limitation movement, driven by intergenerational conflict over service levels and taxation (Button and Rosenbaum 1990).

FUTURE PROSPECTS OF
ACHIEVING REVENUE FLEXIBILITY

Revenue flexibility does not have to be achieved through additional revenues. A growing research tradition has examined numerous microlevel fiscal processes that are important to a county's general fiscal health, including purchasing
(MacManus 1991b), contracting (Cigler 1990), use of analytical techniques (Botner 1991; Poister and Streib 1989); and forecasting (Frank and Gianakis 1990).
States have broadened local investment opportunities. Financing innovations include targeting state revolving funds and bond banks to finance infrastructure.
A group of local governments can diminish differences among their credit ratings by issuing bonds in a pool. Alternative dispute resolution techniques can
yield financial savings (Cigler 1993a, 1993d).

When looking for ways to raise additional revenues, counties must identify which revenue sources are underutilized and which are overutilized (Hy et al. 1992). Taxpayers' reactions to property taxes suggest that they are overutilized as revenue sources. However, other revenue sources may be underutilized. A useful tool in finding the underutilization/overutilization balance is revenue capacity–effort analysis, a methodology developed by the USACIR and refined by Ronald John Hy et al. (1992) for county governments.

County revenue systems are undergoing fundamental change. The outcomes for counties in the 1990s will be less influenced by national and state financial-aid programs and more directly related to the economic base, political leadership, and management capacity of specific counties. Academic research has barely addressed the key issues of county finance, although a wealth of theoretical writing is available.

Until a clearer sense of the county role is forged, efforts to change financing schemes as well as government structure or responsibilities will be fraught with problems. It is arguable that, in the absence of an educational effort focused on taxpayers, state and county officials will continue to have difficulty in devising and implementing revenue options that adequately provide necessary services in equitable ways.

11

Economic Development Strategies among Counties

William J. Pammer, Jr.

ECONOMIC DEVELOPMENT is a major priority among American counties (Marando and Reeves 1991b; Cope 1990). Traditionally, counties did not consider local economic development an important issue because they acted principally as subdivisions of the states. More recently, however, counties have shown an interest in developing local economies. Much of this interest stems from their changing role as local governments. Since the 1980s, for instance, counties have provided more public services than ever before, and economic development is one way they can enhance and diversify their tax base to finance services and local infrastructure.

Research on county economic development, although sparse, has two major themes. First, counties pursue regional economic development to reduce interjurisdictional competition among cities within their boundaries and thereby improve their regional competitiveness (Dodge 1988; Reese 1992; Pammer and Dustin 1993). Second, counties pursue proactive economic development strategies both to market their regions as an outlet for foreign trade and to attract foreign investment (Reese 1992). This chapter explores these themes, with particular attention to economic development strategies that counties pursue. The chapter also presents an exploratory analysis of the effects of supply-side and demand-side strategies on the growth in counties' economic bases. Finally, the chapter concludes with a discussion of the directions that future research might take to advance the knowledge frontier of county economic development.

COUNTIES AND REGIONAL ECONOMIC DEVELOPMENT

As counties approach the twenty-first century, they face major economic challenges. The prospects for workers and communities are worse than in previous decades due to the fact that many business firms have preferred to cut jobs rather than look for other methods of containing costs (Reich 1992). Equally challenging is the fact that economic decline is no longer a central-city problem but a regional concern. Previous research has shown that economic decline is largely a central-city problem caused by the out-migration of middle-class residents and businesses to suburban communities (Juenius and Ledebur 1976; Muller 1975; Howell and Stamm, 1979; Joan K. Martin 1982). Recent trends, however, suggest that the relocation of businesses to other areas of the United States and the world has adversely affected not only central cities but suburban communities as well, thereby affecting county revenues. This concern is especially prevalent among counties with large regional employers (i.e., automotive, aerospace, and biotechnology industries) that are susceptible to fluctuations in national and international economies.

The role of counties in enhancing regional economic development and their success in this area requires county officials to accept a different orientation toward the way economic development has been practiced. The literature characterizes regional economic development as seeking to diffuse interlocal competition by reducing fiscal disparities and promoting coordinated efforts among jurisdictions to attract business and industry (Bahl and Puryear 1976; Gilbert 1990; Dodge 1988; Pammer and Dustin 1993). Primary examples include the Minnesota Fiscal Disparities Program, Hackensack Meadowlands District in New Jersey, and, more recently, the Economic Development and Government Equity (ED/GE) Program in Montgomery County, Ohio. Each of these programs represents a significant departure from the conventional approach to local economic development because they emphasize stimulating interlocal cooperation to promote regional development.

Historically, local economic development initiatives have been parochial in nature, and individual jurisdictions have competed against each other for new businesses. Jurisdictions, for example, have chosen to market their communities through favorable tax treatments (lower tax rates and tax abatement). Such tax differentials can reduce the economic base of neighboring communities, which leads to intraregional tax-base shifting rather than real economic growth. When viewed broadly, economic development implies that the economic stability and prosperity of any single locality is critically linked to the fiscal health and attributes of its neighbors. In practice, regional economic models build on this theme by incorporating tax sharing as a mechanism to promote regional economic development. The underlying principle is that growing communities should contribute a certain percentage of their change in assessed valuation to an areawide pool, which is then redistributed to municipalities that experience a decline in their assessed valuation. The idea is that all localities in a county share (although not necessarily equally) in the distribution of growth.

This view breaks with the tradition of local economic development by offering counties, if they chose to do so, an opportunity to be a catalyst for interlocal cooperation that fosters regional economic growth and stability. Yet, what prerequisites are necessary for counties to assume a regional role in economic development?

PREREQUISITES FOR COUNTIES
TO ASSUME A REGIONAL ROLE

One way to address this question is to recognize the geographic uniqueness of counties as local governments. Unlike cities, villages, and townships, counties include incorporated and unincorporated jurisdictions. Therefore, their policy orientations transcend specific localities. Examples include consolidated and intergovernmental partnerships in solid-waste disposal, code enforcement and inspection, information processing, drug and law enforcement, and, more recently, emergency management (David R. Ward 1987; Bunch and Strauss 1992; Waugh 1994).

Given their policy orientation, counties pursue regional economic development strategies through their participation in intergovernmental partnerships. Equally important, counties are also predisposed to regional economic development because they have larger resource bases than municipalities to facilitate economic development strategies, provide forums for interlocal cooperation, and serve as general-purpose governments representing local interests and having strong local identification. In effect, counties can foster strong cooperative arrangements because they are "conveners or sponsors for the development of intra-county multi-jurisdictional arrangements" (Parks 1990, 2), which could offer a mechanism to coordinate local economic development strategies.

However, counties' role in promoting interjurisdictional cooperation to enhance regional economic development depends on whether county officials understand and accept the relevance of interlocal cooperation to their economic situation. For instance, when faced with the possible relocation of a General Motors plant, coupled with declining revenues and competition from the Columbus, Ohio, and Indianapolis, Indiana, metropolitan areas, Montgomery County, Ohio, opted to explore and eventually formulate a regional economic plan linked to tax sharing (Pammer and Dustin 1993). The plan, commonly referred to as the ED/GE program, merges county-supported economic development projects and tax sharing among cities, townships, and villages (Pammer and Dustin 1993). The plan seeks to insure that each community within Montgomery County "has an equal opportunity to derive some benefit from development outside its boundaries" (Montgomery County 1992). In this case, officials' perceptions of economic vulnerability compelled them to nurture interlocal cooperation.

Another prerequisite to fostering regional economic development is the willingness of county officials to cope with the barriers to interlocal cooperation.

Incorporated and unincorporated jurisdictions (e.g., townships) in counties may be reluctant to accept a regional economic approach. Much of this reticence stems from the historical relationship between county administrations and local governments. For example, cities and villages often distrust county government because they have had unwanted land-use projects such as low-income housing and landfills forced on them.

Another challenge to interlocal cooperation is the possibility of interjurisdictional conflict among suburban areas and central cities. These areas often disagree over who gets what and how much state and federal fiscal aid. Central cities typically argue that they are at a disadvantage because of their declining middle-class population and increased demands for services from dependent populations. Suburban governments typically contend that central cities operate inefficiently and, as a result, use their declining tax base as a way to maximize the receipt of federal and state aid at the expense of suburban communities. For instance, while a tax-sharing model for the ED/GE program was being devised, the city of Dayton, a declining central city, argued that the tax-sharing pool should consider local need, such as per capita income and poverty level. Suburban officials, however, felt that a formula based on these characteristics was biased in favor of Dayton and ignored their needs. Furthermore, suburban communities also felt that Dayton already received favorable treatment through existing intergovernmental revenue transfers. This example illustrates that efforts to promote interlocal cooperation can involve differences among communities, particularly when a tax-sharing approach is the foundation for a regional economic plan.

Suburban–central city differences could also involve conflicts over annexation. For many declining central cities, annexation is an economic development tool to enhance financial portfolios, and it is frequently used by many incorporated suburban governments as well. The annexation debate will be pervasive in states that have township forms of government.[1] A principal concern among townships is that incorporated municipalities, whether central city or suburban, are compromising the political and economic well-being of townships by consuming parts of their economic base. From the perspective of townships, economic development is the ability to preserve their economic base from intrusion by incorporated jurisdictions. Effective interlocal cooperation may hinge on the participation of townships, and regional economic development strategies may therefore have to minimize the practice of annexation or address it in some way. For example, the successful adoption of the ED/GE program in Montgomery County required township participation for two reasons. First, the county needed township tax contributions to generate an areawide pool large enough to facilitate redistribution to communities that experienced a decrease in assessed valuation. Second, the county needed the vote of township trustees to approve the implementation of the program. Therefore, in an effort to increase the possibility of township participation, the ED/GE program required communities that annexed unincorporated areas to make contributions to the pool, under the rationale that incorporated jurisdictions would minimize annexation to avoid large contributions to the areawide pool. Although this approach does not eliminate annexation and this resolution may not apply to every county, it suggests that some accommodation may have to be pursued to facilitate interlocal cooperation and therefore regional development.[2]

A fourth major problem for regional development programs is the perception—if not the reality—that such agreements could threaten officials' political tenure if they result in voter resentment or concern, particularly if the agreements involve the contribution of local tax dollars. The development of the ED/GE program is an example: it was based partly on tax-sharing to promote regional growth and development. Although the proponents of tax sharing recognized its ability to improve the fiscal health of the region (Wolfe 1963; Zodrow 1984), tax sharing introduced a win or lose dimension that was difficult for local elected officials to accept. Although being the recipient of extra revenues has little political risk, the prospect of losing tax dollars can arouse voters, which, in turn, can put elected officials in political jeopardy. Consequently, local elected officials may seek to minimize their contributions, which in the long run may have no significant impact on coordinated efforts for regional growth, or they may opt to not participate because the risks are too high.

How might county governments address the risks associated with regional economic development? More succinctly, how might county governments lay the groundwork for a regional economic-development approach that fosters interlocal cooperation? Perhaps as a first step, counties should delineate their role tactfully when initiating a plan, because, as noted earlier, localities may be skeptical of a county initiative. To overcome this problem a county should choose a course of action that reaches out to other organizations.

LINKAGES

Typically, county governments may have a close working relationship with their chamber(s) of commerce and, as a result, counties may request that their chamber(s) develop a regional approach or least facilitate the idea and components of the plan. In some cases, a chamber may already have an economic-development committee that could research and develop the idea.

Although chambers may constitute a logical starting point for developing a regional economic strategy, it is imperative that they develop a public-private committee that includes key local elected officials and business leaders from different communities and constituencies throughout the county. Broad representation helps in two ways. First, it enables a regional economic-development plan to evolve as a representation of what local officials and business leaders believe is fair, feasible, and reasonable. Second, broad representation helps to mediate differences that may arise among participants, leading to acceptable compromises. For example, during the formulation of the ED/GE program, some jurisdictions disputed the amount of their contributions to the areawide pool that would redistribute dollars to declining communities. To mediate the conflict, county and chamber representatives introduced "hold-harmless" provisions to limit the liability of these communities. By having community representation, local officials were able to discuss the compromise, accept it, and, in turn, support the program.

It should be emphasized that broad, inclusive representation, particularly of all municipalities in a county, must be achieved to avoid any backlash once a regional economic-development plan is adopted. One unintended consequence of the ED/GE program was that four municipalities who were not members of the economic-development committee filed suit against the county, thereby stalling the implementation of the program. Although these communities did not win their suit, this situation could have been avoided had they been asked to be part of the committee. Hence, representation needs to extend across jurisdictions so that local governments can understand the objectives of a regional economic plan and can express their opinions throughout its development.

The inclusion of key business leaders is also critical to the establishment of a regional economic-development plan. Unlike many elected officials, business leaders typically visualize long-term time horizons and appreciate the usefulness of a regional economic approach. As a result, they can help elected officials to focus on the long-term benefit of the enterprise. In addition, business leaders can nurture support for a regional plan through community networks. Moreover, their involvement can lead to financial support for specific projects that promote the region. During the formulation of the ED/GE program, for example, a number of businesses, along with the chamber of commerce, funded an international marketing program and other projects that advanced the region's reputation for aviation technology.

Upon establishing a broad-based committee of key representatives, consensus-building must be implemented when discussing the components of a regional plan. Such consensus can probably be achieved best by using an outside facilitator, perhaps a consultant or local university faculty member trained in the field. A facilitator will be more successful at getting local officials to discuss regional development and the issues surrounding the topic than an interested party because participants will not feel threatened or manipulated.

Regional economic strategies that foster interlocal coordination may involve technical issues that can vary from tax sharing to specific strategies to market new businesses. The technical details of addressing these issues should be left to financial, legal, and chamber professionals. This strategy will prevent the process from slowing if technical aspects are left to community representatives. Most community leaders have neither the time nor the technical expertise to address these issues.

Finally, counties may have to provide local governments with fiscal incentives to participate in a regional economic-development effort, particularly when some localities perceive regional growth as benefiting rivals. As a result, counties may have to use their revenue resources to interest local governments in inter-local cooperative arrangements for economic development. In the case of the ED/GE program, Montgomery County set aside an economic-development fund for local governments totaling $50 million, or $5 million each year for ten years. The funds for economic development came from a portion of a .5 percent sales-tax increase approved by the county commissioners in 1989. In effect, local governments are eligible for these funds if they participate in the tax-sharing strategy that fosters interlocal cooperation. Therefore, if a county is serious about promoting interlocal cooperation for regional development, it may have to provide financial incentives for local governments to participate.

REGIONAL MARKETING AND INTERNATIONAL MARKETS

It was noted earlier that the research literature on counties characterizes them as pursuing proactive strategies aimed at developing markets for regional businesses. Although these strategies do not emphasize the efficiency and effectiveness of the interlocal design, they seek to increase new opportunities for businesses, which, in turn, may yield net increases in employment. Traditionally, marketing strategies have involved attracting foreign investment for communities in the United States. States have been at the forefront of this effort, with the most visible strategy being the trade mission. Indeed, President George Bush, speaking to the National Governors' Association in 1989, observed that states "are becoming our economic envoys . . . restoring American international competitiveness and expanding world markets for American goods and services" (Blaine Liner 1990, 12).

However, counties have also begun to pursue foreign investments. While the data are limited, survey data obtained from the International City/County Management Association (ICMA) for this analysis revealed that approximately 43 percent of those counties who responded were engaged in activities to attract foreign businesses to their communities. Like states, counties also conduct trade missions whose purpose is straightforward—to attract foreign industry to a county. Some trade missions may involve both county and state officials, an approach common in Ohio, where both state and county officials visited Japan and the Far East, eventually leading to the construction of a Honda Plant in Marysville. Other trade missions can involve county officials accompanying individual firms to international trade fairs.

Beyond the trade mission strategy, an export-assistance program (ExAP) can be developed. This approach assists small and medium-sized businesses in exporting a product or service. Montgomery County, Maryland, for instance, established an ExAP through its Office of Economic Development (OED), which assists firms providing up to $1,500 for a market-research study, providing free technical assistance to firms through retired Department of Commerce international-trade experts, offering financial and staff support to firms attending international trade shows, and organizing meetings between foreign firms and local companies that want to do business in a foreign market. In some cases, counties may seek state financial or technical assistance to implement such programs. For example, the OED in Montgomery County, Maryland, initiated discussions with the state of Maryland's Office of International Trade (MOIT) to determine the viability of having market-research studies conducted overseas. The county determined that the market research studies could be completed in a fairly short period of time through MOIT's information base and extensive contacts. The county then negotiated an agreement with MOIT to contract with local service-providers to do the actual studies. In addition, MOIT agreed to train OED staff in counseling companies seeking export assistance.

Typically, ExAPs have an advisory committee work with county staff to review applications submitted by firms and to make recommendations to county staff. In the case of Montgomery County, Maryland, OED convened the International Trade Advisory Committee, a group of seven individuals from the private sector with experience in international trade. These individuals review applications to the ExAP program and make recommendations to the director of OED regarding companies that should receive a market-research study.

Despite the establishment and practice of county market programs such as trade missions and export assistance programs, there is no assessment in the research literature of their impact on the growth of a county's economic base. Blaine Liner (1990) has observed that economic development has not been evaluated by auditors and legislative committees as thoroughly as most other government functions. Perhaps one reason is that the amount of money devoted to economic-development services has been smaller than that allotted to other service functions. Moreover, economic development is fraught with difficulties in identifying appropriate time lags for measuring outcomes, which is also a research dilemma in assessing the impacts of interlocal agreements like the ED/GE program discussed earlier. In short, there must be a period of time that has elapsed before one can assess effects on regional growth. Nevertheless, as the ICMA survey shows, a number of counties use market strategies and it seems valuable to explore their impact on economic growth to draw some preliminary observations about their usefulness in county economic development (Cope 1990).

HOW EFFECTIVE ARE COUNTY ECONOMIC DEVELOPMENT STRATEGIES?

The preceding discussion suggests that proactive strategies, such as seeking out new businesses and markets, are critical to promoting economic development. Indeed, an argument that appears throughout the economic-development literature concerns the trade-off between these strategies (commonly referred to as demand-side strategies) and supply-side strategies among cities and states. According to Peter K. Eisinger (1988), demand-side approaches involve active government participation in developing and identifying markets or industries. Supply-side strategies, however, seek to lower the cost of doing business in a particular location through tax abatements, infrastructure investment, and enterprise zones. Eisinger has criticized supply-side strategies because they tend to increase interlocal competition and the cost borne by communities. The consequences of supply-side strategies are even more profound in a global economy, where capital is more mobile. In effect, supply-side approaches may have a short-term advantage, but there are more long-term consequences because of the costs associated with replacing lost industry.

The emerging cross-sectional research on counties indicates that counties exhibit a higher frequency of demand-side approaches than do cities. For instance, using Eisinger's supply-demand framework, Laura A. Reese (1992) reports that counties have carved a niche for themselves in economic development as regional bodies. They appear to be involved in marketing for regions as a whole and are active in foreign marketing for both imports and exports as outlined above.

SOME HYPOTHESES

Because counties appear to resort to demand-side approaches, it is hypothesized that such demand strategies as soliciting foreign businesses may have a more profound and positive impact on a county's economic base than supply-side strategies such as tax abatement and infrastructure investment. The rationale is that developing new export markets and soliciting foreign businesses permits early and decisive intervention in private investment and helps avoid the head-to-head competition inherent in locational inducements. Therefore, it is expected that active attempts by county leaders to meet with business prospects and to solicit foreign investment will have a significant, positive impact on economic growth.

Other factors clearly may affect the growth of a county's economic base. For example, some literature underscores the public-private venture as the central structural feature of county economic development (Pammer and Dustin 1993). This research alludes to the fact that the union of business and government provides greater vision and expertise. The existence of public-private ventures is also justified on the basis that private investment is critical to the economic health of a jurisdiction (Lindblom 1977; Eisinger 1988). The impact of public-private ventures, however, remains an empirical question. It is hypothesized that the presence of formal public-private partnerships in counties will have a positive impact on a county's economic base.

Another factor that may account for a county's ability to meet economic development goals is the existence of an economic-development plan. Admittedly, such planning has been neither well received nor universally practiced among localities. The absence of economic planning stems perhaps from the historic American suspicion of central economic strategies (Kantrow 1983, 80–84; Wildavsky 1986). Historical predispositions notwithstanding, an emphasis on planned approaches toward economic development has been documented in the case literature on counties (Pammer and Dustin 1993). This emphasis has arisen from the need to use resources efficiently in a highly competitive environment. As a result, a plan can focus long-term resources on a county's comparative advantage vis-à-vis other areas. Planning also allows identification of industries likely to provide significant economic-development benefits. Although empirical evidence of planning among counties is limited, the merits of economic planning in improving county economic growth should be explored. It is assumed that the presence of an economic-development plan may yield some growth in a county's economic base.

Finally, the possible effects of region on growth should be explored. Much of the urban literature suggests that the location of jurisdictions predisposes them to socioeconomic decline or growth. As such, it is hypothesized that counties located in the industrial North may not exhibit as significant growth in their economic base as their counterparts in the South and West because of the decline in manufacturing.

THE 1989 ICMA SURVEY

As noted above, the ICMA's Economic Development Survey of counties provides a database from which researchers can learn more about economic-development strategies. The ICMA surveyed 703 counties throughout the United States and received completed surveys from 131 counties, an overall response rate of 18.6 percent. Despite the small response rate, these data provide valuable insights that may ultimately be confirmed as more data are gathered and analyzed.

The dependent variable, economic growth, is defined as administrators' perceptions of the growth rate in their counties' economic base. This variable was operationalized with a six-point index asking administrators to indicate the extent of growth in their county's economic base during the preceding five years. The six-point index is anchored at one end by a response of rapid expansion (more than 25 percent growth) and at the opposite end by a response of significant (more than 10 percent) decline.[3]

A number of survey items were used to operationalize the independent variables. For example, it was posited that demand-side approaches such as developing export markets, marketing county amenities through promotional and personal contacts with business prospects, and soliciting foreign business would significantly improve a county's economic base. To measure the effects of opening export markets and promotional contacts with business prospects, respondents were asked to indicate whether they meet with business prospects, make visits to prospects, develop export markets, and send brochures to prospects about county amenities. The responses were then used to create an additive index in which higher scores indicated the use of more personal and marketing approaches to attract business prospects. Efforts to solicit foreign business investment were measured by asking administrators if they encouraged economic development by soliciting foreign firms to locate to their county.

Different measures of supply-oriented approaches were also included in the analysis. For instance, respondents were to indicate whether their county used tax abatements to attract business. The use of different infrastructure investments was measured by a composite index to answers to four questions about whether county officials sought to attract new industry by improving sewage collection/treatment systems, improving water treatment/distribution systems, modifying zoning, and improving public-safety services.

The use of an economic-development plan and the establishment of a formal public-private partnership are also assumed to aid in attracting and retaining/expanding industry. To account for the possible effects of these variables, officials were first asked if their counties had an official plan; they were then requested to specify if their county had a formal, incorporated public-private partnership to promote economic development. Finally, region of the United States was also taken into account.

THE STATISTICAL MODEL

Correlation and regression analyses were employed to test the hypotheses. Although regression models assume interval-level measurement, ordinal-level scales and dummy codes have been found acceptable and lend robustness to the model (Labovitz 1971; Blalock 1979, 444). The model estimated is of the form:

Perception of Economic Growth = $a + b_1X_1 + b_2X_2 + b_3X_3 + b_4X_4 + b_5X_5 + b_6X_6 + b_7X_7 + e_i$

where the variables are defined as follows:

X_1 = the use of an economic development plan;
X_2 = index of strategies to open markets;
X_3 = measure of soliciting foreign businesses;
X_4 = the use of tax abatement;
X_5 = the use of infrastructure investment;
X_6 = the existence of a formal public/private partnership
in economic development;
X_7 = measure of geographic region.

Table 11.1 presents the correlation and regression results. As hypothesized, all correlation coefficients between the demand-oriented indexes and the dependent variable are positive. Among independent variables, the demand indexes exhibit the strongest bivariate relationships with perceptions of economic growth. According to table 11.1, the strongest correlation exists between the index of strategies to open export markets/personal contacts with business prospects and the dependent variable ($r = .49$). The supply-side measure of infrastructure investment also exhibits a significant, positive relationship with the dependent variable ($r = .22$), suggesting that greater emphasis on this approach will result in greater growth in a county's economic base.

Tax abatement, a supply-side strategy, does not exhibit a significant, positive impact on the economic base measure. The sign of the correlation coefficient implies that a reliance on abating taxes reduces officials' confidence that there is a corresponding growth in their county's economic base ($r = -.11$). Although the magnitude of this relationship changes in a multivariate context, the sign remains constant.

Turning to the regression results, consistent with the correlations, the index of demand-oriented strategies exhibits the strongest effect on the economic-growth measure. In particular, the standardized beta coefficient for the index of strategies to open export markets/contacts with business prospects is positive and statistically significant (beta = .42). A similar relationship is exhibited by the measure of soliciting foreign business, although its impact on the county economic growth is not as strong (beta = .20). The public-private partnership variable, however, does not exhibit a significant impact on the economic growth measure. Nevertheless, these findings suggest that counties that employ demand-oriented approaches are likely to have officials who are confident about economic growth.

Table 11.1 Regression Analysis of Administrators' Perceptions of County
Economic Growth ($n = 131$)

	r	Standardized Coefficients
Supply-Side Variables		
Tax Abatements	-.11	-.15
Infrastructure Investments	.22*	.07
Demand-Side Variables		
Export Markets Index	.49*	.42*
Soliciting Foreign Business	.40*	.20
Other Variables		
Economic Development Plan	.14	.01
Public-Private Partnerships	.17	.08
Region	-.06	-.07

* $p < .05$
$R^2 = -.28$ $F = 6.83$ $p < .0001$

The impact of the infrastructure investment measure is substantially reduced in a multivariate context, suggesting that this approach does not have a
pronounced impact. Although the literature emphasizes the importance of an
economic-development plan in contributing to a jurisdiction's competitiveness,
its impact on the dependent variable is not statistically significant. Similarly, although the sign of the coefficient is in the expected direction for the measure of
geographic region, this measure does not exhibit a significant impact.

In effect, this analysis, although exploratory and limited, lends some support
to the idea that demand-oriented strategies play a significant role in county economic development. This preliminary analysis highlights the importance of assessing the impact of different strategies on county economic growth.

FUTURE RESEARCH DIRECTIONS

This chapter examined two emerging themes regarding county economic
development. First, counties are actively involved in regional economic development and are motivated in large part by the need to reduce interjurisdictional
competition. Second, counties pursue proactive strategies to attract foreign in-

vestment and develop export opportunities for local industries. More systematic research should be pursued within these broad themes to obtain a better understanding of the uses and impacts of county economic-development strategies. For instance, assessing the impact of such strategies will require the establishment of cause-and-effect relationships between the implementation of strategies and economic growth through the use of cross-sectional designs. However, for this type of research to have theoretical and empirical significance, three criteria must be addressed.

First, comprehensive data sets of county economic-development activities must be developed. In part because research on county economic development is relatively new, no representative data set exists that can be drawn upon to build generalizations applicable to counties in specific regions or nationwide. Achieving this objective is critical, because it affords future research the opportunity to achieve both theoretical and practical significance. Creating such a data set will require the cooperation of both researchers and practitioners. Researchers will have to develop practical and relevant surveys that enable practitioners to respond in an efficient manner, which, in turn, will yield a reasonable response rate to ensure representation and generalizability.[4]

The second criterion is the development of alternative measures of economic growth. For example, further research on this topic will require objective as well as subjective measures of growth. Indeed, officials' assessments of economic growth may accurately reflect what is happening in a county's economic base. Still, the development and use of objective indexes of economic growth (i.e., percentage change in county tax revenues or percentage change in total assessed valuation will help researchers monitor whether subjective judgments of growth resulting from the implementation of specific strategies are consistent with objective trends of economic growth.

The third criterion is the formulation of specific questions to guide research into the use of different economic-development strategies. However, testing new research hypotheses will require that attention be addressed to the former criteria. Nevertheless, one question for future research concerns to what extent counties are resorting to strategic plaaning to achieve economic growth and stability. Indeed, many counties may not consider alternative adjustments to potential changes in the national and international economies. As noted earlier, long-term planning has rarely been accepted in the United States. Thus, perhaps the answer to the above question is self-evident. Nonetheless, counties, like their municipal counterparts, are in an era of economic globalization, and they are becoming more vulnerable to changes in the international economy, a development that will likely require more strategic planning to stay competitive. Therefore, addressing the question posed above could provide valuable answers to additional questions surrounding county economic development. These questions concern the barriers to strategic planning and the factors that influence long-term economic planning. For instance, can formal public-private partnerships act as catalysts for regional economic development? Other research should look more closely at the effects of public-private partnerships on planning to more fully understand them and their effectiveness in helping counties achieve economic-development goals.

Investigators should also address interlocal cooperation to enhance regional economic development. This paradigm is new to many county officials, and future research should therefore explore officials' perceptions of the idea. Do county officials understand the concept of interlocal cooperation? If so, in what way? How did they come to accept the idea? What factors do they see as opportunities and barriers to such cooperation? The answers could offer additional insight about when political and economic conditions offer counties the opportunity to nurture a regional economic-development plan.

Another direction for future research is to investigate the short- and long-term effects of interlocal agreements on regional economic development. For example, what will be the short-term and long-term economic impact of a program such as ED/GE in Montgomery County, Ohio? Will the program produce significant short- or long-term increases in the county's economic base? As noted earlier, a major challenge in assessing the impact of some economic development strategies is the time lag needed for outcomes to be realized. However, to know the true effect of a regional program such as ED/GE, changes in economic growth will have to be monitored for the length of the program.

Equally important, future research must document the types of jobs created by regional economic-development plans and demand-oriented strategies. Are most jobs minimum wage or high wage? In effect, what is the size of the total payroll generated by demand-oriented strategies? Additional research must evaluate the impact of these strategies to establish the differences they really make in the employment base and the overall economic well-being of counties. This research could provide valuable direction to counties about where they should invest their resources to enhance their economic competitiveness. Answers to these questions could advance the knowledge frontier of the American county.

NOTES

1. *Townships* refer to unincorporated subdivisions of counties and exist in most northeastern and midwestern states.
2. If a county finds that the financial benefit of annexing an unincorporated area far exceeds their contribution to an areawide pool, they will still annex.

3. The actual index categories are as follows: 6 = rapid expansion (more than 25 percent growth), 5 = moderate growth (10–25 percent), 4 = slow growth (less than 10 percent), 3 = stable (no real growth or decline), 2 = modest decline (less than 10 percent decrease), 1 = significant decline (more than 10 percent decrease).

4. For example, the only nationwide county economic-development data set to date is the ICMA 1989 data mentioned earlier in this chapter. Although these data are useful for exploratory purposes, the response rate among counties is too low (approximately 18.6 percent) to offer results that can be generalized to all counties throughout the United States. Therefore, future research on this topic must focus on yielding higher response rates among county officials to increase the likelihood of generalizability.

PART V

The Future

12

The American County

Donald C. Menzel

WHAT DOES the future hold for the American county? Will counties become the local governments of the future? Will they be reinvented, revitalized, reengineered, and revolutionized or merely rediscovered and retooled? In many respects, the (arguable) virtues of county governments—proximity to citizens, responsiveness, adaptability, inventiveness, and hybrid structure—may be exactly what is called for in an era of flattened organizational hierarchies, networking, Total Quality Management, privatization, and the blurring of private-public sector boundaries. It might not be so far-fetched, to paraphrase William R. Dodge (1990, 358), to say that if counties did not exist in America, we would have to invent them.

But to suggest that counties are being rediscovered and perhaps appreciated is not to say that we know enough about them and about how we might go about retooling them to insure effective and democratic governance. A major task of this volume is to advance the knowledge frontier of the American county. But how far have we gone? What more is needed? This chapter addresses these questions in a summary fashion, sorting through selected findings and observations proffered throughout the volume.

STRUCTURE/ORGANIZATION

Scholars and public officials alike have long been preoccupied with county structure/organization questions. In general, how does a county government's structure affect organizational performance, and what factors contribute to structural reform or change? Stated more precisely,

1. Under what conditions, if any, do reformed structures result in more efficient government? More effective service delivery? More responsive government? More open and equitable government?
2. Do reformed county governments adopt different public policies than unreformed county governments? Are other factors, such as fiscal stress or

population growth or decline, mediating influences on the types of policies adopted? The philosophy of governing?

3. Under what conditions, if any, do counties with greater discretionary authority (for example, as reflected in home-rule powers and expanded taxation authority) govern themselves more effectively than counties with less discretionary authority?

4. Under what conditions, if any, do counties with elected executives perform more effectively than counties with appointed executives? Or vice versa?

5. Under what conditions, if any, does poor performance contribute to county government structural reform? More generally, what factors motivate counties in some states to reform their structures when counties in other states do not do so? How do social, economic, and demographic variables influence or condition reform efforts and the subsequent performance of county government?

6. Are county decisions to reform influenced by actions of neighboring counties? Are there patterns of influence between and among counties?

7. If regional or metropolitan governance evolves, what role will reformed and unreformed counties play? How will they have to configure themselves to fit into a metropolitan government?

Reforming county government, as several authors in this volume note, does not necessarily mean making county government smaller, more efficient, and reactive. Rather, it means strengthening the power and authority of county officials, especially chief executives, to get the job done—to integrate, coordinate, and empower the county workforce. Reformed counties are expected to be proactive policy making governments. And, as Victor DeSantis and Tari Renner point out in chapter 5 and Susan A. MacManus documents in chapter 4, the trend toward appointing or electing a single chief executive is unmistakable and shows no sign of abating. Similarly, the growing popularity of county home rule is likely to result in greater organizational coherency and integrated decision making. These developments, as James H. Svara's research implies, are likely to spawn county leaders who are particularly strong at coalition building and skillful at adapting to the ambiguities of the formal position they occupy. Appointed and elected county executives will not be authority-driven leaders but will lead through negotiation, persuasion, and empowerment.

The contributors to this volume do not foresee these developments occurring overnight, although some counties are experiencing more change along these lines than are other counties. Rather, change is likely to be incremental, uneven, perhaps chaotic. Inertia always works in favor of piecemeal change, and in the case of counties, it is joined by the built-in resistance expected from row officers who will cling to their political and often fiscal autonomy. The evidence

suggests that reformed counties are rarely totally reformed. Rather, they are typically hybrid structures. For example, among Florida's fourteen charter counties,
most constitutional officers have charter status. The adoption of these starter
charters does not constitute an act of significant change. And, as the National
Civic League notes in the introduction to its *Model County Charter* (1990), the
really big break with tradition comes when a "reorganized county government
brings under council control (and administration by the appointed manager)
functions previously performed by independently elected officers or substantially independent boards and commissions" (xxiii–xxiv).

So, does structure matter or not? The answer is yes, if structure is defined in
terms of the dynamics of authority, leadership, and decision making, and no, if
structure is defined only in terms of forms of government. The authors of this
volume found some evidence, although it is not extensive, that form influences
how much counties spend but has little effect on the types of policies pursued or
the efficiencies effected. Kee Ok Park, for example, found that counties with an
appointed chief administrator or elected executive spent more than those with
traditional commission form of government. This finding, however, was tempered
by the fact that several other variables have a far greater influence on spending
levels. To be sure, no author argues that future investigators should abandon research on structural forms. It may be that more complex research designs are
needed to ferret out the hypothesized relationships between structure defined as
form of government and the consequences suggested in the questions listed
above. And, of course, such designs would need to sort through hybrid forms,
given that many counties have both reformed and unreformed structural attributes.

COUNTY LEADERSHIP

The linkage between structure and performance, although important, may
be no more important than the connection between leadership and performance.
Indeed, it may be even plausible to suggest that leadership can make *the* difference in how well or poorly a county performs across a wide spectrum of tasks
and responsibilities. Although studies of county leaders and leadership are underway (see Svara and Associates 1994), work in this area remains sparse. Much
more needs to be known about how leadership at the county level is exercised.
For example, have power elites or coalitions replaced courthouse gangs of the
past? Similarly, the skills needed to be a successful manager in the often turbu-
lent world of county politics and government must be identified and incorporated into the training and education of county leaders.

Leadership diversity also needs to be considered. In chapter 4, MacManus
documents the trend toward greater leadership diversity in America's large

counties. More women and more racial minorities are gaining seats on county councils and occupying administrative posts. Such diversity could affect policy making and policy outputs.

Some important questions include:

1. Under what circumstances is the quality of leadership more or less important than governmental structure in determining how a county performs?
2. Is leadership at the county level similar or dissimilar to leadership at the city level? Why?
3. Who are the leaders? Is there a power elite?
4. How are constituencies created, especially in mixed electoral systems?
5. How do the skills and knowledge needed to function effectively in county government compare to those needed to function effectively in other local governments? Is the training provided by colleges and universities for municipal managers adequate for county managers? What type of training is offered by state county associations and the National Association of Counties and how adequate is it?
6. Are county leadership roles and styles a function of population size, growth or retrenchment, or rural versus urban differences, or do they result from some combination of these or other variables?
7. Are county councils becoming more diverse bodies? Are more women, racial minorities, and younger Americans gaining office? And if so, how does leadership diversity affect county policy making?

Svara in chapter 7 and Gregory Streib in chapter 8 pull no punches in contending that knowledge of county leadership, especially at the executive level, is woefully inadequate. In chapter 4, MacManus makes an equally strong case for the need to better understand leadership at the commissioner/legislator level. Her data, however, show that increasing numbers of women and racial minorities (particularly blacks) are being elected to county-commission seats in large counties. Among other things, she concludes that county government is an increasingly attractive starting point for the politically ambitious; it is not a political dead end for women, minorities, or others.

Streib also laments the paucity of our knowledge of county leaders and leadership. He contends that leadership at the county level is different than that at the municipal level. For example, he argues that unlike many city managers, county leaders, especially administrators, cannot draw on the same heritage of professionalism, seldom possess the same grants of authority, and therefore must rely heavily on their powers of persuasion and their ability to develop coalitions to succeed. He also issues a call for the academic, professional, and consultant communities to join hands in a genuine effort to strengthen county management. Such a call seems long overdue.

GROWTH IN COUNTY GOVERNMENT

Another theme present in the literature is the growth of counties in terms of bureaucracy and as service providers. In 1960, for example, the full-time county workforce was estimated at 728,000; by 1990, this number had nearly tripled (U.S. Bureau of the Census 1991). Similarly, in 1967 counties were dominant service providers nationwide for forty-one functions (e.g., libraries, hospitals, and so forth). Twenty years later, they were dominant service providers for sixty functions (USACIR 1991c). Such growth prompts many questions:

1. How responsive are growing county bureaucracies in meeting the service needs of their constituents? Are county bureaucracies responsive or unresponsive, affordable or expensive providers of services? Similar questions can be asked about service quality and efficiency.
2. Do counties address inequities in the areas they service? Are they able to service the growing minority populations of suburbia, a population usually found either in poor incorporated communities or in poor unincorporated areas for which the county is the front-line service provider?
3. Who pays for what services? Are some residents (especially city dwellers) taxed more heavily and, therefore, unfairly for county services?
4. Why are more municipalities willing to transfer functions to counties? What difference does this transfer make in the cost and effectiveness of providing public services?

According to Park in chapter 3, county government grows for a number of reasons, most obviously because citizen demands for county services have expanded significantly over the past several decades. Other important influencing variables include population growth as reflected in both suburbanization and exurbs, federal and state mandates, intergovernmental fiscal aid, and geography—the sunbelt phenomenon. At the same time, Park carefully points out that county government growth varies across policy domains. That is, expenditures in the developmental policy field (e.g., roads, sewers, utilities, and so on) result more directly from county wealth (affordability), federal aid, form of government, and region. In contrast, expenditures in the redistributive policy field are driven more by state mandates and demographic features such as age and poverty level. Park's data, although limited to 732 counties in metropolitan areas, can lead to the conclusion that counties are responsive to meeting the service needs of their constituents.

The same conclusion might be arrived at by examining county efforts to diversify their revenue bases. In chapter 10, Beverly A. Cigler shows that counties are searching for and finding alternatives to the traditional property-tax revenue stream. Counties are increasing reliance on user charges, impact fees, and revenue sharing to respond to constituent demands. She also notes that the thrust for tax reform, defined as a broader base and lower, less intrusive rates, has prompted more than thirty states to enact legislation authorizing a county-option sales tax.

WHY COUNTIES CHANGE

Much has been written about the ability of modern organizations to recognize and adapt to changes in their environment. Strategic planning and decision making are heavily predicated on the idea that organizations are able to adjust to and even anticipate changes in their environments. Still, very little is known about how counties as modern organizations respond to changes in their environment (Lewis 1991). Equally sparse are data and information that compare county services and functions. Questions along these lines include:

1. Are counties in increasingly fragmented socio-organizational environments likely to be more or less efficient, effective, responsive, and accountable than counties in less fragmented environments?
2. Are counties in rapidly growing or declining socioeconomic environments able to respond to those changes in a timely and effective manner?
3. How do counties deal with increasingly competitive environments? Privatization, for example, is often held out as a competitive alternative to local government service provision. In addition, does increased competition among city, county, and special district governments result in higher or lower levels of performance?
4. Are some services, such as emergency management or solid-waste disposal, provided in a more effective manner in some counties or states than in others? How might variation in local-government structures, policies, and political cultures influence service delivery (see Waugh 1994)?

As this volume documents, many counties are experiencing considerable change, which is reflected by growing professionalization, more integrated decision making, an expanding menu of services, and more diverse composition of county boards and commissions. As Kenneth A. Klase, Jin W. Mok, and Gerald M. Pops outline in chapter 6, these changes are a function of social, economic, and political pressures that are accompanied both by conflict and by the need to cooperate to achieve economies.

Much change is also being driven by the increasingly important role of counties in the intergovernmental system. As David R. Berman and Tanis J. Salant note in chapter 2, during the 1980s, the vertical intergovernmental system was both more permissive and more coercive. On the permissive side, counties in many states were granted more discretionary authority to conduct their affairs. On the coercive side, counties were forced to undertake expensive functions for which they typically paid out of local taxes. This cost shifting, as J. Edwin Benton argues in chapter 9 and Berman and Salant detail in chapter 2, came from federal preemptions of local authority and the growing practice of mandating services for lower-level governments. Among the most recent illustrations is the National Voter Registration Act of 1993, popularly known as the Motor Voter Act, whose implementation and operational costs are borne heavily by counties.

COUNTIES AS TERRITORIAL DEMOCRACIES

Several decades ago scholars spoke eloquently of the "withering away of the city" and the growth of the "urban political marketplace" (Willbern 1964, 118). The transformation of urban America continues, but what does it mean at the grassroots level? Questions that may take on great significance in the decades ahead as counties, both rural and urban, become more important as territorial democracies include:

1. How democratic are county governments? And can they become, as one scholar has described neighborhood activism in cities, pivotal forces between citizen and state (John Clayton Thomas 1986)?
2. Relative to cities and other units of local government, are counties more heavily influenced by open-government reforms such as sunshine laws? Do such influences enhance or detract from democratic values and practices?
3. Do counties treat their citizens in municipalities differently than those outside incorporated areas? To what extent?
4. What is the extent of county control of municipal incorporation? What is the consequence of more or less county influence over municipal incorporation? Similar questions can be asked of municipal annexation.

Counties, perhaps even more so than municipalities, are becoming open, accessible, and representative political bodies. In chapter 4, MacManus provides considerable evidence along these lines, at least in the context of large U.S. counties. She notes, for example, that the overwhelming majority of large counties (71 percent) elect their legislators from single-member districts or mixed districts—both believed by many observers to be more representative of the citizenry than the at-large electoral method. It is a bit of an irony that the new reform movement is reforming the previously reformed municipal governments by pushing them toward district-based elections and away from at-large elections. MacManus's survey also found that county legislatures are growing rather than shrinking—again, in an effort to promote representativeness. One consequence is that more women and blacks are taking their places on traditionally white-male-dominated county boards. At the same time, more younger candidates are seeking elected county offices.

Campaign and election trends are also pointing in a positive direction toward counties as grassroots democracies. MacManus found that more candidates are running for countywide offices than at previous periods, and many are seeking to get on the ballot via petition. Finally, her survey results leave little doubt that elections in large counties are becoming more competitive.

COUNTIES AS INTERGOVERNMENTAL ACTORS

The emergence of counties as significant service providers and political entities in their own right points to the need to understand more fully how their influence is likely to amplify or attenuate the dynamics of the American federal system. Careful study and attention should be devoted to the changing role of the county in the intergovernmental system:

1. Do counties, especially urban ones wield more or less influence than cities in securing federal aid and support?
2. Are counties forming consortiums or metropolitan-style governments to solve problems and exercise more influence on state and national governments? Are other forms of intergovernmental cooperation emerging (such as interagency networks) that are seeking the same results?
3. Are metropolitan counties dominating or being dominated by central cities or constellations of boards, authorities, and special districts? What is the character of power sharing and competition among counties and district governments and authorities? What are the lines of accountability in thick intergovernmental systems?
4. Are counties an effective forum for working out intergovernmental arrangements among constituent units such as municipalities and special districts? How might their effectiveness be strengthened or weakened by county home-rule powers and special legislation directed at governmental units within a single county?
5. To what extent do county lobbying associations such as the National Association of Counties facilitate or impede intra- and intercounty relationships? How do such associations complement or compete with urban counterparts such as the National League of Cities?
6. Are counties turning service delivery over to nonprofit organizations or private profit-making firms? Insofar as this process is occurring, how is accountability maintained? What are the implications for horizontal intergovernmental relations, especially when cities and counties are contracting with the same nonprofit agencies or private firms?

The role of counties in the intergovernmental system is a topic that every author in this volume discussed in some manner. Counties, like regional councils, are in a true sense intergovernmental bodies. Indeed, they are intergovernmental governments. Perhaps more important, many counties have multiple identities and realities. They can be at once a full-service local government, a quasi-state government, and a regional government. In chapter 2, Berman and Salant note how these multiple roles and identities sometimes cause counties to engage in seemingly contradictory or inconsistent behaviors. On the one hand, as a quasi-state agency they have often been good soldiers in carrying out their duties. On the other hand, counties as full-service local governments have resisted state efforts to encroach on their autonomy and authority and, where significantly limited by state law, have been aggressive in seeking out greater authority and championing the case for home rule. Similar behavior has emerged with regard to mandates. County officials have both welcomed and attempted to avoid new responsibilities imposed by federal and state mandates. And, as Benton notes in chapter 9 with regard to intergovernmental fiscal assistance, county officials have developed a love-hate attitude toward such assistance.

Counties should also be studied as actors in the horizontal intergovernmental system. Berman and Salant assert that counties are major collaborators with other units through contracts and agreements, important participants in regional organizations such as councils of government, and direct providers of areawide services such as solid waste, transit, and health. In chapter 11 William J. Pammer, Jr., also points to the increasingly important role of counties in the horizontal plane by detailing innovative tax-base-sharing ventures between counties and municipal governments in Ohio and describing regional economic development programs in Minnesota and New Jersey. Also, as Cigler details in chapter 10, studies of California and Texas counties show that intergovernmental revenue-sharing agreements between cities and counties can be important vehicles for effecting local governance.

Finally, the mandate issue, which is fundamentally intergovernmental, has had a centrifugal influence on counties. As Benton illustrates in chapter 9, counties cannot escape the inevitable requirements to do more, often with little or no fiscal assistance from higher-level authorities. As Park documents in chapter 3, mandates contribute to higher levels of county expenditures.

Counties, whether they like it or not, are important players in the federal system. Indeed, through their principal lobbying association, the National Association of Counties, they have pressed the U.S. Congress hard for mandate relief. Both House and Senate subcommittees acted favorably on legislation in the summer of 1994. And, on March 22, 1995, President Clinton signed into law the Unfunded Mandates Reform Act of 1995.

FISCAL ISSUES AND PRACTICES

Many counties have broadened their tax bases, relying less on the property tax and more on user fees and other revenue sources. Still, little is known about how counties mix and match finances to provide services and accomplish other important tasks. Studies like that of Herbert S. Duncombe, William Duncombe, and Richard Kinney (1992) are needed to illuminate the approaches, mechanisms, and inventiveness that many believe characterize the financial capacity of county government. Such studies should focus on the following questions:

1. Are counties becoming more financially independent? How do counties deal with state mandates that are often accompanied by few or no new resources?
2. To what extent do counties rebate taxes to municipalities for municipal services that the county does not provide?
3. Are state constitutional restrictions on revenue alternatives increasing or decreasing? If they are decreasing, are counties taking advantage of them?
4. What factors, other than variation in state laws, explain why some counties rely more heavily than others on certain types of revenues (e.g., property tax, impact fees, and so on)?
5. What is the pattern, if any, of fiscal support for certain types of services (e.g., urban services) in contrast to other types of services?
6. How do counties manage federal pass-through monies? To what extent are these funds used efficiently? Rationally? Politically?
7. How successful have counties been in pressuring states to either increase unrestricted state aid or expand county revenue-raising authority?

As Benton reiterates in chapter 9, dollars and mandates have transformed the American federal system. Federal and state fiscal aid to counties and municipalities accounted for 20–30 percent of all local revenue in 1990, even after a decade of federal fiscal cutbacks under the Reagan and Bush administrations. Like the nearly astronomical growth of federal fiscal aid in the 1960s–70s, the growth in costly federal-state mandates imposed on local governments mushroomed in the 1970s and 1980s.

The consequences of the growth and decline of intergovernmental fiscal aid and, more recently, mandates, have been numerous. First, counties have been forced to scramble (and perhaps to be inventive) in an effort to find new dollars or shift existing dollars in such a way as to do more with less. In some instances, they have become entrepreneurial along the lines suggested by David Osborne and Ted Gaebler (1992). Such entrepreneurialism is reflected in county efforts to charge development-impact fees, sell data and other acquisitions, embrace the privatization of marinas and the like, establish enterprise zones, and generally to broaden the revenue base, as Cigler notes in chapter 10. Moreover, as Pammer details in chapter 11, counties have brokered fiscal arrangements with municipal governments in a mutually beneficial effort to strengthen local public economies. Second, conflict rather than cooperation has broken out between large and small counties in some states over state aid distributional formulas.

The entrepreneurial efforts described above, however beneficial, have not come without some trade-offs, one of which is fiscal simplicity. County finances, both on the revenue side and the expenditure side, have become complex, especially in larger counties. That counties (and municipalities) are typically able to balance their budgets is no small feat in the 1990s. Another trade-off has been programmatic accountability in a fiscal sense. Keeping track of what funds are flowing to what programs and how funds are mixed and matched to achieve programmatic outcomes has become a major challenge in its own right.

Finally, Cigler points out in chapter 10 that revenue flexibility does not have to be achieved entirely through adding new revenues. Improved purchasing, contracting, and use of analytical techniques, including forecasting, can contribute to a county's general fiscal health. Furthermore, financial savings can be achieved through other initiatives, including targeting state revolving funds to finance infrastructure, issuing bonds in a pool to influence credit ratings, and even establishing alternative dispute-resolution techniques.

COUNTIES IN THE GLOBAL COMMUNITY

It has become a cliché to say that modern communications and technology have created a globally interdependent world. But little is known about the roles that counties play in the global village. The increasingly important questions include:

1. What types of counties seek commercial and cultural relationships with communities in other nations? How are those relationships developed? Nurtured?
2. Are American counties competing with cities and states for foreign enterprises? If so, what is the character of this competition, and is it beneficial? Is somebody winning and somebody losing? Or is everyone winning?
3. Are there counterparts to the American county in other nations? If so, can meaningful comparisons be drawn?

In describing the emergence of economic development strategies among counties, Pammer rightly contends in chapter 11 that global competition for industrial markets matters to counties as much as to nation-states. County officials are traveling abroad in the hunt for foreign investment. Trade missions to Japan, Europe, and other places are increasingly commonplace. The siting of the Honda plant in Marysville, Ohio, for example, was promoted by joint county-state trade missions to Japan. County-sponsored export-assistance programs represent another means of fostering economic development in the global marketplace. Such programs can include county financing for market research studies for small to medium-sized businesses, technical assistance and information, and organizing meetings between foreign firms and local companies that want to do business in a foreign market.

LOOKING AHEAD

The American county remains something of an enigma whose future is difficult to envision as well as to predict. Fiscal strain, the altered world landscape after the end of the cold war, and the shifts in world trade patterns stimulated by the lowering of trade barriers worldwide are likely to make the ordinary business of running county government (as well as the U.S. government) something more than ordinary.

Counties are not likely to take over municipal governments; there is no evidence pointing to a new wave of city-county consolidations. At the same time, city-county functional consolidation in areas such as emergency medical services and natural-disaster planning is growing throughout the United States. Increasing cooperation is likely to occur in the future as both cities and counties struggle to provide more services to a tax-resistant public. There is also little evidence that counties will break away from states to form new states or regional governments not yet imagined.

These developments and others detailed in this volume also suggest that American counties will be powerful political actors in the decades ahead. The growing professionalization of county workforces will better position counties to shape policy and to receive their fair share of state and federal dollars. The movement toward electing or appointing professionally trained county executives, especially if combined with reductions in the number of elected row officers, will undoubtedly yield more political clout for counties. Then, too, if counties separately or collectively can make a difference in the development of their local economies, political power will surely follow.

The future of the American county is bright, promising, and challenging, although it remains only partially understood. The authors of the essays contained in this volume believe the time has come for scholars and practitioners alike to commit themselves to the task of further advancing the knowledge frontier of the American county. The journey has only begun.

References

Aaron, Henry J. 1975. *Who Pays the Property Tax? A New View*. Washington, D.C.: Brookings Institution.

Abramson, Mark A. 1989. "The Leadership Factor." *Public Administration Review* 49 (November–December): 562–65.

Adrian, Charles R. 1988. "Forms of City Government in American History." In *The Municipal Year Book 1988*, 3–11. Washington, D.C.: International City Management Association.

Aldrich, H. E. 1979. *Organizations and Environments*. Englewood Cliffs, N.J.: Prentice-Hall.

Alford, Robert R., and Harry M. Scoble. 1965. "Political and Socioeconomic Characteristics of American Cities." In *The Municipal Year Book 1965*, 82–97. Chicago: International City Managers Association.

"All-Pro Government Team." 1988. *City and State* (August 29).

Alozie, Nicholas O. 1992. "The Election of Asians to City Councils." *Social Science Quarterly* 73 (March): 90–100.

Ammons, David N., and Charldean Newell. 1988. " 'City Managers Don't Make Policy': A Lie, Let's Face It." *National Civic Review* 77 (March–April): 124–32.

Anderson, William, and Waite D. Durfee. *Intergovernmental Fiscal Relations*. Minneapolis: University of Minnesota Press, 1957.

Anton, Thomas J. 1984. "Intergovernmental Change in the United States: An Assessment of the Literature." In *Public Sector Performance: A Conceptual Turning Point*, ed. Trudi C. Miller, 15–64. Baltimore: Johns Hopkins University Press.

———. 1989. *American Federalism and Public Policy: How the System Works*. New York: Random House.

Aronson, Richard. 1985. *Public Finance*. New York: McGraw-Hill.

Aronson, Richard, and John Hilley. 1986. *Financing State and Local Governments*. Washington, D.C.: Brookings Institution.

Attfield, R. 1983. *The Ethics of Environmental Concern*. New York: Columbia University Press.

Axelrod, Donald. 1992. *Shadow Government: The Hidden World of Public Authorities and How They Control Over $1 Trillion of Your Money*. New York: John Wiley and Sons.

Bahl, Roy. 1984. *Financing State and Local Government in the 1980s*. New York: Oxford University Press.

Bahl, Roy, and William Duncombe. 1993. "State and Local Debt Burdens in the Late

1980s: A Study in Contrast." *Public Administration Review* 53 (January–February): 31–40.

Bahl, Roy, and David Puryear. 1976. "Regional Tax Base Sharing: Possibilities and Implications." *National Tax Journal* 3 (September): 328–35.

Bahl, Roy, and Robert J. Saunders. 1965. "Determinants of Change in State and Local Government Expenditures." *National Tax Journal* 18 (March): 50–57.

Baker, C. Douglas. 1992. "The Role of Governmental Fragmentation on Metropolitan County Expenditures." Paper presented at the Annual Meeting of the American Political Association, Chicago, September 3–6.

Baker, Keith G. 1977. "County Government Expenditure Policy: An Analysis of Change Relationships." *State and Local Government Review* 9 (Winter): 44–48.

Banfield, Edward, and James Q. Wilson. 1963. *City Politics.* New York: Vintage.

Banovetz, James, ed. 1989. *Guidelines on Local Government Management Education.* Report of the ICMA/NASPAA Task Force on Local Government Education. Washington, D.C.: International City/County Management Association.

Beaumont, E., and H. Hovey. 1985. "State, Local, and Federal Economic Development Policies: New Federal Patterns, Chaos, or What?" *Public Administration Review* 45 (March–April): 327–32.

Bell, A. Fleming. 1989. *County Government in North Carolina.* Chapel Hill, N. C.: Institute of Government.

Bennis, Warren, and B. Nanus. 1985. *The Strategies for Taking Charge.* New York: Harper Collins.

Benton, J. Edwin. 1992a. "The Effects of Changes in Federal Aid on State and Local Government Expenditures." *Publius: The Journal of Federalism* 22 (Winter): 71–82.

———. 1992b. "Fiscal Issues and Research on the American County." Paper presented at the Southern Political Science Association, Hyatt Regency Westshore, Tampa, Florida, November 7–9, 1991.

Benton, J. Edwin., and Darwin Gamble. 1984. "City/County Consolidation and Economies of Scale: Evidence from a Time-Series Analysis in Jacksonville, Florida." *Social Science Quarterly* 65 (March): 190–98.

Benton, J. Edwin, and Donald C. Menzel. 1991. "County Service Trends and Practices: The Case of Florida." *State and Local Government Review* 23 (Spring): 69–75.

———. 1992a. "Contracting and Franchising County Services in Florida." *Urban Affairs Quarterly* 27 (March): 436–56.

———. 1992b. "County Service Trends and Practices: The Case of Florida." *State and Local Government Review* 23 (Spring): 69–75.

———. 1993. "County Services: The Emergence of Full-Service Government." In *County Governments in an Era of Change,* ed. David R. Berman, 53–69. New York: Greenwood Press.

Benton, J. Edwin, and Platon N. Rigos. 1985. "Patterns of Metropolitan Service Dominance: Central City and Central County Service Roles Compared." *Urban Affairs Quarterly* 20 (March): 285–302.

Berman, David R. 1992. "State-Local Relations: Mandates, Money, Partnerships." In *The Municipal Yearbook,* 51–57. Washington, D.C.: International City Management Association.

——, ed. 1993. *County Governments in an Era of Change.* Westport; Conn.: Greenwood Press.

Berman, David R., and Barbara Greene. 1993. "Counties and the National Agenda." In *County Governments in an Era of Change,* ed. David R. Berman, 123-34. Westport, Conn.: Greenwood Press.

——. 1993a. "Counties, Other Governments, and the Future." In *County Governments in an Era of Change,* ed. David R. Berman, 135-42. Westport, Conn.: Greenwood Press.

——. 1993b. "State-Local Relations: Patterns and Problems." In *Municipal Year Book 1993,* 87-93. Washington, D.C.: International City Management Association.

Berman, David R., and Lawrence L. Martin. 1988. "State-Local Relations: An Examination of Local Discretion." *Public Administration Review* 48 (March–April): 637-41.

Berman, David R., Lawrence L. Martin, and Laura Kajfez. 1985. "County Home Rule: Does Where You Stand Depend on Where You Sit?" *State and Local Government Review* (Spring): 232-34.

Bingham, Gil. 1986. *Resolving Environmental Disputes: A Decade of Experience.* Washington, D.C.: Conservation Foundation.

Blalock, Hubert M., Jr. 1979. *Social Statistics.* 2d ed. New York: McGraw Hill.

Bland, Robert L. 1989. *A Revenue Guide for Local Government.* Washington, D.C.: International City Management Association.

Blau, Chester I. 1964. *Exchange and Power in Social Life.* New York: John Wiley and Sons.

Bollens, John C. 1969. *American County Governments.* Beverly Hills, Calif.: Sage Publications.

Bosworth, Karl L. 1958. "The Manager Is a Politician." *Public Administration Review* 18 (Summer): 216-22.

Botner, Stanley B. 1991. "Trends and Developments in Budgeting and Finance in Medium Sized Cities in the United States." *Public Budgeting and Finanacial Management* 3 (Special Issue): 443-56.

Bowman, James S. 1994. "At Last, an Alternative to Performance Appraisal: Total Quality Management." *Public Administration Review* 54 (March–April): 129-36.

Bowman, John H., Susan A. MacManus, and John L. Mikesell. 1992. "Mobilizing Resources for Public Services: Financing Urban Governments." *Journal of Urban Affairs* 14 (Index Issue): 311-35.

Boynton, Robert P., and Victor S. DeSantis. 1990. "Form and Adaptation: A Study of the Formal and Informal Functions of Mayors, Managers, and Chief Administrative Officers." *Baseline Data Report* 22 (January–February): 1-12.

Bragg, John T. 1988. "A View from the Commission." *Intergovernmental Perspective* 14 (Summer): 2.

Brasher, C. Nielsen. 1994. "Workfare in Ohio: Political and Socioeconomic Climate and Program Impact." *Policy Studies Journal* 22 (Autumn): 514-27.

Break, George. 1980. *Financing Government in a Federal System.* Washington, D.C.: Brookings Institution.

Bridges, Sara Van Meter. 1991. "A Local Government Perspective on Financing Infrastructure." *Journal of Planning Literature* 6 (November): 202-9.

Bryson, John M. 1988. *Strategic Planning for Nonprofit Organizations.* San Francisco: Jossey-Bass.

Bryson, John M. and Barbara C. Crosby. 1992. *Leadership for the Common Good.* San Francisco: Jossey-Bass.

Bryson, John M., and W. D. Roering. 1988. "Initiation of Strategic Planning by Governments." *Public Administration Review* 48 (November–December): 995–1004.

Buchanan, James M. 1977. "Why Does Government Grow?" In *Budgets and Beureaucrats: The Sources of Government Growth,* by Thomas E. Borcherdins, 3–18. Durham, N.C.: Duke University Press.

Bullock, Charles S. III. 1990. "Women Candidates and Success at the County Level." Paper presented at the Annual Meeting of the Southern Political Science Association, Atlanta, November 8–10.

———. 1993. "Race and Electoral Districting in County Government." Paper presented at the Southwestern Political Science Association, New Orleans, March 18–20.

Bullock, Charles S. III, and Susan A. MacManus. 1990. "Structural Features of Municipalities and the Incidence of Hispanic Councilmembers." *Social Science Quarterly* 71 (December): 665–81.

———. 1991. "Municipal Electoral Structure and the Election of Councilwomen." *Journal of Politics* 53 (February): 75–89.

———. 1993. "Testing Assumptions of the Totality-of-the-Circumstances Test: An Analysis of the Impact of Structures on Black Descriptive Representation." *American Politics Quarterly* 21, no. 3 (July): 290–306.

Bullock, Charles S. III, and A. Brock Smith. 1990. "Black Success in Local Runoff Elections." *Journal of Politics* 52 (November): 1205–20.

Bunch, Beverly S., and Robert P. Strauss. 1992. "Municipal Consolidation: An Analysis of the Financial Benefits for Fiscally Distressed Small Municipalities." *Urban Affairs Quarterly* 27 (June): 615–29.

Burchall, Robert W., James H. Carr, Richard L. Florida, and James Nemeth. 1984. *The New Reality of Municipal Finance: The Rise and Fall of the Intergovernmental City.* New Brunswick, N.J.: Center for Urban Policy Research, Rutgers University.

"Business Fads: What's In—and Out: Executives Latch on to Any Idea That Looks Like a Quick Fix." 1986. *Business Week,* January 20.

Button, James, and Walter Rosenbaum. 1990. "Gray Power, Gray Peril, or Gray Myth? The Political Impact of the Aging in Local Sunbelt Politics." *Social Science Quarterly* 71 (March): 25–38.

Cameron, David. 1978. "The Expansion of the Public Economy: A Comparative Analysis." *American Political Science Review* 72 (December): 1243–61.

Campbell, Harrison S., Jr., and J. Fred Giertz. 1990. "Impact Fees for Developing Infrastructure." *Policy Forum* 3 (1): 1–4.

Cape, William H. 1967. *The Emerging Patterns of County Executives.* Lawrence, Kans.: University of Kansas Governmental Research Center.

Caputo, David, and Richard Cole. 1977. "City Officials and Mail Questionnaires: An Investigation of the Response Bias Assumption." *Political Methodology* 4 (May): 146–55.

Carpenter, Susan L., and W. J. D. Kennedy. 1988. *Managing Public Disputes: A Practical Guide to Handling Conflict and Reaching Agreements.* San Francisco: Jossey-Bass.

Carr, Cathy. 1991. "Los Angeles County Productivity Managers Network: An Alternative to Traditional Productivity Program Management." *Public Productivity and Management Review* 15 (Fall): 47–59.

Cassel, Carol A. "The Nonpartisan Ballot in the United States." In *Electoral Laws and Their Political Consequences,* ed. Bernard Grofman and Arend Lijphart, 226–41. New York: Agaton Press.

Cayer, Joseph N. 1993. "Managing Programs and Services." In *The Effective Local Government Manager,* ed. Charldean Newell, 107–34. Washington, D.C.: International City/County Management Association.

Center for the American Woman and Politics. 1992. "Fact Sheet: Women in Elective Office, 1992." New Brunswick, N.J.: Eagleton Institute of Politics, Rutgers University.

Chang, Stanley Y. 1987. *A Study of the Basic Criteria and Standards for Internal Service Funds.* Lubbock, Tex.: Texas Tech University.

Chang, Stanely Y., and Robert J. Freeman. 1991. "Internal Service Funds: The Neglected Stepchild's Neglected Stepchild." *Government Accountants Journal* 40 (Fall): 22–30.

Childs, Richard S. 1925. *Ramshackle County Government: The Plague Spot of American Politics.* New York: National Municipal League.

Chubb, John E. 1985. "The Political Economy of Federalism." *American Political Science Review* 79 (December): 994–1015.

Cigler, Beverly A. 1990. "County Contracting: Reconciling the Accountability and Information Paradoxes." *Public Administration Quarterly* 14 (Fall): 285–301.

———. 1991. "The County-State Connection: A National Study of Associations of Counties." Paper presented at the Annual Meeting of the American Political Science Association, Washington, D.C.

———. 1993a. "Challenges Facing Fiscal Federalism in the 1990s." *PS: Political Science and Politics* 26 (June): 181–86.

———. 1993b. "Professionalizing the American States in the 1990s." *International Journal of Public Administration* 54 (December): 1965–2000.

———. 1993c. "The Special Problems of Rural County Governments." In *County Governments in an Era of Change,* ed. David R. Berman, 89–106. Westport, Conn.: Greenwood Press.

———. 1993d. "State-Local Relations: A Need for Reinvention?" *Intergovernmental Perspective* 19 (Winter): 15–18.

———. 1994. "The County-State Connection: A National Study of Associations of Counties." *Public Administration Review* 54 (January–February): 3–11.

Clark, Terry N. 1968. "Community Structure, Decision Making, Budget Expenditures, and Urban Renewal in 51 Cities." *American Sociological Review* 33 (August): 576–93.

Clark, Terry, and Lorna C. Ferguson. 1983. *City Money: Political Processes, Fiscal Strain, and Retrenchment.* New York: Columbia University Press.

Cleveland, Harlan. 1985. *The Knowledge Executive.* New York: E. P. Dutton.

Coe, Charles K., and Elizabethann O'Sullivan. 1993. "Accounting for Hidden Costs: A National Study of Internal Service Funds and Other Indirect Costing Methods in Municipal Government." *Public Administration Review* 53 (1): 59–63.

Commission on Intergovernmental Relations. 1955. *A Report to the President for Transmittal to the Congress.* Washington, D.C.: Government Printing Office.

Conlan, Timothy J., and David R. Beam. 1992. "Federal Mandates: The Record of Reform and Future Prospects." *Intergovernmental Perspective* 18 (Fall): 7–15.

Cope, Glen Hahn. 1990. "Successful Economic Development: Meeting Local and Global Needs." *Baseline Data Report* 22 (July–August): 1–11.

Coser, Lewis. 1956. *The Function of Social Conflict.* New York: Free Press.

"Counties and Congress—1993 Review." 1993. *County News.* December 20.

Cronin, Thomas E. 1989. *Direct Democracy: The Politics of Initiative, Referendum, and Recall.* Cambridge, Mass.: Harvard University Press.

Cunningham, James V. 1970. *Urban Leadership in the Sixties.* Cambridge, Mass.: Schenkman Publishing Company.

Dahl, Robert A. 1961. *Who Governs?* New Haven: Yale University Press.

Darcy, Robert, and Charles D. Hadley. 1988. "Black Women in Politics: The Puzzle of Success." *Social Science Quarterly* (September): 629–45.

Darcy, Robert, Susan Welch, and Janet Clark. 1987. *Women, Elections, and Representation.* New York: Longman.

Dearborn, Philip M. 1993. "Local Property Taxes: Emerging Trends." *Intergovernmental Perspective* 19 (Summer): 10–12.

DeBoer, Larry. 1992. "Indiana Solid Waste Management Districts." In *Multicommunity Collaboration: An Evolving Rural Revitalization Strategy,* ed. Peter F. Korsching, Timothy O. Borich, and Julie Stewart, 161–65. Ames: Northwest Central Regional Center for Rural Development, Iowa State University.

Denhardt, Kathryn. 1989. "The Management of Ideals: A Political Perspective on Ethics." *Public Administration Review* 49 (March–April): 187–92.

Denhart, Robert. 1982. "Public Administration: Sub-Field? Profession? Discipline?" *American Review of Public Administration* 16 (Spring): 15–21.

———. 1985. "Romancing the Plan." *Public Management* 67 (July): 9.

Denhart, Robert, and Kevin Prelgovisk. 1992. "Public Leadership: A Developmental Perspective." In *Executive Leadership in the Public Service,* ed. Robert Denhardt and William Sewart, 33–44. Tuscaloosa: University of Alabama Press.

Derthick, Martha. 1970. *The Influence of Federal Grants: Public Assistance in Massachusetts.* Cambridge, Mass.: Harvard University Press.

———. 1986. "Preserving Federalism: Congress, the States, and the Supreme Court." *Brookings Review* (Winter–Spring): 32–37.

DeSantis, Victor. 1989. "County Government: A Century of Change." In *The Municipal Year Book 1989,* 55–65. Washington, D.C.: International City Management Association.

DeSantis, Victor, and Tari Renner. 1992. "Minority and Gender Representation in American County Legislatures: The Effect of Election Systems." In *United States Electoral Systems: Their Impact on Women and Minorities,* ed. Wilma Rule and Joseph F. Zimmerman, 143–52. Westport, Conn.: Greenwood Press.

———. 1993. "Governing the County: Authority, Structure, and Elections." In *County Governments in an Era of Change,* ed. David R. Berman, 15–28. Westport, Conn.: Greenwood Press.

Dock, T. V., and J. C. Wetherbe. 1988. *Computer Information Systems for Business.* St. Paul, Minn.: West Publishing.

Dodge, William R. 1988. "The Emergence of Intercommunity Partnerships in the 1980s." *Public Management* 70 (July): 2–7.

——. 1990. "Regional Problem Solving in the 1990s: Experimentation with Local Governance for the 21st Century," *National Civic Review* 79 (July): 354–66.

Downing, Paul. 1992. "The Revenue Potential of User Charges in Municipal Government." *Public Finance Quarterly* 20 (October): 512–27.

Duncan, John P. 1950. "County Government—An Analysis." In *Oklahoma Constitutional Studies*, 417–48. Guthrie, Okla.: Co-operative Publishing Co.

Duncan, R. B. 1972. "Characteristics of Organizational Environments and Perceived Environmental Uncertainty." *Administrative Science Quarterly* 17 (September): 313–27.

Duncombe, Herbert S. 1966. *County Government in America.* Washington, D.C.: National Association of Counties.

——. 1977. *Modern County Government.* Washington, D.C.: National Association of Counties.

Duncombe, Herbert S., William Duncombe, and Richard Kinney. 1992. "Factors Influencing the Politics and Process of County Government Budgeting." *State and Local Government Review* 24 (Winter): 19–27.

Dunn, D. D., F. K. Gibson, and J. Whorton. 1985. "University Commitment to Public Service for State and Local Governments." *Public Administration Review* 45 (July–August): 503–9.

Dye, Thomas R. 1966. *Politics, Economics, and the Public.* Chicago: Rand McNally.

——. 1981. *Politics in States and Communities.* 4th ed. Englewood Cliffs, N.J.: Prentice-Hall.

——. 1984. *Understanding Public Policy.* 5th ed. Englewood Cliffs, N.J.: Prentice-Hall.

——. 1991. *Politics in States and Communities.* 7th ed. Englewood Cliffs, N.J.: Prentice-Hall.

Dye, Thomas R. and John A. Garcia. 1978. "Structure, Function, and Policy in American Cities." *Urban Affairs Quarterly* 14 (September): 103–26.

Dye, Thomas R., and V. Gray, eds. 1980. *The Determinants of Public Policy.* Lexington, Mass.: D. C. Heath.

Dye, Thomas R., and Thomas L. Hurley. 1978. "The Responsiveness of Federal and State Governments to Urban Problems." *Journal of Politics* 40 (February): 196–207.

Dye, Thomas R., and Susan A. MacManus. 1976. "Predicting City Government Structure." *American Journal of Political Science* 20 (May): 257–71.

——. 1990. "State vs. Local Public Sector Growth: A Comparison of Determinant Models." *Policy Studies Journal* 18 (Spring): 645–57.

Eadie, Douglas C. 1983. "Putting a Powerful Tool to Practical Use: The Application of Strategic Planning in the Public Sector." *Public Administration Review* 43 (September–October): 447–52.

——. 1986. "Strategic Issue Management: Improving the Council-Manager Relationship." *MIS Report* 18: 169–86.

——. 1989. "Identifying and Managing Strategic Issues: From Design to Action." In *Handbook of Strategic Management,* ed. Jack Rabin, Gerald J. Miller, and W. Bartley Hildreth, 169–86. New York: Marcel Dekker.

Ebel, Robert. 1991. A Profile of County Finances. *Intergovernmental Perspective* 17 (Winter), 14–17.

Eichner, Alfred S. 1970. *State Development Agencies and Employment Expansion.* Ann Arbor: Institute of Labor and Industrial Relations, University of Michigan–Wayne State University.

Eisinger, Peter K. 1988. *The Rise of the Entrepreneurial State: State and Local Economic Development Policy in the United States.* Madison: University of Wisconsin Press.

Elazar, Daniel. 1966. *American Federalism: A View from the States.* New York: Thomas Y. Crowell.

Eulau, Heinz, and Robert Eyestonse. 1968. "Policy Maps of City Councils and Policy Outcomes: A Developmental Analysis." *American Political Science Reivew* 11 (December): 456–78.

Fairlie, John A., and Charles M. Kneier. 1930. *County Government and Administration.* New York: D. Appleton-Century.

Farkas, Suzane. 1971. *Urban Lobbying: Mayors in the Federal Arena.* New York: New York University Press.

Farnham, Paul, and Stephen Bryant. 1985. "Form of Local Government: Structural Policies of Citizen Choice." *Social Science Quarterly* 66 (June): 386–400.

Ferman, Barbara. 1985. *Governing the Ungovernable City.* Philadelphia: Temple University Press.

Fix, Michael, and Daphne A. Kenyon, eds. 1989. *Coping with Mandates: What Are the Alternatives?* Washington, D.C.: Urban Institute.

Florida Advisory Council on Intergovernmental Relations. 1991. *1991 Report on Mandates and Measures Affecting Local Government Fiscal Capacity.* Tallahassee: Florida Advisory Council on Intergovernmental Relations.

Fosler, R. Scott. 1991. "The Suburban County: Governing Mainstream Diversity." *Intergovernmental Perspective* 17 (Winter): 33–37.

Frank, Howard A., and Gerasimos A. Gianakis. 1990. "Raising the Bridge Using Time Series Forecasting Models." *Public Productivity and Management Review* 14 (Winter): 171–88.

Fuller, Mark W. 1991. "City-County Consolidation Issues in Colorado: The GRIP Studies." *Public Productivity and Management Review* 15 (Fall): 71–76.

Gabris, Gerald T. 1989. "Educating Elected Officials in Strategic Goal Setting." *Public Productivity and Management Review* 13 (Winter): 161–75.

———. 1992. "Strategic Planning in Municipal Government: A Tool for Expanding Cooperative Decision Making between Elected and Appointed Officials." Paper presented at the First Biannual International Conference on Advances in Management, Orlando, Florida, March 28.

Gargan, John J. 1989. "Strategic Management in City Government: Continuing the Interplay of Rationality and Politics." In *Handbook of Strategic Management,* ed. Jack Rabin, Gerald Miller, and W. Bartley Hildreth, 403–23. New York: Marcel Dekker.

Garland, James C. 1988. "Explaining Government Growth in the U.S. States." *American Political Science Review* 82 (September): 837–49.

George, Alexander L. 1968. "Political Leadership in American Cities." *Daedalus* 97 (Fall): 1194–217.

Gilbert, D. A. 1979. "Property Tax Base Sharing: An Answer to Central City Fiscal Problems." *Social Science Quarterly* 59 (March): 681–89.

Gilbertson, Henry S. 1917. *The County: The 'Dark Continent' of American Politics.* New York: National Short Ballot Organization.

Giles, William A., Gerald T. Gabris, and Dale A. Krane. 1980. "Dynamics in Rural Policy Development: The Uniqueness of County Government." *Public Administration Review* 40 (January–February): 24–28.

Glendening, Parris N., and Mavis Mann Reeves. 1977. *Pragmatic Federalism.* Pacific Palisades, Calif.: Palisades Publishers.

Gold, Steven D. 1989. *Performing State-Local Relations: A Practical Guide.* Denver: National Conference of State Legislatures.

———. 1992. "The Federal Role in State Fiscal Stress." *Publius: The Journal of Federalism* 22 (Summer): 33–47.

Golembiewski, Robert T. 1983. "Toward Professional Certification." *The Bureaucrat* 12 (Summer): 50–53.

Gore, Al. 1993. *Creating Government That Works Better and Costs Less: Report of the National Performance Review.* Washington, D.C.: U.S. Government Printing Office.

Gosling, James J. 1992. *Budgetary Politics in American Governments.* New York: Longman.

Gramlich, Edward. 1977. "Intergovernmental Grants: A Review of the Empirical Literature." In *The Political Economy of Fiscal Federalism,* ed. Wallace Oates, 219–40. Lexington, Mass.: D. C. Heath.

Graves, W. Brooke. *American Intergovernmental Relations.* New York: Charles Scribner's Sons, 1964.

Gray, D. H. 1986. "Uses and Misuses of Strategic Planning." *Harvard Business Review* 64 (January–February): 89–97.

Green, Roy E. 1989. *The Profession of Local Government Management: Management Expertise and the American Community.* New York: Praeger.

Grodzins, Morton. 1966. *The American System: A New View of Governments in the United States.* Chicago: Rand McNally.

Grofman, Bernard, and Chandler Davidson, eds. 1992. *Controversies in Minority Voting.* Washington, D.C.: Brookings Institution.

Gross, Bertram M. 1964. *Organizations and Their Managing.* New York: Free Press.

Gujarati, Damodar. 1988. *Basic Econometrics.* 2d ed. New York: McGraw Hill.

Hadfield, Robert. 1992. Interviewed by Tanis J. Salant, November 16.

Haider, Donald H. 1974. *When Governments Come to Washington.* New York: Free Press.

Halachmi, Arie. 1991. "Information Technology, Human Resources Management, and Productivity." In *Public Personnel Management,* ed. Carolyn Ban and Norma M. Riccucci, 240–53. New York: Longman.

———. 1992. "Evaluation Research: Purpose and Perspective." In *Public Productivity Handbook,* ed. Mark Holzer, 213–25. New York: Marcel Dekker.

Hale, George, and Marian Palley. 1981. *The Politics of Federal Grants.* Washington, D.C.: Congressional Quarterly Press.

———. 1991. *The Politics of Federal Grants.* Washington, D.C.: Congressional Quarterly Press.

Hamilton, Christopher, and Donald T. Wells. 1990. *Federalism, Power, and Political Economy.* Englewood Cliffs, N.J.: Prentice Hall.

Hanson, Susan B., and Patrick Cooper. 1980. "State Expenditure Growth and Revenue Elasticity." *Policy Studies Journal* 9 (Autumn): 26–33.

Harrison, Russell. 1975. "Federal Categorical Grants and the Stimulation of State-Local Expenditures." *Publius: The Journal of Federalism* 5 (Winter): 123–36.

Hawkins, Brett W., and Rebecca M. Hendrick. 1994. "County Governments and City-Suburban Inequality." *Social Science Quarterly* 75 (December): 755–71.

Hawkins, Robert B., Jr. 1976. *Self-Government by District: Myth and Reality.* Stanford, Calif.: Hoover Institution Press, Stanford University.

Hays, R. Allen. 1991. "Intergovernmental Lobbying: Toward an Understanding of Issue Priorities." *Western Political Quarterly* 44 (December): 1081–98.

Hedge, David M. 1983. "Fiscal Dependency and the State Budget Process." *Journal of Politics* 45 (February): 198–208.

Henderson, James. 1968. "Local Government Expenditures: A Social Welfare Analysis." *Review of Economics and Statistics* 50 (May): 153–63.

Hero, Rodney E. 1989. "The U.S. Congress and American Federalism: Are 'Subnational' Governments Protected?" *Western Political Quarterly* 42 (March): 93–106.

Herrman, Margaret S. 1994. *Resolving Conflict: Strategies for Local Government.* Washington, D.C.: International City/County Management Association.

Herson, Lawrence. 1957. "The Lost World of Municipal Government." *American Political Science Review* 51 (June): 330–45.

Hinton, David, and John Kerrigan. 1980. "Knowledge and Skill Needs for Tomorrow's Public Administrators." *Public Administration Review* 40 (September–October): 469–73.

———. 1989. "Tracing the Changing Knowledge and Skill Needs and Service Activities of Public Managers." In *Ideal and Practice in Council-Manager Government,* ed. H. G. Fredrickson, 155–63. Washington, D.C.: International City Management Association.

Hosmer, L. T. 1982. "The Importance of Strategic Leadership." *Journal of Business Strategy* 3 (Fall): 4–21.

Howell, John M., and Charles Stamm. 1979. *Urban Fiscal Stress: A Computer Analysis of 66 U.S. Cities.* Lexington, Mass.: D. C. Heath.

Huelsberg, Nancy A., and William F. Lincoln. 1986. *Successful Negotiating in Local Government.* Washington, D.C.: International City Management Association.

Hy, Ronald John, Cindy Boland, Richard Hopper, and Richard Sims. 1992. "Measuring Revenue Capacity and Effort of County Governments: A Case Study of Arkansas." *Public Administration Review* 53 (May–June): 220–27.

Hyde, Albert C. 1990–91. "Rescuing Quality Management from TQM." *The Bureaucrat* 19 (Winter): 16–20.

Ingram, Helen. 1977. "Policy Implementation through Bargaining: The Case of Federal Grants-in-Aid." *Public Policy* 25 (Fall): 499–526.

International City Management Association. 1978. *The Municipal Year Book.* Washington, D.C.: International City Management Association.

International City/County Management Association. 1990. *The Municipal Year Book.* Washington, D.C.: International City/County Management Association.

Jeffery, Blake R., Tanis J. Salant, and Alan L. Boroshok. 1989. *County Government Structure: A State-by-State Report.* Washington, D.C.: National Association of Counties.

Jenks, Stephen. 1994. "County Compliance with North Carolina's Solid-Waste Mandate: A Conflict Based Model." *Publius: The Journal of Federalism* 24 (Spring): 17–36.

Jones, Larry. 1994. "Senate Panel Urged to Pass No Money, No Mandate Bill." *County News,* May 16.

Juenius, Charles L., and Lyle C. Ledebur. 1976. *A Myth in the Making: The Southern Economic Challenge and the Northern Economic Decline.* Washington, D.C.: Economic Development Administration, U.S. Department of Commerce.

Kammerer, Gladys M., Charles D. Farris, John M. DeGrove, and Alfred B. Clubok. 1964. *City Managers in Politics.* Gainesville: University of Florida Press.

Kantrow, A. 1983. "The Political Realities of Industrial Policy." *Harvard Business Review* 61 (September–October): 73–86.

Karnig, Albert K., and Susan Welch. 1979. "Sex and Ethnic Differences in Municipal Representation." *Social Science Quarterly* 60 (December): 465–81.

Kast, F. E., and J. E. Rosenzweig. 1979. *Organization and Management: A Systems and Contingency Approach.* 3d ed. New York: McGraw-Hill.

Katz, Daniel, and Robert L. Kahn. 1982. *The Social Psychology of Organizations.* 3d ed. New York: John Wiley and Sons.

Kearney, Richard C., and Reginald S. Sheehan. 1992. "Supreme Court Decision Making: The Impact of Court Composition on State and Local Government Litigation." *Journal of Politics* 54 (November): 1008–25.

Kemp, Roger L. 1990. "Metro Areas in the 21st Century: Recognizing and Anticipating the Forces of Change." *Nationl Civic Review* 79 (March–April): 152–57.

Kenyon, Daphne A. 1990. "Reassessing Competition among State and Local Governments." *Intergovernmental Perspective* 16 (Winter) 32–36.

Kessel, J. H. 1962. "Governmental Structural and Political Environment: A Statistical Note about American Cities." *American Political Science Review* 56 (September): 616.

Kingdon, John. 1984. *Agendas, Alternatives, and Public Policies.* Boston: Little, Brown and Company.

Kirchhoff, Bill. 1990. "Babbitt Could Have Been a City Manager." *Public Management* 72 (September): 2–6.

Klay, William E. 1989. "The Future of Strategic Management." In *Handbook of Strategic Management,* ed. Jack Rabin, Gerald Miller, and W. Bartley Hildreth, 44–47. New York: Marcel Dekker.

Kline, James J. 1992. "Total Quality Management in Local Government." *Government Finance Review* 8 (August): 7–11.

Klinger, Ann. 1991. "County Leadership and Models for Change." *Intergovernmental Perspective* 17 (Winter): 45–48.

Knapp, John L., and Tyler J. Fox. 1992. *Special Analysis of City and County Taxes.* Charlottesville: Center for Public Service, University of Virginia.

Kotter, John P. 1990. "What Leaders Really Do." *Harvard Business Review* 68 (May–June): 103.

Kouzes, J. M., and B. Posner. 1987. *The Leadership Challenge: How to Get Extraordinary Things Done in Organizations.* San Francisco: Jossey-Bass.

Koven, Steven G., and Don F. Hadwiger. 1992. "Consolidation of Rural Service Delivery." *Public Productivity and Management Review* 15 (Fall): 315–28.

Labovitz, S. 1971. "In Defense of Assigning Numbers to Ranks." *American Sociological Review* 36 (June): 521–22.

Ladd, Helen F. 1992. "Mimicking of Local Tax Burdens among Neighboring Counties." *Public Finance Quarterly* 20 (October): 450–67.

Ledebur, Larty C., and David W. Rasmussen. 1983. *State Development Incentives.* Washington, D.C.: Urban Institute.

Leonard, Herman B. 1986. *Checks Unbalanced: The Quiet Side of Public Spending.* New York: Basic Books.

Levine, Charles H., and James A. Thurber. 1986. "Reagan and the Intergovernmental Lobby: Iron Triangles, Cozy Subsystems, and Political Conflict." In *Interest Group Politics,* 2d ed., ed. Allan J. Cigler and Burdett A. Loomis, 202–20. Washington, D.C.: Congressional Quarterly Press.

Lewis, Edward B. 1986. "The County Administrator and Productivity: An Examination of Contrasting Styles." *International Journal of Public Administration* 8 (December): 369–90.

———. 1991. "Strategic Management in United States Counties: Precursors and Conditions for Attainment." Paper presented at the Fifty-second National Conference of the American Society for Public Administration. Washington, D.C., March 24–27.

———. 1993. "Precursors of Productivity Improvement Efforts by Appointed County Administrators." *Public Productivity and Management Review* 16 (Spring): 227–39.

———. 1994. "Policy Making/Implementing Activities of Elected County Executives and Appointed County Administrators: Does Form of Government Make a Difference?" *International Journal of Public Administration* 17 (April): 935–53.

Lewis, Edward B., and George Taylor. 1990. "Role and Style Behaviors of United States County Administrators: Scoping Backward and Forward." Paper presented at the Urban Affairs Association Annual Meeting, Charlotte, North Carolina, April 18–21.

Lewis-Beck, Michael, and Tom Rice. 1985. "Government Growth in the United States." *Journal of Politics* 47 (February): 2–30.

Liebert, Roland. 1974. "Functions, Structure, and Expenditures: A Re-Analysis of Recent Research." *Social Science Quarterly* 54 (March): 765–83.

———. 1976. *Disintegration and Political Action.* New York: Academic Press.

Lindblom, Charles. 1977. *Politics and Markets.* New York: Basic Books.

Lindblom, Charles, and Edmund P. Fowler. 1967. "Reformism and Public Policies in American Cities." *American Political Science Review* 61 (September): 701–16.

Lineberry, Robert L., and Edmund Fowler. 1967. "Reformism and Public Policies in American Cities." *American Political Science Review* 61 (September): 701–16.

Lineberry, Robert L., and I. Sharkansky. 1978. *Urban Politics and Public Policy.* 3d ed. New York: Harper and Row.

Liner, Blaine. 1990. "States and Localities in the Global Marketplace." *Intergovernmental Perspective* 16 (Spring): 11–14.

Liner, Charles D. 1992. "Alternative Revenue Sources for Local Governments." *Popular Government* 57 (Winter): 22–29.

Litterer, Joseph A. 1966. "Conflict in Organization: A Re-Examination." *Academy of Management Journal* 9 (September): 180.

Lorenco, Susan V., and John C. Glinewell. 1975. "A Dialectical Analysis of Organizational Conflict." *Administrative Science Quarterly* 20 (December): 489–508.

Lovell, Catherine. 1981a. "Local Government Dependency." *Public Administration Review* 41 (Special Issue): 189–202.

——. 1981b. "Mandating: Operationalizing Domination." *Publius: The Journal of Federalism* 11 (Spring): 59–78.

——. 1983. "Effects of Regulatory Changes on States and Localities." In *The Consequences of Cuts: The Effects of the Reagan Domestic Program on State and Local Governments,* ed. Richard P. Nathan and Fred C. Doolittle, 169–87. Princeton, N.J.: Princeton Urban and Regional Research Center.

Lovell, Catherine, Robert Kneisel, Max Neiman, Adam Z. Rose, and Charles A. Tobin. 1979. *Federal and State Mandating on Local Governments: An Exploration of Issues and Impacts.* Final Report to the National Science Foundation. Riverside: University of California Press.

Lovell, Catherine, and Charles A. Tobin. 1981. "The Mandate Issue." *Public Administration Review* 41 (May–June): 318–31.

Lowery, David, and William Berry. 1983. "The Growth of Government in the United States: An Empirical Assessment of Competing Explanations." *American Journal of Political Science* 27 (February): 665–94.

Luke, Jeff S. 1991. "New Leadership Requirements for Public Administrators: From Managerial to Policy Ethics." In *Ethical Frontiers in Public Management: Seeking New Strategies for Resolving Ethical Dilemmas,* ed. James Bowman, 158–82. San Francisco: Jossey-Bass.

——. 1992. "Managing Interconnectedness: The New Challenge for Public Administration." In *Management in an Interconnected World: Essays in the Minnowbrook Tradition,* ed. Mary T. Bailey and Richard T. Mayer, 13–32. Westport, Conn.: Greenwood Press.

Lyons, William E. 1977. *The Politics of City-County Merger.* Lexington: University Press of Kentucky.

——. 1978. "Reform and Response in American Cities: Structure and Policy Reconsidered." *Social Science Quarterly* 59 (June): 118–32.

Lyons, William E., and David Lowery. 1989. "Governmental Fragmentation Versus Consolidation: Five Public Choice Myths about How to Create Informed, Involved, and Happy Citizens." *Public Administration Review* 49 (November–December): 533–43.

McDonald, John F. 1992. "Enterprise Zones in Illinois." *Policy Forum* 5 (August): 1–4.

MacManus, Susan A. 1986. "Linking State Employment and Training and Economic Development Programs: A 20-State Analysis." *Public Administration Review* 46 (November–December): 640–50.

——. 1991a. " 'Mad' about Mandates: The Issue of Who Should Pay for What Resurfaces in the 1990s." *Publius: The Journal of Federalism* 21 (Summer): 59–75.

——. 1991b. "Why Businesses Are Reluctant to Sell to Governments." *Public Administration Review* 51 (July–August): 328–44.

———. 1992. "Mixed Electoral Systems Offer Opportunities for Representation Diversity." In *Reapportionment and Representation in Florida: A Historical Collection,* ed. Susan A. MacManus, 635–43. Tampa: Intrabay Innovation Institute, University of South Florida Research Foundation.

MacManus, Susan A., J. Edwin Benton, and Donald C. Menzel. 1993. *Personnel Mandate Cost Study: Florida Municipalities: A Survey.* Tampa: Center for Public Affairs and Policy Management, University of South Florida.

MacManus, Susan A., and Charles S. Bullock III. 1993. "Females and Racial/Ethnic Minorities in Mayoral and Council Positions." In *The Municipal Year Book 1993.* Washington, D.C.: International City/County Management Association.

Malone, Claude D. 1986. "The County Administrator: Complexity at the New Frontier." *Public Management* 68 (October): 5.

Marando, Vincent L. 1977. "County Commissioners' Attitudes toward Growth: A Two-State Comparison." *Social Science Quarterly* 58 (June): 129–38.

———. 1981. "Introduction: Targeting State and Federal Resources to Urban Areas." *Urban Interest* 3 (Special Issue): 1–9.

Marando, Vincent L., and C. Douglas Baker. 1993. "Metropolitan Counties and Urbanization." In *County Governments in an Era of Change,* ed. David R. Berman, 71–87. Westport, Conn.: Greenwood Press.

Marando, Vincent L., and Mavis Mann Reeves. 1991a. "Counties as Local Governments: Research Issues and Questions." *Journal of Urban Affairs* 13: 45–54.

———. 1991b. "Counties: Evolving Local Governments, Reform, and Responsiveness." *National Civic Review* 80 (Spring): 222–26.

Marando, Vincent L., and Robert D. Thomas. 1977. *The Forgotten Governments.* Gainesville: University Presses of Florida.

March, James, and Herbert A. Simon. 1958. *Organizations.* New York: McGraw-Hill.

Markusen, Ann R., Annalee Saxenian, and Marc S. Weiss. 1981. "Who Benefits from Intergovernmental Transfers?" *Publius: The Journal of Federalism* 11 (Winter): 5–35.

Martin, Joan K. 1982. *Urban Financial Stress: Why Cities Go Broke.* Boston: Auburn House.

Martin, Lawrence L. 1990. "States and Counties: Adversaries or Partners?: The Florida Perspective." Paper presented at the Annual Conference of the American Society for Pubic Administration, Los Angeles, April 7–11.

Maxwell, James, and J. Richard Aronson. 1977. *Financing State and Local Governments.* 3d ed. Washington, D.C.: Brookings Institution.

Maxwell, John. 1990. "Strategic Management: A Framework for the Management of Change." *Boardroom Files* 9 (Spring–Summer): 22–24.

Mazey, Mary Ellen. 1993. "A Female County Commissioner as a Facilitative Leader: Paula MacIlwaine of Montgomery County, Ohio." In "Mayors and Board Chairpersons: Realizing the Potential of Facilitative Leadership," ed. James H. Svara. Unpublished manuscript.

———. 1994. "The County Commissioner as Facilitative Leader: Paula MacIlwaine, president, Montgomery County Commission, Montgomery County, Ohio." In *Facilitative Leadership in Local Government: Lessons from Successful Mayors and Chairpersons,* James H. Svara and Associates, 63–76. San Francisco: Jossey-Bass.

Mead, Timothy. 1993. "She Was More Than We Expected: Carla DuPuy, Chairperson, Board of Commissioners, Mecklenburg County, North Carolina." In "Mayors and Board Chairpersons: Realizing the Potential of Facilitative Leadership," ed. James H. Svara. Unpublished manuscript.

———. 1994. "Leadership That Exceeds Expectations: Carla DuPuy, Chairperson, Board of Commissioners, Mecklenburg County, North Carolina." In *Facilitative Leadership in Local Governmetn: Lessons from Successful Mayors and Chairpersons,* James H. Svara and Associates, 97–116. San Francisco: Jossey-Bass.

Menzel, Donald C., and J. Edwin Benton. 1990. *Service Trends and Practices in Florida Counties.* Technical Report. Tampa: Center for Public Affairs and Policy Management, University of South Florida.

———. 1991a. "Ethics Complaints and Local Government: The Case of Florida." *Journal of Public Administration Research and Theory* 1 (October): 419–36.

———. 1991b. "Florida County Service Trends and Practices." *Journal of STAR Research* 2 (April): 16–37.

Menzel, Donald C., Vincent L. Marando, Roger B. Parks, William L. Waugh, Jr., Beverly A. Cigler, James H. Svara, Mavis Mann Reeves, J. Edwin Benton, Robert D. Thomas, Gregory Streib, Mark Schneider, and Tanis J. Salant. 1992. "Setting a Research Agenda for the Study of the American County." *Public Administration Review* 52 (March–April): 173–82.

Mields, Hugh, Jr. 1993. "The Property Tax: Local Revenue Mainstay." *Intergovernmental Perspective* 19 (Summer): 16–18.

Mintzberg, Henry. 1990. "The Manager's Job: Folklore and Fact." *Harvard Business Review* 90 (March–April): 163–76.

Mitchell, Jerry. 1992. *Public Authorities and Public Policy: The Business of Government.* New York: Praeger.

Montgomery County, Office of Management and Budget. 1992. *Montgomery County ED/GE Program.* Dayton, Ohio: Montgomery County Office of Management and Budget.

Morgan, David, and Jeffrey Brudney. 1985. "Urban Policy and City Government Structure: Testing the Mediating Effects of Reform." Paper presented at the Annual Meeting of the American Political Science Associaton, New Orleans.

Morgan, David, and Michael W. Hirlinger. 1992. "Reorganizing County Government: Effects on Revenue and Employment." Paper presented at the Annual Meeting of the American Political Science Association, Chicago, September 3–6.

Morgan, David, and John Pelissero. 1980. "Urban Policy: Does Political Structure Matter?" *American Political Science Review* 74 (December): 999–1006.

Mosher, Frederick C. 1968. *Democracy and the Public Service.* New York: Oxford University Press.

Muller, Thomas. 1975. *Growing and Declining Urban Areas: A Fiscal Comparison.* Washington, D.C.: Urban Institute.

Muller, Thomas, and Michael Fix. 1980. *The Impact of Selected Federal Action on Municipal Outlays.* Washington, D.C.: Joint Economic Committee of Congress.

Murphy, T. P., and J. Rehfuss. 1976. *Urban Politics in the Suburban Era.* Homewood, Ill.: Dorsey Press.

Musgrave, Richard A., and Peggy B. Musgrave. 1984. *Public Finance in Theory and Practice.* 4th ed. New York: McGraw Hill.

Myer, Gordon. 1979. "Economies of Size of County Government." *Journal of the Community Development Society* 10 (Fall): 27–36.

Nachmias, Chava Frankfort, and David Nachmias. 1992. *Research Methods in the Social Sciences.* 4th ed. New York: St. Martin's Press.

Nalbandian, John. 1989. "Professionalism in City Management: A New Beginning." In *Ideal and Practice in Council-Manager Government,* ed. H. G. Frederickson, 182–94. Washington, D.C.: International City Management Association.

———. 1990. "Tenets of Contemporary Professionalism in Local Government." *Public Administration Review* 50 (November–December): 654–62.

Nathan, Richard P. 1983. "State and Local Governments under Federal Grants: Toward a Predictive Theory." *Political Science Quarterly* 98 (Spring): 47–57.

Nathan, Richard P., and Fred C. Doolittle. 1987. *Reagan and the States.* Princeton, N.J.: Princeton University Press.

National Association of Counties. 1985. *NACo Survey of Counties.* Washington, D.C.: National Association of Counties.

National Association of Schools of Public Affairs and Administration (NASPAA). 1988. *Standards for Professional Master's Degree Programs in Public Affairs and Administration.* Washington, D.C.: NASPAA.

National Civic League. 1990. *Model County Charter.* Denver: National Civic League.

Netzer, Dick. 1992. "Differences in Reliance on User Charges by American State and Local Governments." *Public Finance Quarterly* 20 (October): 499–511.

Newland, Chester A. 1985. "Decades of Disaffection, Conditions for Confidence in Government." In *The Role of Government in the United States,* ed. Robert E. Cleary, 412. Lanham, Md.: University Press of America.

Nice, David C. 1987. Federalism: The Politics of *Intergovernmental Relations.* New York: St. Martin's Press.

Oakerson, Ronald J., and Roger B. Parks. 1988. "Citizen Voice and Public Entrepreneurship: The Organizational Dynamic of a Complex Metropolitan County." *Publius: The Journal of Federalism* 18 (Fall): 91–112.

———. 1989. "Local Government Constitutions: A Different View of Metropolitan Government." *American Review of Public Administration* 19 (December): 279–94.

———. 1991. "Metropolitan Organization: St. Louis and Allegheny County." *Intergovernmental Perspective* 19 (Summer): 27–30.

Olsen, J. B., and D. Eadie. 1982. *The Game Plan: Governance with Foresight.* Washington, D.C.: Council of State Planning Agencies.

Osborne, David, and Ted Gaebler. 1992. *Reinventing Government.* Reading, Mass.: Addison-Wesley.

Owen, C. James, and York Willbern. 1985. *Governing Metropolitan Indianapolis.* Berkeley: University of California Press.

Pammer, William J., Jr., 1991. *Managing Fiscal Strain in Major American Cities: Understanding Retrenchment in the Public Sector.* Westport, Conn.: Greenwood Press.

Pammer, William J., Jr., and Jack L. Dustin. 1993. "The Process of Fostering Economic

Development through a County Tax-Sharing Plan." *State and Local Government Review* 25 (Winter): 57–71.

Parks, Roger B. 1990. "The County as a Forum for Local Self Governance." Paper presented at the Annual Meeting of the American Political Science Association, San Francisco, August 30 –September 2.

Parks, Roger B., and Ronald J. Oakerson. 1989. "St. Louis: The ACIR Study." *Intergovernmental Perspective* 15 (Winter): 9–11.

———. 1993. "Comparative Metropolitan Organization: Service Production and Governance Structures in St. Louis (MO) and Allegheny County (PA)." *Publius: The Journal of Federalism* 23 (Winter): 19–40.

Pelissero, John P. 1984. "State Aid and City Needs: An Examination of Residual State Aid to Large Cities." *Journal of Politics* 46 (August): 916–35.

———. 1985. "Welfare and Education Aid to Cities: An Analysis of State Responsiveness to Needs." *Social Science Quarterly* 66 (June): 444–52.

———. 1986. "State-City Revenue Sharing Policy: Local Need versus State System Explanations." In *Intergovernmental Relations and Public Policy,* ed. J. Edwin Benton and David Morgan, New York: Greenwood Press.

Perlman, Ellen. 1990. "Education at Top of List for Prince George's Exec." *City and State,* October 8.

———. 1993. "Secretive Governing." *City and State,* March 1.

Peters, Thomas J. 1988. *Thriving on Chaos.* New York: Alfred A. Knopf.

Peterson, John E., and K. K. Edwards. 1993. *The Impact of Declining Property Values on Local Government Finances.* Washington, D.C.: Urban Land Institute.

Peterson, Paul E. 1981. *City Limits.* Chicago: University of Chicago Press.

Peterson, Paul E., Barry G. Rabe, and Kenneth K. Wong. 1986. *When Federalism Works.* Washington, D.C.: Brookings Institution.

Plaut, T., and Joseph Pluta. 1983. "Business Climate, Taxes, and Expenditures and State Industrial Growth in the United States." *Southern Economic Journal* 50 (June): 99–119.

Poister, Theodore H., and Gregory Streib. 1989. "Management Tools in Municipal Government: Trends over the Past Decade." *Public Administration Review* 49 (May–June): 240–48.

———. Forthcoming. "MBO in Municipal Government: Variations on a Traditional Management Tool." *Public Administration Review.*

Pops, Gerald M., and Jin W. Mok. 1991. "Managing Public Organizations under the Conditions of Conflict." Paper presented at the Fourth National Symposium on Public Administration Theory, Washington, D.C., March 21.

Porter, Kirk H. 1922. *County and Township Government in the United States.* New York: Macmillan.

Pressman, Jeffrey L. 1972. "Preconditions of Mayoral Leadership." *American Political Science Review* 66 (June): 511–24.

Redekop, Paul. 1986. "Interorganizational Conflict between Government and Voluntary Agencies in the Organization of a Volunteer Program: A Case Study." *Journal of Voluntary Action and Research* 15 (January–March): 19–31.

Reed, B. J. 1993. "The Changing Role of Local Advocacy in National Politics." *Journal of Urban Affairs* 5 (Fall): 287–98.

Reese, Laura A. 1992. "The Role of Counties in Local Economic Development." Paper presented at the Annual Meeting of the Southern Political Science Association, Atlanta, November 5–7.

Reich, Robert B. 1992. *The Work of Nations.* New York: Vintage Books.

Renner, Tari. 1988a. "Elected Executives: Authority and Responsibility." *Baseline Data Report* 20 (March–June): 1–9.

———. 1988b. "Municipal Election Processes: the Impact on Minority Representation." In *The Municipal Year Book 1988,* 13–21. Washington, D.C.: International City Management Association.

Renner, Tari, and Victor DeSantis. 1992. "The Impact of Political Structures upon Public Policies in American Counties." Paper presented at the Annual Meeting of the Midwest Political Science Association. Chicago, April 9–11.

Rich, Michael J. 1989. "Distributive Politics and the Allocation of Federal Grants." *American Political Science Review* 83 (March): 193–213.

Rivas, Maggie. 1994. "Ineffective Fences." *Dallas Morning News,* January 3.

Rohr, John A. 1989. *Ethics for Bureaucrats: An Essay on Law and Values.* New York: Marcel Dekker.

Rotstein, Arthur H. 1994. "Brady Law Challenger Denies Seeking Fame as a Motive." *Tucson Citizen,* May 30.

Rourk, Richard W. 1993. "Assessment Innovation in Orange County, Florida." *Intergovernmental Perspective* 19 (Summer): 26–28.

Rubin, Barry M., and C. Kurt Zorn. 1985. "Sensible State and Local Economic Development." *Public Administration Review* 45 (March–April): 333–39.

Rule, Wilma, and Joseph F. Zimmerman, eds. 1992. *United States Electoral Systems: Their Impact on Women and Minorities.* Westport, Conn.: Greenwood Press.

Rymarowicz, Lillian, and Dennis Zimmerman. 1988. *Federal Budget and Tax Policy and the State-Local Sector: Retrenchment in the 1980s.* Washington, D.C.: Congressional Research Service.

Sachs, Seymour, and Robert Harris. 1964. "The Determinants of State and Local Government Expenditures and Intergovernmental Flow of Funds." *National Tax Journal* 19 (March): 75–85.

Salant, Tanis J. 1988. *County Home Rule: Perspectives for Decision-Making in Arizona.* Tucson: Office of Community and Public Service, University of Arizona.

———. 1989. *Arizona County Government: A Study of Contemporary Issues.* Tucson: Office of Community and Public Service, University of Arizona.

———. 1991a. "County Governments: Overview." *Intergovernmental Perspective* 17 (Winter): 5–12.

———. 1991b. "Survey of State County Associations Officials." Unpublished manuscript.

———. 1992. "Survey of State County Associations Officials." Unpublished manuscript.

———. 1993. "Shifting Roles in County-State Relations." In *County Governments in an Era of Change,* ed. David R. Berman, 107–22. Westport, Conn.: Greenwood Press.

———. 1994. *An Examination of Tax Revenues Generated by the Navajo Nation in Con-*

conino County, Arizona. Tucson: Office of Government Programs, University of Arizona.

Salant, Tanis J., and Lawrence L. Martin. 1993. "County Constitutional Officers: A Preliminary Investigation." *State and Local Government Review* 25 (Fall): 164–72.

Schneider, Mark. 1989. *The Competitive City: The Political Economy of Suburbia.* Pittsburgh: University of Pittsburgh Press.

Schneider, Mark, and Kee Ok Park. 1989. "Metropolitan Counties as Service Delivery Agents: The Still Forgotten Governments." *Public Administration Review* 49 (July–August): 345–52.

Schott, Richard L. 1976. "Public Administration as a Profession: Problems and Prospects." *Public Administration Review* 36 (May–June): 255–59.

Sensenbrenner, Joseph. 1991. "Quality Comes to City Hall." *Harvard Business Review* 69 (March–April): 64–65, 68–70, 74–75.

Sharp, Elaine B. 1990. *Urban Politics and Administration.* New York: Longman.

Shubart, Ellen. 1992. "Call Him Mr. Ideas." *City and State,* August 24.

Simons, J. W. 1968. "Changing Residence in the City: A Review of Intraurban Mobility." *Geographical Review* 63 (October): 622–51.

Slack, James D. 1990a. "Information, Training, and Assistance Needs of Municipal Governments." *Public Administration Review* 50 (July–August): 450–55.

———. 1990b. "Local Government Training and Education Needs for the Twenty-first Century." *Public Productivity and Management Review* 13 (Summer): 397–404.

Smith, August U. 1989. "Needed: The Integrator Manager." *Personnel* 66 (July): 51.

Smith, Elton C., William I. Sauser, Jr., and Stephen F. Salinger. 1984. *Alabama County Clerk/Administrators: Who They Are and What They Do.* Research Monograph. Auburn, Ala.: Auburn University Office of Public Service and Research.

Snider, Clyde F. 1952. "American County Government: A Mid-Century Review." *American Political Science Review* 46 (March): 66–80.

Sokolow, Alvin D. 1993a. "Legislatures and Legislating in County Government." In *County Governments in an Era of Change,* ed. David R. Berman, 29–42. Westport, Conn.: Greenwood Press.

———. 1993b. "State Rules and the County-City Arena: Competition for Land and Taxes in California's Central Valley." *Publius: The Journal of Federalism* 23 (Winter): 53–69.

Sorkin, Donna L., Nancy B. Ferris, and James Hudak. 1984. *Strategies for Cities and Counties: A Strategic Planning Guide.* Washington, D.C.: Public Technology.

Staley, Sam. 1990. "Tax Base Sharing and Interjurisdictional Competition: Potential and Prospects for the 1990s." Paper presented at the Twentieth Annual Meeting of the Urban Affairs Association, Charlotte, North Carolina, April 18–21.

Stein, Robert M. 1981a. "The Allocation of Federal Aid Monies: The Synthesis of Demand-Side and Supply-Side Explanations." *American Political Science Review* 75 (June): 334–43.

———. 1981b. "The Targeting of State Aid: A Comparison of Grant Delivery Systems." *Urban Interest* 3 (Special Issue): 47–59.

———. 1982. "The Political Economy of Municipal Functional Responsibility." *Social Science Quarterly* 63 (September): 530–48.

———. 1984. "Municipal Public Employment: An Examination of Intergovernmental Influences." *American Journal of Political Science* 28 (November): 636–53.

Steiss, Alan W. 1982. *Management Control in Government.* Lexington, Mass.: Lexington Books.

———. 1985. *Strategic Management and Organizational Decision Making.* Lexington, Mass.: Lexington Books.

Stephens, G. Ross, and Gerald W. Olson. 1981. "The Redistributive Function Federal and State Governments." *Urban Interest* 3 (Special Issue): 33–46.

Stephenson, Max O., Jr., and Gerald M. Pops. 1990. "Managing Conflict in the Policy Process." In *Theory and Research in Conflict Management,* ed. Afzalur M. Rahim, 134–50. New York: Praeger.

Stewart, D. Michael. 1991. "Counties in the Federal System: The Washington Connection." *Intergovernmental Perspective* 17 (Winter): 18–20.

Stillman, Richard J., II. 1974. *The Rise of the City Manager: Public Professional in Local Government.* Albuquerque: University of New Mexico Press.

Stipak, Brian. 1991. "Government Expenditure Levels: Alternative Procedures for Computing Measures." *State and Local Government Reveiw* 23 (Spring): 90–94.

Stone, Donald C., and Alice B. Stone. 1975. "Early Development of Education in Public Administration." In *American Public Administration: Past, Present, and Future,* ed. Frederick C. Mosher, 11–48. University, Ala.: University of Alabama Press.

Stone, Harold A., Don K. Price, and Kathryn H. Stone. 1940. *City Manager Government in the United States.* Chicago: Public Administration Clearinghouse.

Streib, Gregory. 1991. "Strategic Decision Making in Council-Manager Governments: A Status Report." In *The Municipal Yearbook 1991,* 14–23. Washington, D.C.: International City Management Association.

———. 1992. "Applying Strategic Decision Making in Local Government." *Public Productivity and Management Review* 15 (Spring): 341–54.

———. 1995. "Educating Local Government Managers: A National Survey of MPA Programs." *International Journal of Public Administration* 18:915–40.

Streib, Gregory, and Theodore Poister. 1990. "Strategic Planning in U.S. Cities: Patterns of Use, Perceptions of Effectiveness, and an Assessment of Strategic Capacity." *American Review of Public Administration* 20 (March): 29–44.

———. 1994. "Management Tool Update: TQM in City Government." Unpublished manuscript.

Streib, Gregory, and William L. Waugh, Jr. 1990. "Assessing County Officials' Perspectives on Intergovernmental Relations and Local Capacity." Paper presented at the Annual Meeting of the American Political Science Association, San Francisco, August 30–September 2.

———. 1991a. "Administrative Capacity and the Barriers to Effective County Management." *Public Productivity and Management Review* 15 (Fall): 61–70.

———. 1991b. "The Changing Responsibilities of County Governments: Data from a National Survey of County Leaders." *American Review of Public Administration* 21 (June): 139–56.

———. 1991c. "Probing the Limits of County Reform in an Era of Scarcity: A National

Survey of County Administrators and Executives." *Public Administration Quarterly* 15 (Fall): 378–95.

Strum, Albert L. 1982. "The Development of American State Constitutions." *Publius: The Journal of Federalism* 12 (Winter): 57–98.

Svara, James H. 1985a. "Dichotomy and Duality: Reconceptualizing the Relationship between Policy and Administration in Council-Manager Cities." *Public Administration Review* 45 (January–February): 221–32.

———. 1985b. "Leadership Roles in City and County Government." Paper presented at the Annual Meeting of the Southern Political Science Association, Nashville, Tennessee, November 3–5.

———. 1987. "Mayoral Leadership in Council-Manager Cities: Preconditions versus Preconceptions." *Journal of Politics* 49 (February): 207–27.

———. 1988a. "The Complementary Roles of Officials in Council-Manager Government." In *The Municipal Year Book 1988,* 23–33. Washington, D.C.: International City Management Association.

———. 1988b. "Council-Manager Relations and the Performance of Governing Boards in North Carolina Cities and Counties." *Popular Government* 54 (Summer): 27–32.

———. 1989. "Characteristics, Contributions, and Values of City and County Managers in North Carolina." *Popular Government* 55 (Fall): 11–19.

———. 1990a. "Leadership in Cities and Counties: Comparing Chairpersons and Mayors of Council-Manager Governments." Paper presented at the Annual Meeting of the American Political Science Association, San Francisco, August 30–September 2.

———. 1990b. *Official Leadership in the City.* New York: Oxford University Press.

———. 1993a. "Achieving Effective Community Leadership." In *The Effective Local Government Manager,* ed. Charledean Newell, 19–52. Washington, D.C.: International City/County Management Association.

———. 1993b. "The Possibility of Professionalism in County Government." *International Journal of Public Administration* 16 (December): 2051–80.

Svara, James H., and Associates. 1994. *Facilitative Leadership in Local Government: Lessons from Successful Mayors and Chairpersons.* San Francisco: Jossey-Bass.

Swain, John W., and Jay D. White. 1992. "Information Technology for Productivity—Maybe, Maybe Not: An Assessment." In *Public Productivity Handbook,* ed. Marc Holzer, 194. New York: Marcel Dekker.

Swiss, James E. 1992. "Adapting Total Quality Management (TQM) to Government." *Public Administration Review* 52 (July–August): 356–62.

Szanton, Peter. 1981. *Not Well Advised.* New York: Russell Sage Foundation.

Tarlock A. Dan. 1987. "State versus Local Control of Hazardous Waste Facility Sitting." In *Resolving Local Conflict,* ed. Robert W. Lake, 137–58. Newark, N.J.: Center for Urban Policy Research, Rutgers University.

Teitelbaum, Fred, and Alice E. Simon. 1979. *Bypassing the States: Wrong Turn for Urban Aid.* Washington, D.C.: National Governors' Association.

Thernstrom, Abigal M. 1987. *Whose Vote Counts? Affirmative Action and Minority Voting Rights.* Cambridge, Mass.: Harvard University Press.

Thomas, Clive S., and Ronald J. Hrebenar. 1990. "Interest Groups in the States." In *Politics in the American States: A Comparative Analysis,* ed. Virginia Gray, Herbert Jacob, and Robert B. Albritton, 123–58. 5th ed. Glenview, Ill.: Scott Foresman.

Thomas, John Clayton. 1986. *Between Citizen and City.* Lawrence: University Press of Kansas.

Thomas, John P. 1982. "County Home Rule: A Fiscal Perspective." Ph.D. diss., cited in Blake R. Jeffery, Tanis J. Salant, and Alan L. Boroshok. 1989. *County Government Structure: A State-by-State Report.* Washington, D.C.: National Association of Counties.

———. 1987. "A Perspective on County Government Services and Financing." *State and Local Government Review* 19 (Fall): 119–21.

———. 1991. "Financing County Government: An Overview." *Intergovernmental Perspective* 17 (Winter): 10–13.

Thomas, K. W. 1976. "Conflict and Conflict Management." In *Handbook of Industrial and Organizational Psychology,* ed. M. D. Dunnette, 889–935. Chicago: Rand McNally.

Thomas, Robert D. 1981. "Targeting and Federalism: Components of a Policy Dilemma." *Urban Interest* 3 (Special Issue): 10–20.

———. 1991. "Counties in Transition: Issues and Challenges." *Intergovernmental Perspective* 17 (Winter): 41–44.

Thomas, Robert D., and Suphapong Boonyapratuang. 1993. "Local Government Complexity: Consequences for County Property-Tax and Debt Policies." *Publius: The Journal of Federalism* 23 (Winter): 1–18.

Thomas, Robert D., and Vincent L. Marando. 1981. "Local Governmental Reform and Territorial Democracy: The Case of Florida." *Publius: The Journal of Federalism* 11 (Winter): 49–63.

Thompson, Frank J. 1993. "The Challenges Revisited." In *Revitalizing State and Local Public Service,* ed. Frank J. Thompson, 309–27. San Francisco: Jossey-Bass.

Thompson, James. 1967. *Organizations in Action.* New York: McGraw-Hill.

Thompson, Joel A. 1987. "Agency Requests, Gubernatorial Support, and Budget Success in State Legislatures Revisited." *Journal of Politics* 49 (August): 756–79.

Tiebout, Charles. 1956. "A Pure Theory of Local Expenditures." *Journal of Political Economy* 64 (December): 416–24.

Todd, Barbara. 1991. "Counties in the Federal System: The State Connection." *Intergovernmental Perspective* 17 (Winter): 21–25.

Ukeles, Jacob D. 1982. *Doing More with Less: Turning Public Management Around.* New York: Amacom.

Urban Data Service. 1988. "County Form of Government—1988" (survey). Washington, D.C.: International City Management Association.

Ury, William, Jeanne Brett, and Stephen Goldbert. 1988. *Getting Disputes Resolved: Designing Systems to Cut the Costs of Conflict.* San Francisco: Jossey-Bass.

U.S. Advisory Commission on Intergovernmental Relations (USACIR). 1978. *State Mandating of Local Expenditures.* Washington, D.C.: USACIR.

———. 1981. *Measuring Local Discretionary Authority.* Washington, D.C.: USACIR.

———. 1982. *State Mandates: An Update.* Washington, D.C.: USACIR.

———. 1984. *Regulatory Federalism: Policy, Process, Impact, and Reform.* Washington, D.C.: USACIR.

———. 1985. *Intergovernmental Service Arrangements for Delivering Local Public Services: Update 1983.* Washington, D.C.: USACIR.

———. 1987. *The Organization of Local Public Economies.* Washington, D.C.: USACIR.

———. 1988a. *Local Revenue Diversification: Local Income Taxes.*

———. 1988b. *Metropolitan Organization: The St. Louis Case.* M-158. Washington, D.C.: USACIR.

———. 1989. *Local Revenue Diversification: Local Sales Taxes.* Washington. D.C.: USACIR.

———. 1990a. *Mandates: Cases in State-Local Relations.* Washington, D.C.: USACIR.

———. 1990b. *State Fiscal Capacity and Effort.* Washington, D.C.: USACIR.

———. 1991a. *The Allegheny County Case.* Washington, D.C.: USACIR.

———. 1991b. *The Changing Public Sector: Shifts in Governmental Spending and Employment.* Washington, D.C.: USACIR.

———. 1991c. "Counties." *Intergovernmental Perspective* 17 (Winter): 1-51.

———. 1991d. *Interjurisdictional Tax and Policy Competition: Good or Bad for the Federal System?* Washington, D.C.: USACIR.

———. 1992a. *Metropolitan Organization: The Allegheny County Case.* Washington, D.C.: USACIR.

———. 1992b. *Significant Features of Fiscal Federalism.* Vol. 1. Washington, D.C.: USACIR.

———. 1993. *Federal Regulation of State and Local Governments: Regulatory Federalism: The Mixed Record of the 1980s.* Washington, D.C.: USACIR.

U.S. Bureau of the Census. 1988. *County and City Data Book.* Washington, D.C.: U.S. Government Printing Office.

———. 1989. *Census of Governments, 1972-1987: Finance Statistics* (computer file).

———. 1990a. *County Government Finances 1989-1990.* Washington, D.C.: U.S. Government Printing Office.

———. 1990b. *Finances of County Government: 1987 Census of Governments.* Washington, D.C.: U.S. Government Printing Office.

———. 1990c. *Statistical Abstract of the United States.* Washington, D.C.: U.S. Government Printing Office.

———. 1991. *County Government Employment: 1990.* Series GE-90-4. Washington, D.C.: U.S. Government Printing Office.

U.S. General Accounting Office. 1988. *Legislative Mandates: State Experiences Offer Insights for Federal Action.* GAO/HRD-88-75. Washington, D.C.: U.S. Government Printing Office.

Vines, Kenneth. 1976. "The Federal Setting of State Politics." In *Politics in the American States,* ed. Herbert Jacob and Kenneth Vines, 3-48. 3d ed. Boston: Little, Brown.

Wager, Paul W., ed. 1950. *County Government across the Nation.* Chapel Hill: University of North Carolina Press.

Walker, David B. 1986. "New Federalism: 1981-86." *SIAM Intergovernmental News* 9 (Winter): 1-3.

Ward, David R. 1987. "Snow White and the 17 Dwarfs: From Metro Cooperation to Governance." *National Civic Review* 76 (January-February): 16-26.

Ward, Peter D. 1981. "The Measurement of Federal and State Responsiveness to Urban Problems." *Journal or Politics* 43 (February): 83–101.

Waugh, William L., Jr. 1988. "States, Counties, and the Questions of Trust and Capacity." *Publius: The Journal of Federalism* 18 (Winter): 189–98.

———. 1994. "Regionalizing Emergency Management: Counties as State and Local Government." *Public Administration Review* 54 (May–June): 253–58.

Waugh, William L., Jr., and Ronald John Hy. 1988. "The Administrative, Fiscal, and Policymaking Capacities of County Governments." *State and Local Government Review* 20 (Winter): 28–31.

Waugh, William L., Jr., and Gregory Streib. 1990. "County Officials' Perceptions of Local Capacity and State Responsiveness after the First Reagan Term." *Southeastern Political Review* 18 (Spring): 27–50.

———. 1993. "County Capacity and Intergovernmental Relations." In *County Governments in an Era of Change,* ed. David R. Berman, 43–52. Westport, Conn.: Greenwood Press.

Weaver, Kenneth L. 1992. "Rural County Government Reform: The Montana Case." Paper presented at the Annual Meeting of the Western Political Science Association, San Francisco.

Weeks, J. Devereux, and Richard W. Campbell. 1993. "County Revenues." In *Handbook for Georgia County Commissioners,* by J. Devereux Weeks and Paul T. Hardy, 159–77. 3d ed. Athens University of Georgia.

Weissert, Carol S. 1981. "State Legislatures and Federal Funds: An Issue of the 1980s." *Publius: The Journal of Federalism* 11 (Summer): 67–84.

Welch, Susan, and Timothy Bledsoe. 1988a. *Suburban Reform and Its Consequences: A Study in Representation.* Chicago: University of Chicago Press.

———. 1988b. *Urban Reform and Its Consequences.* Chicago: University of Chicago Press.

West, Jonathan P., Evan M. Berman, and Michael Milakovich. 1993. "Implementing TQM in Local Government: The Leadership Challenge." *Public Productivity and Management Review* 17 (Winter): 175–89.

West, Jonathan P., and Charles Davis. 1988. "Administrative Values and Cutback Politics in American Local Government." *Public Personnel Mangagement* 17 (Summer): 207–22.

White, Herbert G. 1990. "Managers and Leaders." *Library Journal* 115 (June 15): 51.

Whittaker, Carol L. 1993. *County-Tribal Relations: Gaining Perspective.* Tucson: Office of Government Programs, University of Arizona.

Wildavsky, Aaron. 1986. "Industrial Policies in American Political Cultures." In *The Politics of Industrial Policy,* ed. Claude Barfield and William Schambra, 15–32. Washington, D.C.: American Enterprise Institute.

Willbern, York, 1964. *The Withering Away of the City.* Bloomington: Indiana University Press.

Williams, O. P. 1967. "Lifestyle Values and Political Decentralization in Metropolitan Areas." *Social Science Quarterly* 48 (December): 299–310.

Williams, O. P., H. Herman, C. S. Liebman, and T. R. Dye. 1965. *Suburban Differences and Metropolitan Policies.* Philadelphia: University of Pennsylvania Press.

Wilson, Thomas D. 1966. "Elected County Chiefs." *National Civic Review* 10 (November): 561–68.

Winnie, Richard, Harry P. Hatry, and Virginia B. Wright. 1977. *Jobs and Earnings for State Citizens: Monitoring the Outcomes of State Economic Development and Employment and Training Programs.* Washington, D.C.: Urban Institute.

Wolfe, M. A. 1963. "Taxation and Development." *Planning* 29: 107–17.

Wolkoff, M. J. 1992. "Is Economic Development Decision-Making Rational?" *Urban Affairs Quarterly* 27 (March): 340–55.

Wright, Deil S. 1969. "The City Manager as a Development Administrator." In *Comparative Urban Research,* ed. Robert T. Daland, 203–48. Beverly Hills, Calif.: Sage Publications.

———. 1988. *Understanding Intergovernmental Relations.* Pacific Grove, Calif.: Brooks/ Cole Publishing Company.

Wrightson, Margaret. 1986. "From Cooperative to Regulatory Federalism." *SIAM Intergovernmental News* 9 (Winter): 4–6.

Zeller, Florence. 1975. "Forms of County Government." In *County Yearbook,* 27–33. Washington, D.C.: International City Management Association.

Zimmerman, Joseph F. 1983. *State-Local Relations: A Partnership Approach.* New York: Praeger.

———. 1987. "The State Mandate Problem." *State and Local Government Review* 19 (Spring): 78–79.

———. 1990. "State Mandates and Restraints on Local Discretionary Authority." *Comparative State Politics* 11 (December): 49–56.

———. 1991. *Federal Preemption: The Silent Revolution.* Ames: Iowa State University Press.

———. 1992. *Contemporary American Federalism: The Growth of National Power.* New York: Praeger.

Zodrow, George. 1984. "The Incidence of Metropolitan Property Tax Base Sharing and Rate Equalization." *Journal of Urban Economics* 15 (March): 210–29.

Contributors

J. Edwin Benton is an associate professor of political science and public administration at the University of South Florida. He holds a master's degree from the University of South Carolina and a Ph.D. from Florida State University. He is co-editor of *Intergovernmental Relations and Public Policy*. His research has centered on local government structure, finance, and service delivery and has appeared in the *Social Science Quarterly, Public Administration Review, Urban Affairs Quarterly, Publius, State and Local Government Review, Journal of Urban Affairs,* and *Public Opinion Quarterly*. He is currently completing a book on county government services.

David R. Berman is a professor of political science at Arizona State University, where he specializes in state and local government, politics, and public policy. He holds a master's degree and a Ph.D. from American University. Among his works is the edited volume *County Governments in an Era of Change* (1992).

Beverly A. Cigler is a professor in the School of Public Affairs at the Pennsylvania State University, Harrisburg. She holds a master's degree and a Ph.D. degree in political science from Penn State. In 1994, she received the Society for Public Administration's Section on Intergovernmental Administration and Management's Donald Stone Award for distinguished scholarship in intergovernmental relations.

Victor S. DeSantis is an assistant professor of political science at Bridgewater State College, Massachusetts. He holds a master's degree and a Ph.D. from American University. He previously served as manager of statistical analysis for the International City/County Management Association. He has published numerous works on local government structure and operations in the *Public Administration Review, State and Local Government Review,* and the *International City/County Management Association Municipal Yearbook*.

Kenneth A. Klase is an assistant professor of public administration at West Virginia University, where he specializes in public budgeting and financial management. He holds an M.B.A. from Auburn University and a doctorate of public administration from the University of Georgia. His most recent publications have appeared in *Public Budgeting and Financial Management* and the *International Journal of Pubic Administration.* His current research focuses on local government fiscal stress, county conflict, and the financial management of water and wastewater treatment facilities.

Susan A. MacManus is a professor of public administration and political science at the University of South Florida, where she specializes in state and local government finance, budgeting, politics, and government. She received a master's degree from the University of Michigan and a Ph.D. from Florida State University. She has published numerous articles on local government structures in the *Journal of Politics, American Politics Quarterly, Social Science Quarterly, Urban Affairs Quarterly, Journal of Urban Affairs, State and Local Government Review, Western Political Quarterly, American Journal of Political Science, National Civic Review,* and the *International City/County Management Association Municipal Yearbook 1993.* Her latest books are *Reapportionment and Representation in Florida: A Historical Collection* (1991) and *Doing Business with Government* (1992).

Donald C. Menzel is a professor of public administration and political science at the University of South Florida. He holds a master's degree from Miami University (Ohio) and a Ph.D. from Penn State University. He has published widely in journals such as the *Public Administration Review, Administration and Society, Journal of Public Administration Research and Theory, Urban Affairs Quarterly, Journal of Urban Affairs, Public Personnel Management, Western Political Quarterly, Policy Sciences,* and *State and Local Government Review.* He is currently conducting research on the ethical environment of local government managers and ethical issues in the public administration academy.

Jin W. Mok is an associate professor of public administration at Kookmin University in Seoul, Korea, and was formerly on the faculty at West Virginia University. He holds a master's degree and a Ph.D. from West Virginia University. He has published articles in *Political Studies Review* and the *Policy Studies Journal.*

William J. Pammer, Jr., is an associate professor of public administration at the University of South Florida, where he specializes in local government budgeting, financial management, and economic development. He received a master's degree from the University of Akron and a Ph.D. from the University of

Oklahoma. His articles have appeared in the *Social Science Quarterly, Urban Affairs Quarterly, Review of Black Political Economy, State and Local Government Review,* and the *International City/County Management Association Municipal Year Book 1992.* His most recent book is *Managing Fiscal Strain in Major American Cities* (1990). His current research focuses on how local government procurement practices affect minority business participation in government contracting.

Kee Ok Park is an assistant professor of government at the University of Virginia. He holds a master's degree and a Ph.D. from the State University of New York at Stony Brook. His recent articles on local government expenditures have appeared in the *Public Administration Review* and the *Urban Affairs Quarterly.* His research interests include urban policy and administration, public policy in general, and research methods.

Gerald M. Pops is a professor of public administration at West Virginia University. He holds a law degree from the University of California, Berkeley, and a Ph.D. from the Maxwell School of Citizenship and Public Affairs at Syracuse University. He was a legislative analyst in California and a U.S. Air Force judge advocate before entering academia. He has published widely in the fields of administrative law and justice, ethics, public-sector labor relations, and conflict management. His most recent book is *The Case for Justice* (co-authored with Thomas J. Pavlak).

Tari Renner is chair of the political science department at Illinois Wesleyan University. He holds a master's degree and a Ph.D. from American University. He formerly served as the senior statistical analyst and director of survey research at the International City/County Management Association and as an associate professor at Duquesne University. His research interests include electoral behavior, election systems, and urban forms of government and their policy and representational consequences.

Tanis J. Salant is assistant director for the Office of Government Programs at the University of Arizona. She received a master's degree in public administration from the University of San Francisco and a doctorate of public administration from the University of Southern California. She has published numerous books and articles on county government, including a national study on the shifting roles in county-state relations. She has published recent articles in *Public Administration Review* and *State and Local Government Review.*

Gregory Streib is an associate professor of public administration at Georgia State University. He received a master's degree in public administration and a

Ph.D. from Northern Illinois University. He has published articles in *Administration and Society, Public Productivity and Management Review, Public Administration Review, American Review of Public Administration,* and other public administration journals. He has also contributed several articles to the *International City/County Management Municipal Year Book.* His current research interests include the development of strategies for reducing the health-care costs of local governments and local government applications of merit-pay techniques.

James H. Svara is a professor of public administration and political science and director of the public administration program at North Carolina State University, where he specializes in city and county politics and government. He holds a master's degree and a Ph.D. from Yale University. He is the author of numerous articles published in *Public Administration Review, Journal of Politics, Administration and Society,* and the *Urban Affairs Quarterly.* His most recent book is *Facilitative Leadership in Local Government: Lessons from Successful Mayors and Chairpersons* (1994).

John P. Thomas is the Executive Director of the American Society for Public Administration. He has served as Executive Director of the National Association of Counties and the State Association of County Commissioners of Florida. He received a Doctor of Public Administration degree and a Master's of Public Administration degree from the University of Southern California and holds a Master of Arts degree in political science from the University of Toledo. He is a member of the National Academy of Public Administration and has written numerous articles on local government.

Index

Political cultures, 15, 89; individualistic, 85, 87; moralistic, 85, 87; traditionalist, 85, 87
Poor mouthing, 24
Pops, Gerald M., 15–16
Porter, Keith H., 4
Portland, Oregon, 100
Posner, B., 134
Prelgovisk, Kevin, 135
Prince Georges County, Maryland, 114
Privatization, 181, 203. *See also* Public-private partnerships
Professional associations, 131, 137. *See also* County associations
Professionalization: administration, 4; of county government, 46, 84, 109, 123, 206; managers, 101
Progressive Era, 4, 7, 63
Property taxes, 168
Public choice theory, 55
Public policy: allocational policies, 35, 39, 41, 49; developmental policies, 39, 41, 49; outputs, 80
Public-private partnerships, 193–96, 198

Quality of life, 49, 170

Reagan administration, 156, 161
Reagan-Bush administrations, 152, 154, 160–61
Reese, Laura A., 192
Reeves, Mavis Mann, 13, 38–39, 41, 81, 112
Reformed governments, 42, 46, 81, 100
Regional economic development, 185–86, 198
Regionalism, 8, 12, 100
Regional sprawl, 169
Renner, Tari, 15, 68, 70
Republicans, 64, 66, 79 (n. 4)
Research agenda for counties, 8, 9, 18
Revenues: flexibility, 166, 171, 182; intergovernmental, 69–70; property taxes, 168; revenue sharing, 170. *See also* County revenues
Rhode Island: counties in, 42; state-local relations, 156
Rice, Tom, 37
Rigos, Platon, 10
Rosenzweig, J. E., 96
Row officers, 8, 17. *See also* County constitutional officers
Rural: areas, 110; counties, 30, 88, 98
Rymarowicz, Lillian, 168

Sachs, Seymour, 151
St. Louis, Missouri, 11

Salant, Tanis J., 12, 14, 208–10
Saunders, Robert J., 151
Schneider, Mark, 12, 38, 49, 83–84, 90
Shelby County, Tennessee, 114
Slack, James D., 133
Snider, Clyde F., 6
Sokolow, Alvin D., 77, 118, 180–81
South Carolina: fiscal note statute, 22; state-local relations, 156
Southern counties, 41, 90
Special districts, 14, 18, 31, 48, 59, 95, 179, 208
Staley, Sam, 180
State colleges and universities: role in county management, 131–32
State-county relations, 162. *See also* Federalism
Stein, Robert M., 40, 151, 155
Streib, Gregory, 16–17, 110, 134, 140–41, 143, 207
Suburban-central city differences, 187
Suburbanization, 15, 47, 77, 207
Sunbelt states, counties in, 43
Sunshine laws, 209
Svara, James, 16, 104, 123–24, 204, 206
Szanton, Peter, 132

Tax abatement, 185, 192, 194–95
Tax base sharing, 179–80; shifting, 185
Tax increment financing, 17, 176
Taylor, George, 12
Technical assistance, 130, 191
Tennessee, counties in, 167
Tenth Amendment, 23
Term limits, 53, 62, 68. *See also* Elections
Texas: county boards, 66; mandates, 25; purchasing and bidding practices, 11; school districts, 86
Thomas, John P., 168, 176–77, 181
Thomas, Robert D., 9–10, 118, 127 (n. 2–3)
Tiebout, Charles, 38
Tobin, Charles A., 156
Totality-of-circumstances test, 61–62. *See also* Elections
Total Quality Management (TQM), 17, 142–44, 203
Townships, 6
Training, in county management, 131

Unfunded Mandates Reform Act of 1995, 23, 211
Unincorporated areas, 30, 48, 80
Unionization, 99
United States Congressional Budget Office, 156

rw: devolution
Div School course on liturgical year
clear warren count
turn in help
re-framing Skocpol
call janusry
e-mail Eng. Rev. conf

Samuel C. Bushnell, 1905
" I come from the city of Boston,
The home of the bean + the cod,
Where the Cabots speak only to Lowells,
And the Lowells speak only to God. "
American arbitration assn,
    http://www . a dr. org
    lermundi.org/mediators.html